Virtue of Honor

Acquiring Truth

*Giving a Voice
to Childhood Trauma*

Joanne Richardson

ADVANCE PRAISE FOR *VIRTUE OF HONOR*

"**Virtue of Honor. Acquiring Truth — Giving a Voice to Childhood Trauma**, is a breathtakingly honest and deeply moving account of resilience, faith, and the power of truth. Joanne Richardson doesn't just share her story—she invites you into the rawest moments of her life, where pain meets grace and darkness gives way to light. Her courage to confront complex PTSD, childhood trauma, workplace and domestic abuse, and choose healing with painful physical disabilities will inspire anyone who has ever felt too broken to believe that restoration is possible. This is more than a memoir—it's a beacon of hope."

Michelle Prince, CEO, Performance Publishing

I had no idea what to expect from this book—probably gossip from an ex C-suite corporate America executive. But what I learned is how broken our system is and how deeply this affects those who generally don't have a voice in corporate America: women. Joanne's story is visceral. From childhood trauma to corporate trauma, it's eye-opening how ignorant we are about trauma. And if you are a trauma victim, this book will open your options to healing. Yet it's engaging, exceptionally well written, and page after page takes you on a roller coaster of emotions, reflection, and a deeper understanding of human nature. Broken, but beautiful. Lastly, this book makes you fall in love with Jo—the underdog who, despite all the odds and life's severe circumstances, emerges purified, rectified, and in peace. And so can you.

Andy Costa, Emmy Winner, DP, PMP

Performance Publishing
McKinney, TX

Copyright © 2025 by Joanne Richardson
All Worldwide Rights Reserved.

All rights reserved. No part of this publication may be reproduced, stored in a retrieval system or transmitted, in any form or by any means, electronic, mechanical, recorded, photocopied, or otherwise, without the prior written permission of the copyright owner, except by a reviewer who may quote brief passages in a review.

ISBN:
978-1-961781-26-9 (paperback)
978-1-967451-00-5 (hardcover)
978-1-967451-01-2 (ebook)

Library of Congress Control Number: 2025915823

I never set out to tell this story, although it has been on my heart for years. I spent years burying the truth beneath survival, pushing forward, and never looking back. But the past has a way of demanding to be heard. It lingers in the quiet moments, in the spaces between breaths, in the memories that refuse to fade. This is not a tale of victimhood—it's a reckoning. A testimony of faith, betrayal, resilience, and the relentless pursuit of truth. It's about standing tall when the world tries to break you, about finding peace in the outcome.

Dedicated to my secret keepers, —Mona Lisa and Wanda, the strongest warriors I know.

⚠ READER ADVISORY

··

This memoir does not shy away from the hard truths. It confronts emotional and spiritual abuse, betrayal, complex trauma, loss, and the long, bloodied road to healing. The reflections within are raw, unapologetic, and unfiltered by tradition or expectation.

You will encounter grief, self-betrayal, abandonment, and despair—but you will also encounter a greater truth: that redemption is real, that healing is possible, and that Christ meets us in the deepest valleys.

This is not an easy journey. It was never meant to be.
Proceed with care. Breathe when you must.
But know this as you turn each page:
You are not alone. And no matter how dark it gets, hope is already breaking through.

TABLE OF CONTENTS

Foreword xv
Preface 1
⚠ Content Warning: Suicide and Extreme distress 1
Trickery 2
Introduction. Behind the Curtain 5
Who Am I? 8

ACT 1

Chapter 1. Right Decisions 11
    Sabino 11
    New Environment 13
    Complex PTSD (Childhood Trauma) 16
    Gaining Tools 20

Chapter 2. Identity and Image 23
    Childhood 23
    The Farm 33
    Saying No 37
    Loneliness 39

Chapter 3. Schooling 43
    Sociality 43

Chapter 4. Broken 51
    ⚠ Content Warning: Sexual Assault 51
    Predators You Know 52
    Finding Comfort 54
    In The Spirit of Hope 54
    What the Blood Didn't Take 56

Chapter 5. Anorexia **57**
    ⚠ Content Warning: Anorexia 57
    Frozen Desperation 58
    My First Real Secret 58
    Hard Truth 60
    Starvation, Shame, and Survival:
    A Trauma-Informed View of Anorexia Nervosa 62

Chapter 6. Fear **65**
    ⚠ Content Warning: Suicide and Deep Emotional Pain. 65
    Dark Window 66
    Eye of the Beholder 67
    Protection 69
    Fortitude 72

Chapter 7. Motherhood **77**
    Harvesting 77
    Being a Mother 78
    Generational Trauma 81
    Canceled 83
    Story of the Lost Son 85

Chapter 8. Early Mistakes **89**
    Saying "I Do" again 89
    Idolatry 91

Chapter 9. Early Work Path **93**
    Resilience 93

Chapter 10. New Horizons **97**
    Fake It 'Till You Make it! 99
    My First Whale 100
    Workaholic's Handbook 107
    The Lord's Prayer 112

Chapter 11. Gluttony **115**

Chapter 12. Living in Blindness 119
    Rock Bottom 120
    My Secret Keeper is Dead 121
    Shopping 122
    Quick Fix 123

Chapter 13. Lust 125
    ⚠ Content Warning: Sexual Content, Despair,
    and Redemption 125
    Gateway Drug 127
    Hedonism 127
    Complacency 128
    Debauchery 129
    Sex 130
    View From the Web 131
    Repentance 134
    Folly 135

Chapter 14. Wrath 139
    ⚠ Content Warning: Abortion, Despair, and Redemption ... 139
    Unnamed 140
    Abortion 142

Chapter 15. Greed 145
    The Price of Wanting More 145
    Glass Houses 147
    Work, Work, Work 148
    The Fish-A-Roo 150

Chapter 16. Escape 155
    ⚠ Content Warning: Domestic abuse, Suicidal Ideation
    and Despair 155
    Taking the Doctor's Advice 156
    Out on a Limb 158
    Unemployment 161
    Sloth 162
    Dreaming of Angels 163
    Finding Strength 165
    The Move 167
    You Get What You Ask For 170
    Pride 173

ACT 2

Chapter 17. Faith of a Child 177
   Sowing of the Seed 177
   Testimony of Christ 182
   The Word 185
   Engaging and Following The Spirit 188

Chapter 18. Hope 191
   Watering the Mustard Seed 191
   Woman in White 192
   Turing on a Dime 196
   Acquiring the Truth 199
   A Deeper Look—An Uncomfortable Truth 200
   My Imposter 202
   Imposter Syndrome 203

Chapter 19. Time of Trials 207
   Sucked Back In 208
   Writing on the Wall 211

Chapter 20. A Heart for God 217
   A Mirror to Your Heart 222
   Scarlett's Sinner Corner 233

Chapter 21. All That Glitters Is Not Gold 241
   Prudence 245
   Persistence, Resilience, and Faith 247

Chapter 22. Posterior Tibial Tendon Disfunction (PTTD) 249
   Year of the Foot 249
   Facing My Pride 252
   Reconstruction Foot Surgery 253
   Preparation 256
   Pain 257
   Fibromyalgia 258
   Fibromyalgia and Complex PTSD 259

Chapter 23. Into the Storm 263
   Thinking Clearly 263
   Heartbreak 264

Asking for Help 267
Perspective 268
Armor of God 270
Living in Faith 273
Healing and Recovery 275

Chapter 24. Pride Disguised as Light 279
Education 279
Turn of Events 281

Chapter 25. Running 287
Just Blake 288

Chapter 26. Chastity 295

Chapter 27. My Career 299
Appreciation 299

Chapter 28. Inside the Gilded Birdcage 303
Butterfly Effect 306
Groundhog Day 311
Used Up 313
Physical Abuse in the Workplace 316
Burning Bridges 318
Honest Evaluation 322
Corporate Whistleblowing 323
Justice 327
Spiritual Warfare in the Workplace 329

Chapter 29. I Am a Woman 333
Sexism 336
Corporate Chauvinism 339
The Women 344

**Chapter 30. CPTSD Coping Mechanisms vs.
Survival in a Toxic Workspace** 347
Breaking the Cycle: Healing After Workplace Trauma 350
Vomit 351

Chapter 31. Suicidal Ideation 355
Lost in the Wilderness 356
Serpent in My Garden 357

ACT 3

Chapter 32. Healing 361
    Full Circle 361
    View from Gethsemane 363

Chapter 33. Doubt 367
    How Much Is Too Much? 367

Chapter 34. Course Correction — Breaking Strongholds 373
    Anger 373

Chapter 35. Trust in Christ's Plan 379
    Pride 379
    Placing Trust in My Heart 382
    Self-Reflection: A House Swept Clean 386
    Stopping the Insanity 388
    A Life No Longer Borrowed 390

Chapter 36. Are Your Secrets Living Thru You? 393

Chapter 37. It's Been an Honor 399

Chapter 38. The Table is Set 403

Chapter 39. Freedom 409
    To Be Me 409

FOREWORD

Courage is never quiet. It speaks when silence would feel safer. Joanne Richardson's Virtue of Honor: Acquiring Truth is that kind of courage—unflinching, raw, and profoundly authentic. She does not hide behind safe words or polished surfaces. She opens her life, scarred and redeemed, and invites us to step into the shadows she once lived through so that we might see the light she has found.

As I read Joanne's story, I felt my own heart stirred. Memories surfaced from my childhood—moments I had buried, lessons I hadn't fully realized had shaped me. Her honesty made me braver to face my own. That is the gift of this book: Joanne's voice does not only tell her story; it makes space for ours.

One of the most urgent truths in these pages is the reminder that trauma left unhealed never truly disappears. It seeps into families, workplaces, communities, and even churches. We cannot pretend it away. Joanne refuses to minimize the lasting wounds of abuse and betrayal, yet she also refuses to be defined by them. She shows us that confronting our mental health is not weakness—it is strength. Healing begins with truth, and truth demands courage.

What strikes me most deeply is Joanne's determination to own her story. To own your story is to refuse shame. To name your truth is to strip the enemy of his greatest weapon—silence. Joanne embodies this risk, and in doing so, she extends to us an invitation: to walk our own rugged inward roads, to confront the hard places, and to discover that God's grace is strong enough to meet us there.

This book is not just an autobiography—it is a testimony. It is a mirror for those who need to face what they've been running from, and a beacon for those who long for freedom. Joanne's faith runs throughout, a steady witness to the God who redeems.

This is more than a book to read—it is a book to wrestle with. Let Joanne's words stir you, challenge you, and lead you toward the same freedom she has found. My prayer is that you will not close these pages unchanged.

Marya Patrice Sherron,
KI Productions & Publishing

PREFACE

CONTENT WARNING:
SUICIDE AND EXTREME DISTRESS.

....

This chapter contains discussions of suicide, trauma, and deep emotional pain. These topics are presented with honesty and rawness, reflecting real experiences. If you are struggling or find these themes distressing, please take care while reading. You are not alone—if you need support, reach out to a trusted friend, faith leader, or a professional resource.

If you or someone you know is in crisis,
help is available:

☎ National Suicide Prevention Lifeline: 988 (U.S.)

☎ Crisis Text Line: Text HOME to 741741

Your life matters. ♥

TRICKERY

Oct. 2022. I'd been crying for hours. Weeks, actually. I've been running and numbing myself with family obligations, work, and travel to hide the pain. Tonight however, I have nowhere to run. I cannot get a hold of my emotions since mom died. I am praying and begging Christ to stop the pain. I'm sobbing for comfort. Begging for peace and to be set free. Begging Him to take me home. This world is too hard—I am not strong enough. I feel like all the intentional "cuts' that have been administered to me over the years are now open and streaming blood down my body. All the abandonment. All the scorn. All the rejection. All of my failures—the pain is so intense I can barely breathe. I feel like I have been shredded from the inside out. I am broken. I have lost hope.

I was suffering in a grave of despair. The Serpent was in my garden.

I recognized evil's voice in my head from years of hearing it as he fed me lies upon lies. Although this time, the fact he was so close terrified me.

"Get the ice and razor blades. Make it deep. The pain will be gone." A familiar request. Tonight, the comforting thought of death seemed relieving. I was just done.

This voice is one of destruction and lies. Ideas spin in your head and offer the comfort of escapism. This voice rejoices in your struggles and offers reprieve by leading you deeper and deeper into despair, offering a way out.

"No!" I said out loud. "I know who you are. Be gone!"

Having a serpent in my garden terrified me. I made the call at midnight and started my healing.

PREFACE

> ISMs: Broken. Desperation. Abandonment.
> Suicidal ideation. Empty. Pain.
>
> Heavenly Virtue: Hope

I was praying for help. I was praying for peace. I was praying to end the pain.

My prayers were answered that night in my garden.

"And the Holy Spirit helps us in our distress. For we don't even know what we should pray for, nor how we should pray. But the Holy Spirit prays for us with groanings that cannot be expressed in words. And the Father who knows all hearts knows what the Spirit is saying for the Spirit pleads for us believers' harmony with God's own will.

And we know that God causes everything to work together for the good of those who love God and are called according to his purpose for them. For God knew his people in advance, and he chose them to become like his Son, so that his Son would be the first born, with many brothers and sisters. And having chosen them, he called them to him. And he gave them right standing with himself and he promised them glory."

Romans: 8: 26-30

INTRODUCTION

BEHIND THE CURTAIN

This is me ... I have a light within me. Pompous as this may sound, I've known this light my whole life. I shine brighter than others most of the time, and that causes all walks of life to be drawn to me or instantly repelled.

I was born and raised in Missoula, Montana, in the big green house on the corner of McDonald Street my dad built in 1961. For 59 years, that home meant security. I attended school and then college at the University of Montana, raised my family, and built a life surrounded by mountains, rivers, and an endless Big Sky. It was home. But life wasn't always serene.

I married at 18, raised three sons, and spent 11 years running a home daycare. At 39, I made an abrupt shift into senior corporate sales leadership at Fortune 100 companies. I went from wiping noses to closing multimillion-dollar deals. My success came from intellect, trade, and my innate ability to connect with people. This shift was more than a career change—it was a transformation of identity.

For 23 years, I thrived in the high-stakes world of Corporate America, but the relentless demands came at a price. That world offered wealth, power, and prestige, but it also drained my peace. At 49, I accepted Christ as my Savior. Faith didn't erase my battles, but it armed me with truth. My personal life mirrored the chaos of my career.

I spent 29 years in marriage—two men, different on the surface but alike in their need for control. One was brooding and jealous; the other, flamboyant and emotionless. Both worked tirelessly to manage my thoughts, drive, finances, and confidence. They weren't my refuge; they were my cage. Their control only deepened my need to prove myself—to be seen and heard.

I am a natural leader—an intense ENTJ. I ask questions, analyze situations, and demand clarity. I am also empathic, attuned to emotions and motives. I build trust, make people feel valued and understood. I give what I need in return but rarely receive it.

My memory is like moving pictures. Events, conversations, and settings are neatly organized in my mind. I never needed notes. It made me formidable in business but uneasy to those who wished I'd forget. But this sharp recall came at a cost.

These memories, though a gift, are also trauma flashbacks. My questioning nature was a survival tactic—hyper-vigilance to stay ahead, anticipate needs, and demand honesty. If someone tried to hide the truth, I dug deeper.

People-pleasing is self-betrayal—the daily act of erasing yourself to accommodate others. Yet, this skill made me exceptional in business. I turned pain into profit and trauma into talent. But success never filled the void.

> "People-pleasing is self-betrayal—the daily act of erasing yourself to accommodate others. Yet, this skill made me exceptional in business. I turned pain into profit and trauma into talent. But success never filled the void."

To quiet the emptiness, I sought acceptance in reckless ways. My career, wealth, and success provided me endless opportunities for excess, and I explored them. But the void remained.

Then my life changed. I had always believed in Christ but never committed to Him. I thought I was a Christian—I prayed in trouble, attended church on holidays, and assumed I was fine. But I was blind.

Had you pressed me about saving faith, I would have fought you. I thought belief was enough. I didn't see that the light I carried was His, that I had misused His gifts to distract myself from truth.

Grace was my turning point. It showed me the difference between knowing Christ and truly following Him. It reframed my struggles, giving them purpose.

My testimony is a battle call—to examine your life and see the truth in your circumstances. The line between success and failure is thin. My story offers hope.

Never a victim. I am a survivor. A warrior.

He caught me when I fell.

WHO AM I?

I have led a life of adventure, success, and achievement—more good times than bad. I've laughed more than I've cried. I've danced more than I've crawled. At one point in my life, I thought I had all the worldly success a person could have—I'd put in years of running on a gerbil wheel, moving at the speed of light, going everywhere and nowhere fast. But beneath the surface, there were secrets buried so deep I didn't even realize they were mine. My secrets had become my normal way of surviving life.

I had willingly let my secret life run my life.

Perception is a powerful thing.

I've held many monikers: daughter, sister, wife, mother, aunt, grandmother, friend, leader, mentor, missionary, teammate, teacher. Then there are the other names: cheater, liar, worthless, crazy, bossy, aggressive, abandoner, stupid. Lucky.

This is my Prodigal Daughter story—Luke 15:11-32—a journey from brokenness to wholeness, from shame to healing, from a wasted life to one renewed by Christ's mercy. It's a book of hope, exposing life's snares with raw honesty and a desire for truth.

If you believe suffering only happens in obvious places, this book may challenge your thinking. If my words make you uncomfortable, take that discomfort as an invitation to reflect, not a judgment. If the nonlinear structure frustrates you, know that life itself is messy and unsorted.

I've spent years asking myself: Why can't I catch a break? Why do I always fight to keep it together? Why am I never right, even when my instincts scream otherwise?

Why is my sword always up and ready for battle? Why can't I trust myself? Not trusting others is one thing—but not trusting *yourself*? That's an entirely different thing.

The truth is that those who hold you down fear your potential and your strength. They avoid accountability, deflect responsibility, and thrive on keeping you small and ineffective. Because potential scares people. Because the truth scares people out of hiding. But here's what I've learned: Your voice is the most powerful weapon you have in your arsenal. It unsettles people—as it should.

> "The truth is that those who hold you down fear your potential and your strength. They avoid accountability, deflect responsibility, and thrive on keeping you small and ineffective. Because potential scares people. Because the truth scares people out of hiding. But here's what I've learned: Your voice is the most powerful weapon you have in your arsenal. It unsettles people— as it should."

The Truth is the only way to be free.

This is my truth—the good, the bad, and the deeply flawed. I refuse to hide in the shadows. I will speak boldly, not just for me, but for anyone who feels silenced. For anyone who needs a way out.

I'm a woman from a small mountain town who crossed into raging waters and is now forging a new path. I'm far from perfect—but I don't have to be.

This is my story.

Act 1

CHAPTER 1

RIGHT DECISIONS

SABINO

Sitting on a flight headed to Dallas. But this is no regular trip. I'm returning after having spent 35 days in a trauma recovery treatment center. I'm thoroughly enjoying a Diet Pepsi and a bag of M&M's. I'm deprived of sugar but clearheaded. I understand myself better than any person should after getting a complex PTSD diagnosis. It's truly life-changing to understand childhood trauma's effects on one's perspective, daily interactions, and reactions.

I take inventory: I'm hopeful, at peace, well fed, have normal anxiety levels, and I'm pretty much over the visceral pain of mom's death and the 59 years of assorted emotional and physical abuse I now understand. For $75K, you too can achieve a hard reset. A momentary reprieve from the gerbil wheel of life. A second chance at getting it right—or in my case, a fourth or fifth chance.

I'd be lying if I didn't admit this break was long overdue. Life had cascaded about three years prior, and I'd been under extreme stress with work, family, and physical pain. To alleviate some of the pressure, I overworked, slept, isolated myself, smoked, drank, and ignored all the signs—until finally my body gave out under the weight of the duress. Numbing yourself and running doesn't work.

I basically crawled into the center. I had high blood pressure, anemia, and a vitamin deficiency. I was malnourished, severely dehydrated, and clinically depressed. My persistent brain fog and anxiety had me climbing up the walls. I had quit self-care such as baths, teeth brushing, cooking, and cleaning for weeks before I noticed the pattern. I was also exhausted beyond comprehension. Being bone-tired takes on a new meaning when you get to this point. It is not the first time I've been in this mental or physical state.

It had been a hell of a three years: two stressful family weddings, two sons expelling me from their lives, one stressful job switch, my brother Blake's death, my friend Wanda's death, and then mom died. On top of that, I hated the career I had once loved and was again on my way out. Couple that with intense dissociation, and you've got a great recipe for internal combustion. The pain just had to stop.

NEW ENVIRONMENT

Life inside the center felt like a warm cocoon. All the residents were just like me (in different but similar ways). They had addictions, childhood, sexual, and religious trauma, mental disorders, and mixed diagnoses stemming from prolonged self-abuse. There were no egos, posturing, or social classes. Check your masks at the door because you have no chance of holding onto anything under the guide of these trained, world-class therapists. Vulnerability is the only game that's allowed.

On the first day, I was struck by how nice and caring everyone was. From the staff to the residents, it was overwhelming. Had I been around a lot of angry, non-caring, sad folks all these years? How many smiles and hellos can one person get in a day? Or the next day? And the next? It was crazy. It seemed I became one of them by day three.

During that first week, I also felt the effect that three meals a day had on my system. It was amazing. I had forgotten how important food is. Medication taken on time also works very well. Early bedtime, early to rise was another revelation. How did I forget such things? Discussions were all at a personal and educational level. The residents were all highly educated and successful in their own right and had valuable insights to add to every conversation. Top that with a true nurturing attitude toward one another, and what is created is an atmosphere of love and healing. Is this what treatment centers are all about? Nah—it's just Sabino.

Located in beautiful Tucson, this center—which was once a boys' school—has created a magical world. Free of outside influences, it offers a place to feel safe in your pain. It is accepting. Inviting. Comforting. And extremely different from any community I had ever experienced. I'm convinced no one could ever come here and walk away the same.

The first step was to get me back on my meds for fibromyalgia, eat, and get all the sleep I needed. Next came 400+ hours of therapy, group discussions, physical activity, and enough water to drown a horse. Throw in massages, brain mapping, acupuncture, horse riding, chakra balancing, yoga, brain remapping, neurofeedback, hypnosis, accelerated resolution therapy (ART), breathwork, eye movement desensitization and reprocessing (EMDR) treatments, and learning new tools to try to pry the past emotional trauma from my mind, body, and soul.

Seems it's working. I learned I could trust myself. I learned what love and respect are and what they are not. I confirmed that I am indeed a powerful and tenacious woman—a woman who rubs some people the wrong way and drives the weak crazy. I learned I am allowed to be just me.

We worked on my abandonment fears first. Through EMDR and ART, I went back and soothed my younger self. I offered my young self, love and understanding as I processed many past traumas. The experience was life-altering. Feeling my own inner child's pain was both exhilarating and exhausting. Years of feeling unloved and unwanted took a backseat. I was able to soothe her tears, caress her hair, and administer hugs—all in my mind. It helped break down the fears and restore a semblance of closure. It provided me understanding.

The second step was about releasing the pain revolving around my mom and accepting her death, and the pain tied to losing my family home and the security it brought. This was accomplished through one-on-one therapy as well as through a grief group. I began to understand that I had held very deep shame of her denial of me. I mourned the fact that hope was gone with her death. I could never show her my worth and clearly grew to understand that all my efforts were not my failure but hers. Healing tears instead of wounded tears helped me cross over to a better place with her death.

I had Christian counsel once a week. It was fabulous. We talked about which trial I was experiencing in Joseph's life—I felt I was coming out of prison and feeling sunshine for the first time in years.

I get to be me. I am allowed to fully understand and trust myself.

The story of Joesph can be found in Genesis chapters 37-50.

COMPLEX PTSD (CHILDHOOD TRAUMA)

I was given a crash course on complex childhood trauma. I understood—in a very limited knowledge base—post-traumatic stress disorder (PTSD), but I'd never heard of complex PTSD. Second to accepting Christ, the diagnosis cleared my eyes and helped me to acquire the truth.

To be diagnosed with C-PTSD under ICD-11, a person must first meet the core diagnostic criteria for PTSD (World Health Organization [WHO], 2018).

PTSD was formally added to the *Diagnostic and Statistical Manual of Mental Disorders* (DSM-III) in 1980, primarily in the context of war-related trauma. By the time of the DSM-5's publication in 2013, the definition expanded to include a variety of traumatic experiences—not only combat, but also accidents, assaults, and natural disasters (American Psychiatric Association [APA], 2013). Traditional PTSD symptoms are typically linked to a single traumatic event or a few events. These symptoms fall into four main clusters:

1. Intrusions and re-experiencing. For me, this presented in nightmares, flashbacks, and intrusive thoughts tied to self-identity and personal worth.
2. Arousal and reactivity. A state of heightened nervous system arousal—always being on guard, needing your back to the wall, jumping at loud noises, irritability, trouble sleeping or concentrating.
3. Avoidance. Don't want to talk about it. Don't want to think about it. Push it down. Hide. Run. Numb. Don't seek treatment. *I'm good. I'll be good.*
4. Negative changes in cognition and mood. Persistent negative beliefs about yourself, others, and the world. Emotional numbness. Shame. Hopelessness.

Complex PTSD is different. It results from chronic, repeated interpersonal trauma, often beginning in early developmental years, and typically within caregiving or attachment relationships (Herman, 1992; van der Kolk, 2005). C-PTSD is not currently recognized in the DSM-5, which is the standard used in the United States. Instead, it is formally recognized by the World Health Organization in the ICD-11. Due to this, many U.S. insurance companies do not yet cover trauma treatment under a C-PTSD diagnosis—an unfortunate barrier to care.

Complex trauma involves sustained, repetitive exposure to interpersonal trauma—typically within caregiving relationships—and significantly impacts affect regulation, self-perception, and relational functioning (Ford & Courtois, 2020). This trauma may include, but is not limited to, physical, sexual, and emotional abuse, as well as abandonment, chronic adversity, neglect, bullying, loss, and exposure to violence. In most cases, these experiences begin in early childhood, during critical developmental windows (Teicher & Samson, 2016). Because the brain is still forming, this abuse has a more penetrative and neurologically disruptive impact on brain development. *You have been programmed adversely.*

In addition to the core PTSD symptoms, C-PTSD includes three distinct symptom clusters:

Disturbances in self-organization (DSO):

a) Affective dysregulation—difficulty managing emotions and physiological responses.
b) Negative self-concept—chronic feelings of worthlessness, shame, or guilt.
c) Relational disturbances—challenges in forming or maintaining close relationships due to mistrust, detachment, or fear of intimacy.

Author and therapist Pete Walker, who has lived experience with C-PTSD and specializes in recovery from childhood trauma, describes these adaptations as "emotional flashbacks"—sudden regressions into states of fear, shame, or despair triggered by relational cues, even in adulthood (Walker, 2013). His work is especially helpful for those recovering from covert emotional neglect and narcissistic abuse.

The funny thing about brain scans is they don't distinguish between physical and emotional pain. The same neural circuits are activated (Eisenberger & Lieberman, 2004). My scan entering Sabino was bright red, representing an overwhelmed, dysregulated system. My scan leaving was a beautiful, calm blue. The peace of knowing the truth had begun reversing decades of ingrained trauma responses and rewiring my brain toward healing.

References:

- American Psychiatric Association. (2013). *Diagnostic and Statistical Manual of Mental Disorders (5th ed.)*. Arlington, VA: APA.
- Eisenberger, N. I., & Lieberman, M. D. (2004). Why it hurts to be left out: The neurocognitive overlap between physical and social pain. *Trends in Cognitive Sciences*, 8(7), 294–300.
- Ford, J. D., & Courtois, C. A. (2020). *Treating Complex Traumatic Stress Disorders in Adults (2nd ed.)*. Guilford Press.
- Herman, J. L. (1992). *Trauma and Recovery: The Aftermath of Violence—from Domestic Abuse to Political Terror*. Basic Books.
- Teicher, M. H., & Samson, J. A. (2016). Annual research review: Enduring neurobiological effects of childhood abuse and neglect. *Journal of Child Psychology and Psychiatry*, 57(3), 241–266.

- van der Kolk, B. A. (2005). Developmental trauma disorder: Toward a rational diagnosis for children with complex trauma histories. *Psychiatric Annals*, 35(5), 401–408.
- Walker, P. (2013). *Complex PTSD: From Surviving to Thriving: A Guide and Map for Recovering from Childhood Trauma*. Azure Coyote Press.
- World Health Organization. (2018). *International Classification of Diseases 11th Revision (ICD-11)*. Geneva: WHO.

GAINING TOOLS

No shame—at 60, I finally barged through the open door to the path of healing.

Finding truth at any age is empowering. Discovering it at the tail end of a roller coaster ride that included a wild career, abusive romantic relationships, and complicated entanglements with close family/friends is beyond frustrating.

Perspective is a mind-blowing tool when you're diagnosed with childhood complex trauma. When I first got the diagnosis and dug in with trained phycologists to better understand my mental illness and how it shows up in my emotions and reactions to life's difficulties, I experienced a wave of relief. And then another wave of acceptance. I am not going insane, I realized. I've been programmed to accept abuse from others. Made to believe others' feelings about myself were true. I am not unlovable.

I am not unreasonable. I am reasonably questioning and setting professional and personal boundaries. I have a right to my feelings and thoughts even if you disagree. I know I have been deceived. I see through all of it. Finally. Clarity.

My first reaction was: How did I not know? A minute of shame and then a wave of relief and acceptance. Then I realized I needed to understand how my mind was broken and how to erase a lifetime of backwards thinking. How did I ever succeed in life covering up all this trauma? Why didn't I see the abuse and stand up for myself sooner? Where was my voice?

So angry at myself.

Anger was a new emotion. I somehow had never learned that anger is an emotion to be felt, recognized, and explored. I had only learned to push it away.

I learned cognitive tools for how to calm my over-zapped brain and nervous system. Daily meditation, Muse biofeedback, breathwork, and journaling. I learned the truth of how I have been a survivor of extreme emotional punishment, sexual and physical abuse. I learned to understand myself and discovered why I was always searching for acceptance. I learned to set stronger boundaries and hold them. Truthfully, I learned to love and trust myself; I learned I hadn't been imagining being treated indifferently throughout my entire life.

Realizing I had been programmed to believe lies about myself had intrinsic value. I was assured I had no individual importance. I was told that I was nothing, my feelings were unimportant, and I was too demanding of my own way. I didn't understand my place or my role in any situation. I didn't understand how to just be happy in my environment. I didn't understand I was inferior. I didn't understand that I couldn't speak up or make a phone call to move around an issue and find the truth. I couldn't ask for accountability.

Until I realized: Yes, I can.

CHAPTER 2
IDENTITY AND IMAGE

CHILDHOOD

I was the last child born in my family. The only girl—eight, nine, and 10 years younger than my brothers. I entered a family of six children: my three siblings and my mother's three half-siblings. It was a generational household, layered with complexities I didn't understand until much later.

Mom was raised very poor, growing up in the Dakotas before moving with her family to California during the Great Depression. My grandmother Amelia had a tumultuous life—several husbands, lovers, and six children. Times were hard. Amelia lost her first and second husbands, and by the time she was in her late 40s, she had her last child. My mom, at 14, ran away with a man who beat her. She returned home to marry a drunk, divorced him, and by 21, married my dad in Missoula.

My dad was born in Deer Lodge, Montana, to a Milwaukee railroader and a strong, silent, God-fearing mother. A mathematical genius, he was upright and disciplined. To make ends meet, his mother ran the railroader's boarding house, where he and his siblings lived. At seven, he cleaned out animal railroad cars for five cents a day. He fished, hunted, and lived simply during the Depression. Later, he and his three brothers all fought in World War II. Remarkably, all four returned home alive.

Within a few years of marrying, my parents had three boys. Dad worked at the lumber mill, and Mom stayed home. When Amelia was diagnosed with bone cancer, Mom nursed her until it became too difficult. Amelia moved to a convalescent home, leaving my parents with a deal: to inherit her house and land if they took in her three youngest children, aged seventeen, fourteen, and twelve. The extra property, which was many acres around the homestead, would be sold to pay medical bills. The deed was for $1 with compliance of guardianship.

Times were hard on my folks when I was born. Dad had just started his own business as a machinist, and mom was the bookkeeper, secretary, maid, cook, and chief bottle washer. My brothers resented my mother's half-siblings for coming into the house and causing distractions. But I loved the older kids and considered them my brothers and sister. My crib was in my "sister" Sheryl's room, and for a while I even slept in her bed. The big kids were in Vietnam or going to law school. My sister eloped and left abruptly a month after my eighth birthday. The big brothers graduated from high school when I was in the fourth grade.

We had no faith in our family. There was no discussion of God, Christ, or the Bible. Mom had a bad experience with religion and spat on faith. No bible school for me to learn about Christ or have peers. When the boys left for the Army, Navy, or to work in the shop and live on their own, mom was finally free. I was now alone with her and without interference or intervention from others. At age 10, I became her *relentless* target—the child she resented and ridiculed. The child paraded around in front of her friends. The child that was never comforted when my sister who had raised me left my bed. The child she gossiped about.

My youngest memories consisted of me always being a nuisance. I was always just tolerated until they could put me to bed, or I was quietly distracted. I demanded too much from my mother, who had nothing to give to an irritating, inquisitive child. My siblings were busy scouting, racing jeeps, participating in theater, or working at the shop.

I was home experiencing the war mom called daily life. I learned very young (3-4) to stay out of her way. Be seen and not heard—that was how I stayed out of her ire. I also learned I was not wanted—too demanding of my own way and too needy to be cared after. By the time I could walk, I knew I was too unworthy to be loved by her. By the time I could run, I knew my voice in any situation was not appreciated. My entire existence had to be squashed. I was just too much. I was invisible and needed to stay that way. I learned my place quickly and was reminded of it daily.

There was an open hostility surrounding mom in all things she did and said. She was cold, resentful, and judgmental. She pitted her children against one another. She doled out praise just to suck you in and then punched you in the gut when you let your guard down. Appearance was everything, and reality and truth were things to be feared and hidden. I have very few good memories aside from the ones that involved my brother Blake or sister Sheryl. Since we shared a room, graduating from crib to her bed, I would wait for her to get home from work in the mornings. She rubbed my back and sang "Lemon Tree" to me. She was simply fascinating to me because she was so graceful, loving, and different from mom.

My other brothers were non-existent. They fought, scuffled, and made cutting remarks to each other. One stuttered horribly and was mercilessly teased. One used to trap me on the floor and tickle me until I peed or fought like hell, crying, kicking, and screaming to get away while others watched laughing. Other times they touched when no one was watching. To this day, I can't tolerate tickling or being held down without being triggered.

I never felt safe in my home. I felt on edge, anxious, transparent, and resented. Oppression. Stay small. My mother made it clear that I was not good enough. "That I shouldn't think so highly of myself." Always under her judgment and scrutiny. And to my siblings, I was a spoiled brat. Disinterest in my life, but the same scrutiny on my shortcomings' that mom applied.

Looking back on those years, the most vivid image I have is of Mom's distorted, angry face as she hurled cruel remarks and threats at me. The underlying message was clear: I wasn't worthy of being her daughter. I was a disappointment—expected to accept that verdict, never question it, and keep my shame to myself. Don't embarrass her. Don't ask why. Stay small. Swallow everything down and never let it show.

Dad was different. He cherished me. He worked long hours in the shop, but when he was home, I always had a place in his lap. He told me I could do anything I wanted when I grew up. That I was smart. Capable. My favorite memories involve watching him operate the lathe and work on projects. I would get just close enough, with my oversized welder's mask on, to watch his every move. He took to drawing chalk lines on the floor so I wouldn't get so close that the hot metal sparks burned my shins or put holes in my little socks or dresses. That upset mom. No one wanted to upset mom. But all in all, I have very few memories of this time. Photos show I chased rabbits in my poncho with tights as the new shop was being built. I remember one brother falling off a 30-foot roof. I remember the concern administered to him. But I can't remember which brother it was.

When I was four, pleasing mom became a full-time job. Reading her moods and leaning in or backing away became second nature. I rode my bike to the store to get her cigarettes. I liked this big girl's responsibility, and the payoff was $.50 of penny candy. In 1968, that amounted to a large bag of candy. But most importantly, I did something to please her.

I learned to dust with the grain, fold clothes her way, and set holiday tables just so. Preparing for her bridge club was my joy—until my enthusiasm or the ladies' compliments became too much for mom, and I'd be shut out.

She liked to sit down to a bowl of sunflower seeds. I would pour her a bowl so I could sit by her while she ate them. When I got older, I could have my own, but for the time being, her letting me sit by her was enough. For hours and days on end, I would play in a corner with my

IDENTITY AND IMAGE

Barbies. I made their clothes out of scrap material and saved Jello boxes and made furniture for them. The world of make-believe became my escape. If it wasn't Barbies, it was playing with my Fisher-Price city and airport. I had all the little people, cars, luggage carriers, and tiny suitcases. I'd dream for hours about getting on that airplane and going to fabulous places. Everything was organized, and my imagination took care of the rest.

Oftentimes I played with Lisa. Lisa had been my friend since the age of three. Our brothers had scouted together. We also lived on the same block, eight houses away from one another. She was my sister in arms. She lived the same life, but different. We were each other's rocks from an early age. I would disappear for hours at Lisa's house until dad walked down and called me home. Lisa never wanted to play at my house. Mom made her uncomfortable. No one was ever home at Lisa's, so playing for hours was easy and calm.

31

Mom would tell her friends repeatedly how I played by myself for hours without interrupting her. She bragged about her silent, self-reliant daughter. I wonder if she ever considered that I was actually staying away from her judgment and anger. Why would a little girl play in the furthermost corner of a house with her back turned to the world for days on end?

If I wasn't inside, I would be out playing matchbox cars and marbles or spending hours making mud pies. Mom never checked on me during any of these activities. The point was, I wasn't making her mad if I was busy being silent and playing by myself. If I didn't ask for anything or require anything from her, then I was invisible to her. And I was safe.

My play area would always be neat and tidy. I was not one to take up space. If the call was directed to pick up, I wanted to be able to do it quickly. I was safe not communicating with others. Being left alone became my only concern.

At a young age, my mother took to slapping me across the face in secret when she got upset with me. Before that, it was the red belt with the buckle forward as she or dad called out the number of whips. It was dad and mom, in front of the others, applying discipline. It was out in the open if a child was being disciplined. All the kids got the belt. It didn't seem odd until it did. It was rare until it was not.

I wasn't always the cause of her mood, but I was the only one around to catch her ire. Her slaps were full force, filled with rage, and hurt like hell and left bruises. They would come in succession—one, two, three, and then four. I couldn't cry if I tried. The anger I felt stayed tightly buried within me. I'd stand there letting her blast away.

You ruined your tights—bam.
You are too young to say big words—bam.
Who are you to not eat the food I prepared for you—bam.
You're spoiled, always wanting more—bam.
You're ruining your hair with lemon juice—bam.
You're not appreciative of what I give you—bam.
If abortion had been legal, you wouldn't be here—bam.
You are too stupid to doubt my words—bam.
You'd be nothing without me—bam.
You're a slut. You're getting fat. You're not smart. You're not expected to do much—bam.

THE FARM

My happiest childhood memories were at the farm.

Dad's brother, Uncle Bob, and his wife, Aunt Myrna, had created something of a magical haven out in Huson, Montana. From the moment my bags were unloaded, the weight of my world lifted. I could stay for weeks on end, playing with my cousin Kathleen as if time didn't exist.

We climbed the old barn—despite clear warnings not to—and discovered nests of barn kittens tucked into the hay. I had never held such tiny, vulnerable creatures before. That thrill was unmatched. Every day, I'd ask Kathleen if it was early enough to go gather the chicken eggs; she would simply roll her eyes, already used to the routine, and chuckle at her city cousin. Feeding the horses and cows didn't feel like a chore—it felt like joy.

She was the country mouse, and I was the city mouse.

Kathleen was my closest confident. We told each other our secrets and had nicknames for each other like sisters. Our grandmother, with her careful hands and heart, had crocheted stuffed poodle dolls for just the two of us one Christmas. Kathleen named hers Pierre. I named mine Jock. We carried them everywhere, cradling them like babies. She loved Barbies and mud pies and imaginative games just like I did. We played together for days on end, and we hardly ever disagreed.

The farm was its own kind of playground—one built from nature instead of fences. Uncle Bob made us a zip-line in between two ponderosa trees that we had to use a ladder to grab hold of. Hay bales at our feet stopped our arrival and prompted us to stick our feet out. I learned quickly not to play behind straw, farm equipment, or be mischievous—especially when Uncle Bob was home from his Milwaukee railroad engineering job.

Aunt Myrna was magical. She'd walk us down to the creek and teach us how to float on our backs through the shallow rapids. There was a light in her—a flash of playfulness that made everything feel safe and full of wonder. She trusted us.

Aunt Myrna would head back up to the house and leave Kathleen and me to play by the water, then whistle when lunch was ready or to beckon us home. You could hear her whistle a country mile away. Sometimes she'd surprise us by reappearing in her swimsuit, ready to join the fun because dinner had already been prepared. That level of trust was foreign to me—so was the clarity of her boundaries. She made them known, and I honored them—not out of fear, but because I respected her.

Kathleen and I were both the youngest in our families. She had been born 11 years after her siblings, and I always felt a mirrored connection with her. We were the tagalongs at family gatherings—the "twins" who didn't mind sticking together.

She had an older sister, Aline, who I also cherished deeply. Aline radiated Christ like no one I had ever encountered. She had a voice like an angel. When she sang hymns, your thoughts fell silent. Her words didn't just rise in song—they pierced through to the soul.

My love of gardening was planted during those farm days. Aunt Myrna and Uncle Bob worked the soil side by side, growing a massive, thriving garden. Uncle Bob had built elaborate trellises, and together they canned and jellied whatever the land provided them. All of it was stored in the underground root cellar beneath the kitchen. I loved going down there—it was damp, musty, and earthy.

The steps were steep. You had to wear shoes. It all felt like a secret world.

The food was always good, always enough. The dinner table was never a place of tension or judgment. If I didn't like what was being served, I wasn't punished or scolded. Instead, Aunt Myrna would smile and make me my favorite: sourdough oatmeal pancakes with warm maple syrup. There was no power play. Just kindness.

What I didn't realize then—but understand now—is that their home was grounded in Christ. That side of the Richardson family didn't just *talk* about Jesus; they lived it. Peace was the natural outflow. Joy was ever-present. Comfort wasn't forced—it was freely given.

I remember lying on the floor with Kathleen, our backs pink and sore from the sun, and Aunt Myrna rubbing lotion into our skin. But it wasn't just lotion; she gave us backrubs until we fell asleep. I had never been touched like that—never received such tender, undeserved care.

As I began to stir from that nap, I overheard a conversation between Uncle Bob and Aunt Myrna. She whispered, "I feel so sorry for her because I know she isn't ever loved on like this." And Uncle Bob responded simply, "We can only pray."

That kind of love—the kind you don't have to earn, the kind that sees you, touches you gently, and offers you peace—is the kind of love Christ gives. The farm didn't just give me memories. It gave me glimpses of what it feels like to be held in trust, surrounded by peace, and known without having to perform. It was a foreshadowing of the deeper love I would come to know in Jesus.

Sometimes God plants us in small places so we can experience a bigger truth: that even in a broken world, He is still showing us His heart through the hands and lives of others. That farm was holy ground—not because of the soil or the house, but because of the Spirit that lived within it.

Thank you, LeenKath, for unselfishly sharing your mother with me.

Love, AnneJo

SAYING NO

The kitchen smells like toast, coffee, and cigarettes. It was comforting to me, as that is all I've ever known. Mom drinking her coffee, reading the paper in her pink robe and dad making toast is the most common memory I have. September, age 15, I came out of my room for breakfast dressed all cute for my school day. She took one look at me and her body contorted with rage.

"Who do you think you are to mix and match outfits I bought for you? You ungrateful little bitch, always needing to be so independent." Bam.

I was stunned. She had bought me these clothes. They were all hanging neatly in my closet in my bedroom with the blue walls, blue curtains, blue carpet, and frilly white with blue flowered bedspread. Perfect. Calm. Each night, I'd play dress-up, planning tomorrow's outfit like a private escape. Real-life Barbie, controlling one small piece of my world. I had been making her happy dressing up for her. I thought I was pleasing her. After all, she could see how hard I was trying. I had expressed gratitude and praise for her generosity. But how much can you really do?

My anger rose out of the root of my soul, and I struck back. I snapped inside. "No, mother, not this time. In fact, never again."

My hand slapped her face with as much force as I could muster. I was surprised by the quickness with which I delivered the retaliation. Her eyes said it all. First, I saw fear. Second, unbridled rage. She came at me with another slap, and I caught her hand and twisted it down. I looked her dead in the eyes, and I told her she could never hit me again. I turned and walked out the door.

I sobbed all the way to school. Not because she slapped me, but because I had slapped back. I was ashamed of striking her and at the same time very proud of myself for telling her no. Hitting her felt good. I meant it to hurt. I'd had enough.

That night, there was hell to pay with dad, who lectured me about hitting my mother. She had conveniently not told him about all the other slaps and all the pain she'd inflicted upon me over the years. And I didn't dare tell. She acted like she was the innocent one. Funny—as I recall it now, she made it seem like I had wronged her. She was far from innocent, far from hurt, and far from concerned for my feelings. Yet she sat there all dejected and red-eyed while I received my lecture from dad. It was decided that no one was allowed to slap anyone. Fine by me. She got a taste of my fire and must have not wanted it again because the slapping stopped. I have never slapped another person. It's a chicken-shit thing to do, and all because you can't control your emotions.

Mom slapped because she could. She slapped when she felt she was losing her edge—her control of another.

She slapped sober, which made it more offensive. She slapped to ease her own stress and frustrations of her life. She slapped with rage. She slapped because she liked it.

I wasn't the only one she slapped—but I was probably the only one that struck back.

The one that made the most sense:

"You rejected me as a baby." Bam. The old lady finally said the truth.

LONELINESS

My first major depression came at the age of 17. Odds are I had been in a depressed state for years, but this one was different. It was dark, and suicidal ideations started forming in my mind. The need to escape.

Mom had golfed every day for the past 11 years. As a little girl, she would let me tag along instead of hiring a babysitter. When I got tired, she would let me ride on her golf bag carrier. When I got older, she left me home or insisted I babysit for one of her golfing friends.

The loneliness of being home alone was isolating. But being at home with mom was also stressful. Only at night, when dad was there, was there a feeling of peace. Mom picked on him those nights instead of me. I asked for help to speak with someone, and mom took it personally. That really caused strife. Ultimately, I was not allowed to ask for help from a therapist and was told to buck up. She took me shopping instead of asking questions.

My friends—and ultimately my boyfriends—became my escape. Mom liked it when I wasn't home. She didn't have to worry about having me alone at home. I got my car at 15 as a hand-me-down from my brother, started working fast food jobs at 16, and married at 18 all to get free from her. I took what she gave me and asked for more. Damn right—because I deserved more. If I wasn't allowed to have any emotionality, sympathy, love, or respect, I would certainly have material goods. Her money was her idol. If throwing some of it my way to keep me quiet was the easiest path, she took it.

I started smoking cigarettes and weed at 12 and occasionally drank alcohol when I could manage to buy it. Hanging with friends became all I cared about. I didn't grow up in the same house as my brothers, in which they went scouting or fishing or on family outings. I grew up with dad working and mom golfing. Alone.

I grew up in a resentful household. Mom and dad struggled and argued. The passive hostility was often deafening. Mom was finally free to live her life. Dad was securing our livelihood in the shop. I was the tween they still had responsibility for, standing in the gap.

I was a ripe target. I just needed to be loved. Needed to feel worthy of being loved. And I was so lonely.

On my 16th birthday, a new boyfriend called to officially ask me out. I had friends over at the time to celebrate with cake and ice cream when he rang. The group started singing happy birthday as I spoke on the phone with great exuberance. Looking back, I didn't realize the signs: him drilling me on who was over, all because he heard male voices in the background. When you're 16 and a senior, star athlete calls, you don't ask many questions—and you certainly don't make demands. Little did I know I had stepped into the worst emotional scenario of my life.

He was the son of a dad from the rough part of town. He was a gifted athlete and had a nice, easy presence to him. He had a great laugh, was impossibly good looking, and took his high school popularity, good grades, and athleticism in stride. He made me feel important, protected, and loved. Within three months, he quickly took over my social life, steered my relationships clear of all males (and ultimately girls, too), and subtly guided me away from my parents' influence. He instilled in me the idea that no one would ever love and cherish me like he did, and that he would never hurt me.

Again: I was 16. I was young, easily influenced, untainted by life, and easy pickings for him. On December 22, 1979, three months after we met, he took my virginity. I was all too happy to give it up in a cold camper in his grandfather's backyard. It was uneventful—no surprise given our youth and inexperience. The most telling sign of what was to come was the way he searched for the blanket with my blood on it. He had to find evidence of my broken hymen to ensure I was telling the truth about my innocence. I think that was the only time he felt confident about my level of commitment to him. He reduced me to proof—not a girl to love, but a claim to validate. My blood became the evidence he needed to believe me. That blanket meant more to him than I did. It was the blueprint for control, and I didn't see it yet. I did not have consensual sex again until my honeymoon.

At 16, my life was controlled by someone else. I was married at 18, and I knew I had made a mistake. At 20, I dropped out of college to keep the peace. At 21, I became a mother. This was my childhood.

CHAPTER 3

SCHOOLING

SOCIALITY

School was a conundrum for me. In fact, being in groups of people still is a conundrum to this day. How do you know how to go along with the flow when you've been programmed to believe you are invisible? Mom started me in the first grade when I was four years old. That I had not lost any baby teeth didn't seem to concern her at all. Not surprisingly, I had to repeat first grade. In a snap, I lost my little peer group I had started with and faced public humiliation. Mom said it was because I was so small and not bright enough. Dad just hugged me.

I remember snippets of kindergarten in the basement of a Lutheran Church and my year in my first year only because of Artie, who had been my playmate alongside Lisa walking to school. There is one memory that is vivid in my mind. In 1968 in Missoula, winter was hard, freezing, and full of snow. The school regulations at the time stated that little girls had to wear dresses and boys got to wear trousers.

My dad had just started his business, and with seven mouths to feed, extra cash was tight. I remember going to the fabric store with my mother and selecting patterns and materials for jumpers that created 12 different outfits, all of which my mother sewed. The jumpers included a dress that was long enough to hit the floor when you kneeled on your knees. Thing is, when you got to school, you had to remove your pants (if you were a girl) and put them in a big box that had everyone's snow gear.

The caveat was I had an outdoor, lined, adorable pair of pull-on pants that I could wear walking to school and during recess if it was cold. The idea was appealing because I could walk to school without the horrible leftover, massive, boys blue snow pants. I could look like a girl.

I remember walking into first grade with my new outfits on. I had essentially designed them and sat near my mother while she sewed each and every fancy little pocket and alternating material patchwork. These flourishes made the jumpers interchangeable with all the other tops and bottoms. I was prideful. Exuberant, even. I was pleasing

Lisa and I on first day of school. Circa 1967

my mom with compliments and accolades for her sewing abilities. I sat by her for weeks sewing and encouraging her with ideas. My closeness to her body and creativity was never permitted. She gave me joy, but somehow, I knew mom felt shame. Shame in how little money they had. Shame her daughter would be dressed differently than the JCPenney and Sears catalog store-bought clothes my classmates wore. Shame she had to sew. Shame she wasn't keeping up with her friends. Shame against my dad that he couldn't provide. Anger she was responsible for so many kids. Anger she had to sew at all for this little girl she didn't want.

On a random winter day, my mother got a phone call. She was to come down and speak with the teacher and the principal because of my wardrobe. My mother went into the meeting, and she knew this principal well. The teacher, at least 30 years old, told her I couldn't wear pants to school anymore. My mother, perplexed, said, "Is Joanne not taking off her pants and putting them in the box with the snow clothes before she starts her day?" The teacher replied, "Yes, she is. But I don't like her attitude as she breezes in the door. She has a level of authority when she enters the room in her pants that I find it upsetting."

Now, mom had a lot of personalities, but her first instinct was always to be a fighter. Recounts of her retelling the story were always the same. She said she simply looked at the teacher and told her that her own self-confidence was her problem, and then she cast her eyes on the principal and said, "What are we going to do about this?" The principal replied that these were indeed Missoula County school rules, and that no girls could wear pants at school. My mother looked him in the eyes and said, "Oh, so it's you who enjoys watching little girls' underwear as they twirl on the monkey bars and swing high."

The next day, I was allowed to wear my jumpers to school and decide if I wanted to take my pants off during the day or not. In fact, all the Missoula County schools changed the rules shortly afterwards. The old broad had balls. Even though she wanted me to be invisible, she wanted everyone else to notice me. Even though she had denied all my feelings, she felt entitled and parental when it came to changing rules that protected me. Looking back on this story, which I've heard one million times, makes me wonder what in the world I did as a five-year-old to upset grown adults. Was my desire to dress warm and stylish on my walk to school in my homemade clothes so awful? Was the fact that I essentially designed little costumes at such a tender age so reprehensible that I needed to be knocked down a peg? To be scorned? For my actions to be called into check? Did my personal existence bother everyone? My gosh, even from a young age I had an impeccable fashion sense. At five, I also had confidence that was palpable and upsetting to adults.

The following year we were rich enough to buy store clothes. I asked her to sew again, dreaming of the outfits in my mind. But she said, "We can afford better clothes." I was so disappointed. I loved my clothes—I had so many aspirations for new designs. No one ever made fun of me for my clothes at school. No one, except the adults.

In fifth grade, at the age of nine, in 1972, mom and I both got called in. This time the teacher told her I was bossy. Too independent. I completed projects easily but with an attitude. I didn't respect authority, and other children saw my attitude and copied me. "She tries to lead my class. She rolls her eyes at me when I dress her down. She knows what she's doing. She has no respect for me," this teacher said.

My mother, who could smell the alcohol on this teacher, noticed how her ruddy skin, bright dyed red hair, and orange lipstick clashed with her cigarette-stained teeth. And in that moment, my mother told her she didn't respect her either.

She told her to go get the principal so we could discuss the fact she was teaching children drunk. She told her to leave me alone and never call us in again. She looked at me and said, "Joanne, should we go?" And I said yes.

Then it was the summer of 1977. I was 14. My mom was shopping and found a chic boutique that was going out of business. The selections left were all sizes 00–2. She came home and picked me up and then purchased 15 bags of adult styles. Executive cut blazers, silk blouses, and tailored trousers made of wool, cotton, and linen. Sweater sets, dresses, skirts, silk scarves, and leather belts. It was extravagant of my mother to lavish me in such a way, but I clearly remember some prices on the blazers were as low as $2.99. This was my first shopping experience. I was prideful that my mother made such an effort for me. Her face was happier than mine when we shopped that day. To have her fawn over me in such a way changed how I thought about myself.

That night, I put on a fashion show for my father to help justify my mother's expenses. But still he became very overwhelmed and slightly outraged at my mother's indulgence. These clothes were beautiful. Very adult. Very put together. Perfect on my pre-adolescent figure. I remember leaving the room as my mother was passionately explaining to him what a good deal it was and how little it cost. At the time, I felt ecstatic about having such a wardrobe but ashamed that my father thought I'd been spoiled.

In the end, I took what was offered. She bragged to her friends for months about that sale and her stylish daughter. She paraded me around to her bridge club if I made the mistake of coming home directly after school on bridge day. She told them about the crazy deal she got. Acted like she always treated me well. Like she was the doting mom. But then the act ran stale. Then I was ungrateful and spoiled for having such a wardrobe. She began to criticize me when I intermixed the styles to look like a teenager. She critiqued how I carried myself and my appearances most ruthlessly when I wore just overalls or Levi's 501s and a sweatshirt.

At the age of 16, we were called in one last time. It was my high school homeroom teacher this time. We sat there while the teacher tore down my wardrobe and told mom I walked into class dressed better than all the teachers. She said it was my attempt to exhibit authority and confuse the class about who was in charge. She told mom I needed to dress like a normal teenager. Mom again took my side. She told the teacher her sense of style did, in fact, need some work. "Leave my daughter alone," she said. "If the teacher can't afford a nicer wardrobe than a 16-year-old, then maybe she needs a new job." To my surprise, my mother never mentioned what a good deal she had got on all the clothes.

In retrospect, these teachers should have embraced me. They should have offered me more encouragement. But instead, I repelled them. Take the clothes off—it didn't matter. It was the confidence I exhibited when I walked through my life that unnerved them. They should have allowed the rest of the little girls to lead by my example. They could have endorsed me, but they felt I needed to be knocked down. They should have taken the time to get to know what was under this little girl's chest. They should have offered more supportive ways to enhance my budding leadership and self-confidence. But they didn't like my attitude, didn't like the authority that I demanded as I walked in the door. They didn't see the value in me.

What I didn't realize until years later was that my mom's defense of me had nothing to do with me. Being called in by the teachers gave mom a chance to domineer others and be nasty and controversial. It gave her bragging rights for her own ego—pride to impress all her friends. She might have been right; she might have been wrong. Either way, I was just her pawn. She never asked why I was having issues in school. Why I was having difficulties with those in charge. Or why I felt I needed to look perfect to be accepted.

Getting along with others at school was difficult. I had my pack of Becky, Beth, and Lisa, but not much beyond that. The popular girls didn't like my confidence or my attitude. I wanted to be popular and everyone's friend, but I balked at conforming to their view of how I should act, look, and respond to situations. I didn't like not being invited to places even though my friends were. I wouldn't make myself small to make them more comfortable. If I had other ideas of what we should do or how we could do it, it always fell on deaf ears.

And then there were the boys. The popular boys in my grade didn't like me much better than the girls. Their coolness or athletic performance did not impress me. Trying to fit in became a chore.

Try to be nice.
Be agreeable.
Don't show anyone up.
Don't be super smart.
Take the bait we feed you.
You'll fit in if you're just a face in the crowd.
Don't be yourself if you want friends.

I didn't want to follow any of those rules. It's not that I wouldn't—I couldn't. I didn't think like others. So I followed my own rules. I set my own standards. I went looking to fill a void of rejection so deep it had no limits. I searched in all the wrong places.

I later discovered that embracing a mental illness diagnosis of complex childhood PTSD is peaceful and powerful. I can clearly look back at the course of my life and see trauma markers at all ages. I can see the early abandonment, isolation, emotional/ intimacy abuse, learning to fawn, fighting to be recognized, troubled relationships, reckless behavior, troubled family dynamics, and, most importantly, emotional boundary setting.

I just wish I could have figured it out earlier. But now the coulda, shoulda, and woulda don't control me—my future does.

CHAPTER 4

BROKEN

CONTENT WARNING:
SEXUAL ASSAULT

The following chapter contains a candid and unfiltered account of sexual assault. It explores the emotional, psychological, and spiritual impact of such trauma with raw honesty. While my intent is to speak truthfully about my experience, I recognize that this topic can be deeply painful and triggering for some readers.

If you have experienced sexual violence or are sensitive to this subject, please read with care. If at any point this becomes overwhelming, I encourage you to step away, seek support, and return when you feel ready.

This is not just a story of pain, but of survival, faith, and the power of reclaiming one's voice. You are not alone.

PREDATORS YOU KNOW

....

It is 1980 and I am 16. It's the end of the school picnic at Lolo Hot Springs. A group of friends believing we would always be so young and free. It's a beautiful, fun day filled with swimming, BBQ, and laughter.

My date has been asking to have anal sex for weeks, even though we are not having intercourse. "It's not really sex—you won't get pregnant. It's no big deal," he says. Today he has reached the point of begging, bullying, and shaming me into showing how much I love him. His persistence has intensified to a point where I am visibly shaken. He suggests we take a walk into the woods to have a moment to reconnect.

Once in the woods, he again starts insisting that this is something I must do to prove my commitment to him. He loves me, he says. I start crying, letting him know this is not something I am willing to do. He persists, and I cry harder. In my emotional state, he brings me over to a tree, pulls down my white shorts and undies, spits in his hand, and takes my innocence.

Life stands still. I focus on my little white tennis shoes and white bobby socks. My mind crashes, and I go numb. The crying has stopped. My mind is frozen, suspended in nothingness. The rough motion against the tree bark leaves cuts and bruises on my thighs and hands. I focus on the tree bark. It looks like a puzzle to me—how all the oval bark grows in an endless pattern. I hear the sounds of a forest interrupted by the wail of relief at the moment of ejaculation. Mercifully, I know it is over. My cute little red shirt with red and white heart buttons has debris all over the front. I wipe the blood and jism off my thighs with a few handfuls of pine needles. He soothes my tears, telling me how much he loves me. He tells me that this is our secret. He tells me we are going to be just fine. I believe him.

After the assault, walking hand in hand back to the group, I am in shock, ashamed, and guilty. My knees are trembling, and I have lost all my steady composure. My bright smile is gone. My natural glow is now ashen. One of the senior boys looks at me and says, "How'd you like it, Jo?" He winks. The emotions are crushing. I felt the world fall out from under my feet. I was shattered and so ashamed and embarrassed that his buddies knew. I felt disgraced and mocked. A joke for others' amusement. I am ashamed of my new reputation. Repulsed. My date, standing right by me, sees my reaction to the senior boy and throws the evilest look towards him I have ever seen. I turn and leave. Guess he didn't want me to know that it wasn't because he loved me.

Once home, I frantically wash my blood-stained white shorts with toothpaste in the bathroom sink for fear my mom will see them while doing the laundry. I throw the underwear away. Tell no one. Push the shame down and continue life as normal. Ask mom for a new toothbrush the next morning. Tell her a cold is going around.

ISMs: Wrath. Dismissed. Abandoned. Used. Hated. Disposable. Denial. Shame.

FINDING COMFORT

I did an odd thing that night after my bath. I went in and snuck a pair of my mother's underpants and jammies (which smelled of her perfume and smoke) and laid in bed in a fetal position praying I wouldn't get pregnant. Somehow wearing her scent made me feel comforted. Somehow, I needed my mother's closeness. I think I wore her clothes because I needed her. Because I needed to be held. I needed to feel close to something that reminded me I was still a little girl.

I understood later, what I did that night wasn't odd—it was instinctual. It was the purest attempt a child could make to reclaim safety, to reach for connection in a world that had just shattered. There's no shame in what I did. It's more remarkable that even in the middle of unspeakable trauma, my body and soul *knew* what I needed—*her*. A mother.

I felt dirty for days after; I thought others could see my shame through my clothes. I tightened my mask and went forward.

IN THE SPIRIT OF HOPE

I read an old friend's book[*]—a friend who was also with us that day at Lolo Hot Springs—and in disbelief learned that the same thing had happened to her in the backseat of a car while another senior boy was driving. Her predator,

---

[*] In the Spirit of Hope. Kimberly Hope Anderson. https://a.co/d/46zNDuX

the same boy who winked at me, was more charitable, as he stopped at a convenience store to grab Vaseline. Seems there was a competition of some sort amongst these buddies for the end of the school year.

I was 16. Barely 100 pounds. He was 18 and weighed close to 200 pounds in lean adolescent muscle. I didn't stand a chance. I didn't have a voice. I didn't know pain. I didn't understand life. I didn't know I had a choice. I didn't know any better. I just wanted to be loved. I let him do it. I didn't fight—I didn't walk away. Shame.

I didn't know I could tell. I had no one to tell—and still be safe.

He was the only one that made me feel safe. I was deceived. At 16, he said he loved me. What did he love? I was a broken, sad, unloved, innocent little girl. But boy did I have potential to become trainable. And I was so lonely. So alone. Someone wanted me.

Through an ART session, I relived the moment and all aspects of the trauma associated with it. Through the process, I was able to comfort my young self with adult compassion and acceptance. I told her this shame did not belong to me or her. I was able to love that scared little girl. It was a shame that never belonged to me, but that I had held on to tightly. The guilt belonged to someone else, but it had been hiding in my deepest, darkest memories.

This experience shaped my life for many years. This wasn't the only time in my life I felt broken, but this assault is where my personal value as a woman was destroyed. Or better said, where I gave all my power over to another to keep them loving and wanting me. This is where I learned that love came at a cost. Love meant sacrifices and hostility. Love meant total allegiance to expectations of compliance.

WHAT THE BLOOD DIDN'T TAKE

At Sabino I'd come to understand what happened to me was not love. It was evil disguised as tenderness.

And the silence I was forced to keep was never my shame to bear.

The enemy tried to steal my identity before I even knew who I was.

But God—He saw. He always saw. And He never looked away.

> *"Nothing in all creation is hidden from God's sight."*
> **Hebrews 4:13**

When I laid that memory at the foot of the cross, I didn't pretend it wasn't real.

I named it. I wept it out. I gave it to Jesus piece by piece.

And do you know what He did?

He didn't tell me to forget.

He told me *I was never the one to blame.*

> *"Christ didn't wipe the story clean—He wrote truth through it."*

He didn't wipe the story clean—He wrote *truth* through it.

He showed me that the blood that was taken from me is not the blood that defines me.

His blood is.

And that blood restores what was stolen.

CHAPTER 5

ANOREXIA

CONTENT WARNING: ANOREXIA

The following chapter contains raw and unfiltered reflections on anorexia, severe emotional distress, and the physical and spiritual toll they take. These experiences are shared with honesty and without dilution, capturing the weight of suffering, struggle, and survival.

If you have battled disordered eating or overwhelming distress, please read with care. My intent is not to glorify pain, but to shed light on its reality—and the redemption that follows. If at any point this becomes too heavy, I encourage you to pause, breathe, and return when you're ready.

Above all, this is a testimony of resilience, faith, and the grace that sustains us through even the darkest valleys.

FROZEN DESPERATION

I am rolling in the leaves with my two adorable, toe-headed babies. We are smiling, laughing, throwing leaves in the air, and tackling each other with the pure, honest enthusiasm only conveyed when you are in the presence of joy. Bonner Park, with its thick canopy of trees, is loaded with families on this beautiful spring Sunday. I'm alone with my boys. Hours before, I openly cried in church while I managed a three and one-year-old alone. Worse, I am lonely, sad, and constantly stalked to the point of despair. I am 24. I have a beautifully packed picnic blanket, bright toys, and Tonka trucks for the sand. I pull out the boys' perfectly balanced lunch while I allow myself only grapes, which I know will pass right through me with a handful of laxatives. I weigh 95 pounds. I'm impossibly depressed, oppressed, and nervous as a cat on a roof because I know my husband is cruising around the park and parking just down the street to ensure that no one is speaking to me.

> ISMs: Secrecy. Desperation. Depression.
> Imprisoned. Ashamed. Obsessive thoughts.

MY FIRST REAL SECRET

Anorexia.

Living in active trauma and feeling out of control in every aspect led into my need of self-denial. I was living in a cage someone had placed around me, and I felt hopeless.

Then one day my focus shifted, and weight became my enemy. The thought of success became a project, a goal. Numbing and running to quiet the noise in my head.

I couldn't express my frustration and anger outwardly, so I turned it inward. I am capable. I do have determination. I do have control of my household—and myself.

Being a small girl, it was almost too easy to push away a plate or claim I wasn't hungry. No one suspected the truth. I had babies back-to-back, lost most of the weight, and worked my tail off with the daycare and gardening. I baked constantly, prepared elaborate meals, and took joy in watching others eat. Little did anyone know I rewarded myself with a bite of this or that—but only if I had passed days of brutal mental "tests." Each one harder and harder to maintain. Always tightening, never slipping back. I celebrated each denial of food and loss of a pound as a victory. I felt pride and self-gratitude for each hungry night in bed.

I excelled in cooking wonderful food for my family, daycare, camping adventures, scouting events, or holiday meals. Family or not, I overfed everyone.

I felt pride watching the clock to determine the next bite I had deemed myself worthy of. I was merciless on myself. Merciless.

I allowed myself "meals" only after strict calorie intake and fierce workouts. I granted myself permission to eat a bite only after passing many daily tests. I felt joy feeding my daycare babies and pride for not indulging at McDonald's when I met other moms on play dates. I gardened and mowed the lawn with a push mower in the heat of the day to burn extra calories, not even allowing myself water. That way, I could rest assured knowing nothing was going in, only out. I played games in the backyard and kept my babies and daycare outside activities as much as was possible. Caravans of wagons and bikes to the park, picnics and games, arts and crafts in the backyard, take naps. Have a snack and hit the swings or play toys inside. Nice life from the outside looking in.

When others began to comment, I had dropped to 98 pounds from 131. This just intensified my need to restrict. Whatever "I" was doing was working. For the first time, I felt in control. I felt empowered. I felt defiant. I had a secret. My spouse grew uneasy with the attention I was receiving and asked me—*just once*—to eat. He never brought it up again. I'm not certain how long I would have continued had it not been for my father.

HARD TRUTH

On Easter in 1988, we were all having brunch at the Rocking Horse. It was a day I had allowed myself to eat after weeks of restrictive tests that I had successfully passed. I weighed 93 pounds. I was in a beautiful green pantsuit that showed off my body but still camouflaged the weight loss. Dad and I were in line, and he brought "it" up.

"Joey, you need to start eating," he said, his voice low but firm. The look in his eyes—the pain on his face that gripped me to the core. And in the buffet line.

"Dad don't worry. Look at all this food on my plate—I'm fine," I replied, smiling it off.

He pulled my shoulder.

"Joey," he said, this time looking me dead in the eye. "I know what it looks like and feels like when your body is starving. You start eating—or you will die."

He intentionally patted my bony shoulder as he stepped out of line, and I saw his eyes fill with tears. Tears I never expected. Tears that hit me harder than any words could. The look in his eyes, such pain and such love. Dad was so brave.

That night, lying in bed, I had my first encounter with Christ. I closed my eyes and said a prayer for help. I was praying to leave this world. To be free. Almost immediately, I felt my entire body shudder. It was as though I had turned on a spotlight inside my mind. Warmth. I felt the fragility in every part of me. My ribs resting on my spine with nothing in between—a vision so vivid it felt real. I felt the hunger, the emptiness, the hollowness that had consumed me. It was a terrifying feeling. Truly terrifying. And then comforting of my soul, an awakening. A knowing—a conviction to stop abruptly.

A commitment crossed my lips. I promised to regain my strength and start feeding my body. I was 91 pounds at my lowest. I never again played games with food.

I knew Christ had been there when I called Him. He was always there—just within my grasp. I heard His words, I felt His conviction and changed my diet, but never gave Him any thanks. I just kept walking in shame.

ISM: Pride.

STARVATION, SHAME, AND SURVIVAL: A TRAUMA-INFORMED VIEW OF ANOREXIA NERVOSA

....

Anorexia offers a comforting thought of control over your entire existence. Acceptance. Programmed that a person's weight represented their happiness, restriction represented achievable goals. It represented power. It made me happy and gave me something to look forward to—my own rules.

Eating disorders are rarely about self-obsession; they are a cry for stability and a way to cope with unresolved pain. Starving myself wasn't just about weight—it was about survival. It was about silencing my thoughts, numbing the pain, and creating a barrier between me and the world.

between me and the world. The demon of anorexia wasn't born from seeking vanity; it was born from wrath. My own pride of thinking and thriving on the lies that told me I deserved this. To be small. To be invisible. To be voiceless. The lies that told me I had no worth unless I controlled everything—even my own hunger.

Yes—this way of thinking is that perverse.

> "The demon of anorexia wasn't born from seeking vanity; it was born from wrath. My own pride of thinking and thriving on the lies that told me I deserved this. To be small. To be invisible. To be voiceless. The lies that told me I had no worth unless I controlled everything—even my own hunger."

Trauma and anorexia are like twisted partners in crime. Trauma strips you of control, of safety, of self-worth, leaving you broken and scrambling to survive. Anorexia steps in, offering this illusion of control—counting calories, shrinking your body, exercising to extremes, punishing yourself for existing. It's a coping mechanism that feels like power at first but ends up being another chain. CPTSD puts you in this constant loop of fear, shame, and hypervigilance. You're disconnected from your body, treating it like the enemy because you would do anything to escape the uncomfortableness of your own skin.

By following strict diets, the fear and the circumstances of your life quiets down for a little while. But that's the trick. It doesn't last. Trauma survivors disconnect from their bodies, and anorexia just helps you dissociate even more. Your body becomes the enemy, just like your mind already feels. And the shame? It's like gasoline on a fire. You punish yourself because you don't feel worthy of even being alive. You create this perfect storm of control, perfectionism, and self-hate while your trauma loops in the background like a broken record. You're hypervigilant, trying to control every bite because everything else feels out of control. And the worst part? Your brain and body are so starved they can't even process what's real anymore, so you're stuck in this vicious cycle of self-destruction that feels like survival. Breaking free means facing the trauma and feeding the body at the same time, but until you do, the lies and the loop just keep you there.

CPTSD isn't just about the memories; it's the way they live inside you, hijacking your thoughts, distorting your reality, and convincing you that control equals safety.

If you are in this endless cycle, please step out of it. Find your strength. Ask for help. Believe you need help.

Believe you are worth help.

CHAPTER 6
FEAR

CONTENT WARNING:
SUICIDE AND DEEP EMOTIONAL PAIN.

This chapter contains discussions of suicide, trauma, and deep emotional pain. These topics are presented with honesty and rawness, reflecting real experiences. If you are struggling or find these themes distressing, please take care while reading. You are not alone—if you need support, reach out to a trusted friend, faith leader, or a professional resource.

If you or someone you know is in crisis,
help is available:

📞 National Suicide Prevention Lifeline: 988 (U.S.)

📞 Crisis Text Line: Text HOME to 741741

Your life matters. ♥

DARK WINDOW

I was 33. The boys were sleeping peacefully in their beds. I was in a quiet house as he was out for the evening at a fishing event, and I had 36 pills of Demerol and a full bottle of vodka. I had a hip fracture from a skiing accident a week earlier. It was a yard sale crash that occurred while my friends and I were racing to the lodge for a beer. The mask of happiness of the girls' ski weekend seems far in the distant past.

I stood at the kitchen sink, emptied the pills into my hands, and the tears began to fall. Determined to commit suicide, I began to pray. I asked for forgiveness, asked Christ to keep my babies safe, asked to be allowed to leave this desolate existence, asked to be permitted to experience peace. I stood at the kitchen sink for hours, looking at my reflection in the dark window. I was praying but never expected an answer.

But then I had an infusion of strength. I heard the words, "This, too, shall pass. You are leaving him. You are safe. You are loved. I am here." But more importantly, I felt my mind shift with an atmosphere of love, tranquility and warmth.

I looked down at my hands; they were filled with nothing but white powder. I must have rolled those pills from hand to hand for hours. I turned on the water and washed it all down the sink. I sat at the table and waited for him to get home. It hit me: I could not remember the last time I wanted him home. His mere presence had ruled my life for 18 years and weighed like a caul around my neck. Now I was sitting and waiting for him, feeling light and at peace with my decision. It was divorce, not death, which separated me from him. But it was Christ that made my choices and provided me with strength. Even though I was separate from Christ in my relationship with Him, He was not separate from me. He knew right where to find me.

ISMs: Despair. Worry. Broken. Suicidal ideation. Neglected. Manipulated. Afraid.

Heavenly Virtue: Hope.

EYE OF THE BEHOLDER

At this point, I have $44 to my name and a lot of bills. I had been feeding my boys pancakes for breakfast, lunch, and dinner for a month. I had no staples in the house left. I'm washing clothes with baking soda. I'm scrounging around the house looking for change to buy some milk. It costs $1.17 a gallon and I have $0.90 in my purse. Look by the washing machine. There's always change down there.

I search frantically because I need some milk for the boys. I feel I have no one to turn to—but this is something I can't admit. I find a quarter and a dime encrusted with old laundry soap. I sit down and cry on the cold cement basement floor. I have more than enough.

My basement—I've cried here many times before. It's my space. Unfinished floor joists are visible as well as stud walls with fiberglass insulation showing its fun pink fluff.

I can cry here—no one will find me. No one looks for me down here.

I get ready, drop the boys at my mom's, and tell her I'm going grocery shopping. She is sure I'm failing.

I go to the store looking shiny and beautiful, without a care in the world. Off-white corduroy pants, red sweater, and long blonde hair in a French braid—cascading and looking like a waterfall. It's a small town, and I ran into an old friend. She has boys my age. Her basket is overflowing with food for Christmas dinner. She has treats, meat, eggs, two gallons of milk, cereal, and a beautiful poinsettia. I can't take my eyes off that flower; *I used to have full carts like that. I want a poinsettia for my fireplace. I want food for my pantry. I hope I can feed my children again—like I used to. I want treats for my boys. I want to cook a wonderful dinner for my family. I am humbled at what I have given up to move forward.*

Envy swells within me. I start to cry in the store.

Poor Sue. She thinks I'm crying because I'm sad I'm getting a divorce around Christmas time. She encourages me. She is so kind to me. A moment of compassion. She says things will get better; I am strong. She has no idea my

This is what $44 looks like

boys and I are starving. She doesn't know about the child support guidelines stating that until the divorce is final the father doesn't have to pay support—unless he wants to. She doesn't know he's stalking me in his police cruiser, threatening me and invading my personal space. She can't tell by my appearance that I am hungry, scared, and tormented. I'm too tough to let anyone know that.

I am scared. And I haven't admitted it to myself.

I buy a gallon of milk and drive away.

ISMs: Broken. Worry. Desperation. Pride. Fear. Shame.

… Phooey—resilience in spite of myself.

PROTECTION

When a woman decides to leave an abusive or controlling relationship, the moment she fully breaks away is often the most dangerous. Many don't realize that abuse isn't just physical—it's emotional, psychological, and even institutional. Those who have spent years manipulating through intimidation don't give up easily.

For the abuser, the loss of control feels like an injustice. It's not about love that drives them back into spaces where they no longer belong—it's entitlement. They believe they are owed something, that their presence, their emotions, and their demands still carry weight. To them, consent is irrelevant and boundaries are merely inconveniences. The home, the body, the mind of the one they once claimed as "theirs" should still answer to them. And when they realize that power is slipping away, desperation replaces reason.

In the quiet of the night, she may wake to find a looming shadow, a presence where no one should be behind locked doors. Some men feel entitled to access their former partners, refusing to respect their decision to leave. They use every tool at their disposal—manipulation, intimidation, emotional breakdowns—to reassert control. In that moment, fear is expected. Panic is understandable. Sometimes, strength is found in the unexpected.

She does not react with terror. Instead, she meets the storm with an eerie calm. Not by her own strength, but by Christ's. Where fear should have taken root, there was peace. Where anxiety should have overwhelmed her, there was steadiness. She moves with a certainty that is not her own, because the Lord is her defender. She rises not in panic, but with assurance. She kneels on the bed and opens her arms to offer comfort. Rather than fueling his rage, she does something unpredictable—she disarms him with a presence so steady that he collapses into it. He cries, shakes, and denies reality. His ego, shattered, refuses to accept that his control is slipping away. She soothes him to escape by appeasing him like she has always done.

When morning comes, she does what so many must do—take protective steps. Locks are changed, warnings are issued, law enforcement is notified. The harassment doesn't stop immediately; after all, men who feel entitled to power don't relinquish it without resistance. But she stands firm.

This is how abuse escalates. This is what control looks like.

But this is also what victory looks like.

Abusers don't always strike. Sometimes, they enter your home uninvited. Sometimes, they use emotional outbursts as a weapon just as effective as a clenched fist or a firearm strapped to their belt. They convince themselves that their actions aren't criminal and that their desperation justifies their violations.

But the truth is simple—no one has the right to violate your boundaries. No one has the right to control your decisions. And no one has the right to make you fear for your safety.

Thank God she wasn't afraid. Because Christ was there first.

She was not alone that night. The presence of evil had entered her home, but the presence of God was greater. There is no shadow that can live and loom larger than the Almighty. No entitlement, no manipulation, no force of human will can stand against the power of Christ in a soul that belongs to Him.

So, when the man stood over her, believing he had the right to be there—he was wrong.

When he assumed she would fear him—he was wrong.

When he believed she still belonged to him—he was wrong.

She had already been claimed—she belongs to Christ.

> *"The Lord is my light and my salvation —*
> *whom shall I fear? The Lord is the stronghold of my life —*
> *of whom shall I be afraid?"*
> **Psalm 27:1**

Heavenly Virtue: Justice

FORTITUDE

Fortitude is courage in pain and adversity. It is bravery to escape abuse and bravery to know there is a better way of living. I possessed the fortitude to believe I was worthy of more. I possessed the bravery to lead a better life. A life without insanity, without manipulation and fear.

If you are currently in an abusive relationship, get out. Get help. Find your courage and go make a new life free of abuse. Don't be afraid. Don't consider other ways to get out. Don't stay numb. Don't make excuses for your partner's actions. You and your actions are not the reason for the abuse you're experiencing.

If you are or have been a victim of longtime partner sexual, violent, or emotional abuse, just know that the shame and guilt do not belong to you. You were chosen because your abuser viewed you as strong and confident or weak and vulnerable and someone that needed breaking. The younger and more naive you are, the better. They manipulated you into believing their lies of your shortcomings and overall lack.

Manipulation of your emotions starts early in a relationship and is intended to keep you from thinking clearly. This type of abuser works to break you down bit by bit through means of oppression, possession, jealousy veiled by love, scorn, shame, and clouding or denying your ability to make independent decisions until they own you in their own depraved form of slavery. If you have known them since childhood, the pervasion is more intense because during this time your brain and reactions are still forming patterns of thought surrounding your personal identity.

Abuse of this form just compounds your trauma survival tactics to another level. You just want to be—no, need to be—loved. You don't even know they caught you in their snare until you are in so deep that you can't see a way out. They do this with love bombing and by using your vulnerability and need to be loved and taken care of emotionally to their advantage. They hook you.

They are predators in the worst form.

They mean to cause you pain. They mean to control you because they have low self-esteem and feeding off you is all they live for. It makes them feel better about themselves. Your tears build them up. Your objections exalt their forcefulness over you. It provides them with power they can't gain elsewhere. Without your identity, they don't have one on their own.

"You scare them. They feel your power. They feel your appetite for life, and that terrifies them. That's why they keep you scared, rejected, and walking on eggshells. Their rules will always change and get stricter, even if you are doing everything their way. The game only intensifies when they have you beaten down."

It will not get better. It's not a phase. It's not a one-time thing. It's not their drinking. It's not their job. It's not because they love you and want what's best for you. It is not because of the sad story of their upbringing. It's the way they like it. It makes them feel great. They do not have remorse because they have no empathy for anyone but themselves. You are a pawn. You are their pawn.

Get out. Now.

When you leave, they will try to destroy you. Then they will try to shame you and cast doubt on you even more. They will cut deep and then slash with resentful abandon. You're too stupid to support yourself. Look at you—you don't even have a job. Good luck starving. You won't make it one week without me. No one will ever love you like I do. You are insane. You are unwell. You're sick. It's the Prozac you're taking that's making you think this way. You won't do any better than me. I'm the best you will ever get. You are lucky I even want you. Your friends all agree with me. You're not the girl I married. Just look at you. You are a pitiful excuse for a mother. You will be wined and dined and 69'd, but no one will ever love you.

You're not taking my kids away. I will tell them about you. I will tell them you are a whore. I will tell them you destroyed our family. I will tell them how selfish you are. I will tell them anything I want to make them abandon and hate you. Who are you to leave? Little miss perfect, my ass. I mean, really, take a hard look at yourself. You are pathetic. You are delusional. Who are you to think you can leave me?

Their rage will be worse than ever before. And when that fails, the begging will start. They will write regret-ridden letters, promise to change, plead for another chance.

When you do not relent, they will switch tactics again. You're too stupid to support yourself. You won't make it. No one will ever hire you. You are a horrible person. You are pitiful. And when that does not shake your resolve, their worst fear will be realized—you will leave them behind and thrive without them.

For you, my hope is that you still leave. Strong. Supported by a strength that holds your resolve. Possessing this strength can make you feel alive for the first time in a very long time. It's okay to choose yourself. To put yourself first. It's not selfish. It's not to hurt them. It's simply to actively choose yourself. To choose a better life—one without fear, scrutiny, and mocking. To choose a better life for your children in which they can view their mother as strong and whole. To live in peace and free from a fearful, desolate life.

Do you know why they fight so hard to keep your rotten self from leaving?

It's because all this time, they were afraid you would leave them. They always knew you were better than them. They feared your strength, your resilience, your ability to survive what they threw at you. And now, as you walk away, they know the truth—they were never strong enough to break you. They will spend the rest of their lives blaming you for their failures, trapped in the past while you move forward into the life you deserve.

Well done, my faithful servant.

Make a move now if any of this rings clear. If you recognize the pattern, please seek support. Do it. Make a change. It's called bravery, not weakness. Get out and live the life you've been dreaming of.

> *"Don't give what is holy to unholy people. Don't give pearls to swine! They will trample the pearls, and then turn and attack you."*
>
> **Matthew 7:6**

CHAPTER 7

MOTHERHOOD

HARVESTING

I love planting season! I like to make a yard beautiful and fill it with flowers. I'm feeling low because we have no money to buy plants. There is barely enough money for food, let alone plants.

I bring my babies to a popular home supply retailer and load a cart full of plants to my heart's desire. I am generous and enthusiastic as I encourage the boys to pick out plants.

I smile as I shop and as I push my cart out to my station wagon and fill it. I return the cart with a 100-watt beaming smile. I go home and plant my stolen plants with the boys.

I continued to do this practice to one degree or another until I was saved by Christ. The only thing I have ever stolen.

ISMs: Stealing. Image. Entitled. Total lack of respect. Desire. Temptation. Easy.

BEING A MOTHER

Being a mother has been one of my greatest rewards and heartbreaks. True gifts. All my children are beautiful and special. Heart swelling. My children were knitted in my womb before the world was created, at Christ's hand. Just like me. Just like you. They were ordained to be my children. They ARE of me. I AM of them. I respect the choices they make. But in reality, their choices aren't any more or less important than mine.

Motherhood gave me a chance to rewrite my childhood. To truly love another person without initial rejection. It gave me a chance to feel accepted. It was intoxicating to experience from a trauma standpoint. Love was dangerous. Love always wanted something in return. You had to work for love.

You prepare for them, feel their first kick, and rejoice at their first breath. You know the day, time, weight, inches, and experience of each birth in your heart. Lightning hits your soul when you hold each baby for the first time. I feel the connection and future needs. I feel their hunger.

Maternal instinct kicks in. You nurse and take care of another person like you've never known you could. Careful care and the gentleness of your gift becomes your entire essence. You are fiercely protective and proud of every achievement, from the first attempts at crawling to graduations and marriages. You know the curve of their jaws and their individual gait from the back. You understand their style, intelligence, and physicality well before the age of three. You know their moods by the look in their eyes. You know when they are hurt and when they need a hug. You know when they lie—to you or to others. You know if they are easily frustrated or stubborn, mature or childish in nature. Calm or anxious. Do they throw things, collapse into tears, bite others for control, shut-down with depression, or hold steady in storms? Mothers see it all. Eventually you know the child, but you might not like what you see. You may not like the differences in personality traits and habitual learned behaviors. But you still keep talking and offering wisdom onto each of them differently.

As a mother, you also influence them a great deal. Good or bad, they watch you and learn from you. They see your goodness and ugliness. They see your drive, fight, immediate instinct, friends, and circle of influence. They see who you trust and don't trust. They see your faults and strengths. And they take from you just as hungrily as they did when they nursed.

Sometimes they gorge themselves. They take too much and end up suffering—or take too little and fail to thrive. Give nothing, take what was offered, just as I did with mom. Or they learn fast and hard that you are not each other's cheerleader in all things. They feel your intolerance for differing opinions. When you don't remember things the same way. When you don't respond the same way. When you don't appreciate their teasing. They are experts in deciphering emotions and triggers, and they play into both. They have learned how to praise and tear down.

No two are alike. Different temperaments since birth. Luck of the draw? God-given traits? Nurture or nature. Or is it all deeper than that?

Is a calm or strife-filled pregnancy a consideration in personality? Is an emotionally/physically healthy pregnancy a plus? Can the baby feel the resentment? Can the baby hear the words being said? Does the baby inside me feel my internal struggle? My shame? My cage?

The home where my children were raised was a contradiction. On the outside, it was a charming green house with dark green shutters and an adorable garden—a picture of warmth and stability. But inside, it was a battleground of anger, resentment, jealousy, and selfishness—emotions that seeped into every corner and left scars that no amount of paint or flowers could hide.

When I moved to Dallas in 2002, I left them with their dad. Called his bluff about wanting the boys and ripped the cord and ran. I took his power away by giving it all back to him. Within three months, they had started to choose Texas high schools and colleges to graduate at. No courts, no more threats, no more control over me.

My abandonment caused deep wounds. For this, I am beyond sorrowful ... it wasn't my intention. I was selfish. I hurt a lot of people when I left—my *dad*, mom, friends, and teammates. I ran. I hurt my boys the most. My ex was never going to let me live in peace in Missoula. I had faith I was moving forward. I knew the path I needed to take to get free. The same path I am on today. Lots of bridges crossed. Many more to cover.

GENERATIONAL TRAUMA

I gave my complex trauma to my children. Not because I wanted to. Not because I didn't love them enough to protect them from it. But because trauma doesn't ask for permission—it seeps into the cracks of everything, even love. Even the best intentions.

I wanted to give them everything I had—unconditional love, acceptance, safety. I wanted to be the mother that I had needed, the one who would have fought for me, held me through my storms, and never made me feel like I had to earn her love. I wanted my love to be enough to rewrite my childhood, to rewrite our story. Trauma has its own script, and I was still tangled in it.

My fear, my hypervigilance, my inability to fully trust—it all spilled onto them, whether I spoke it or not. They felt it. They saw it. A mother's fear is a child's first lesson in danger. They lived in an emotional battleground and experienced it daily. They watched how I reacted to the world, how I read between the lines of people's intentions, how I measured a room before I entered it. They learned when to be silent and when to cut. They learned how to anticipate a storm before it hits and create their own.

I taught them strength, but I also taught them survival. There's a difference. Strength is standing tall, rooted in who you are, unwavering. Survival is knowing when to fight and when to run. I had mastered survival. I thought I was teaching them resilience, but really, I was teaching them how to read people's moods before they even spoke. How to brace for rejection before it came. How to guard their hearts with walls so high that love had to prove itself before it could enter.

I see myself in them, and I don't always like what I see. I see this stubbornness that isn't just independence, it's a shield. I see the quick wit that doubles as a weapon. I see the way they struggle to accept love without suspicion, the way they push people away before they can be hurt. I see the fire in them, and the same fire that carried me through my own pain. But I also see the exhaustion of carrying something so heavy, so early.

And the anger. Oh, the anger. Not the kind that erupts. The kind that simmers beneath the surface, waiting for the right trigger, the right betrayal. The kind that just isn't about the moment but about everything that came before it. The kind that remembers. I passed that down, too.

They learned from me how to fight for themselves, but they also learned what it looks like to run. When I left, they learned that love could be abandoned. That love could leave. No matter how much I told them it wasn't about them, no matter how much I tried to make them understand why I had to go, a child doesn't separate the leaving from the left. They only know that one day, I was gone.

I thought I was giving them freedom by leaving. I was. But I was also giving them wounds. I thought I was protecting them from more chaos. I was. But I was also proving their worst fear—that love can walk away.

That's the part that crushes me the most. Not that I left. Not that I had to go. But in doing so, I planted the seed of abandonment in them, the very seed I spent my whole life trying to uproot from myself.

Did I break the cycle, or did I just reshape it into something else? I don't know. Maybe it's both. Maybe trauma never truly leaves a family—it just shifts form. Maybe my leaving just wasn't an escape—it was a wound I knowingly inflicted, one I would spend the rest of my life trying to repair.

But this, I know: I love them. Not perfectly. Not without damage. But I love them with a depth that reaches beyond blood, beyond distance, beyond choices. And if love alone could heal, they would never hurt a day in their lives.

But love isn't always enough. And that is my deepest sorrow.

CANCELED

In today's millennial cancel culture environment, one could say I've been canceled by my youngest sons. Pink slipped. Shown the door. No words. No explosions. No demands. Light switched off.

Five years of silence.

It's been kind of peaceful.

Christ's directive is to live in gratitude for all we have been given. I have been given life. I have been given the opportunity to give life. For that is the charity of God. He gives us our heart's desires and rejoices in our delight. He gave me the right sons. He gave them the right mother.

I thought I was pleasing them by always going over the top in meeting or exceeding their demands. I wanted them to love me. I wanted them to care about me. If they wanted something, they got it. I wanted them to include me. I liked seeing them smile and having fun. I felt material gifts and experiences were better than the gift of myself. I certainly do not impress them. I craved real connection, but they had no interest in my life or thoughts. After all, who was I? I was the one in the family everyone made fun of. The butt of every joke. The one they called only when they needed money or a gift. The one their father despised. I was just trying to be a good mom. Trying to make everything perfect for them and soothe their worries.

A wet noodle, spoiling, overachiever, planner, bending over backwards mother's influence is no better than how I had been raised. Self-abandonment. Actually, it's worse. I thought I could give them the affection and admiration I felt for my father—and I thought it would be reciprocated.

At first, the pain was unbearable. I looked for any flicker of hope, any returned text or call. It seemed I cried for months at the drop of the hat. I would go into the bedroom and smell my youngest's coat that he left behind. I would pull out the baby pictures and cry. I would beg my oldest son to tell me the truth behind their abandonment. I would search for reasons— something, anything. I reached out and realized I'd been blocked. I cried some more.

At Sabino, I realized the truth. It's just another form of emotional abuse. Me crying in pain is all on me. It's all emotionality driven as a weapon—one side to punish, the other side to mourn.

I stopped playing the game once I understood that their silence held no power over me. I am not ashamed. I am not burdened by their departure. I am stronger. I now know what love is, and what love is not.

When I stopped reacting and turned it over to the Lord, I accepted this hardship, and understood this silence is for my own good. I found extreme peace in the situation.

Trials are when the Lord is with you the most.

> *"And we know that God causes everything to work together for the good of those who love God and are called according to his purpose for them."*
>
> **Romans 8:28**

In time, perhaps they will want a mother again …

If my story resonates because you have been cast out as well, I hope my peace can penetrate you. None of us are powerful enough to change the course of time, but we can hold faith that the Lord knows what He's doing.

Heavenly Virtue: Charity

STORY OF THE LOST SON

Life is complex! Especially as a mother.

As I laid next to my mother as she was dying, holding her in my arms, I thought of myself in her womb. It was odd thinking about it laying there, so adult and aware, that I was once inside of her. Purposely created. I pictured myself as a forming baby, and of my birth, I felt gratitude. Love. Appreciation for her contribution.

> "You made all the delicate, inner parts of my body and knit me together in my mother's womb. Thank you for making me so wonderfully complex! Your workmanship is marvelous—and how well I know it. You watched me as I was being formed in inner seclusion, as I was woven together in the dark of the womb. You saw me before I was born. Every day of my life was recorded in your book. Every moment was laid out before a single day had passed."
>
> **Psalm 139:13-16**

I ran from my mother for five years. Never said goodbye when I left Missoula. Silence. It took a lot of strength to do. But I did and I returned when I was ready. Forgiveness is the best gift the Lord gives us. Forgiveness is for yourself, and through Christ's sacrifice He receives His Joy when we accept it. Forgiveness asked for, but not received by others, does not need to hold you in sorrow. Forgiving yourself is a true gift from God as He has forgiven you. That is true charity.

I have often wondered if my sons would return to me as the lost son did to his father and ask for forgiveness—as I did for my mother. But I have also learned that forgiveness must exist even in silence.

The story of the lost son. The prodigal son. The ultimate story of running.

> "A man had two sons. The younger son told his father, "I want my share of your estate now, instead of waiting until you die." So, his father agreed to divide his wealth between his sons. A few days later the younger son packed up all his belongings and took a trip to a distant land, and there he wasted all of his money on wild living.

About that time, his money ran out, a great famine swept over the land, and he began to starve. He persuaded a local farmer to hire him to feed his pigs. The boy became so hungry that even the pods he was feeding the pigs looked good to him. But no one gave him anything. When he finally came to his senses, he said to himself, At home even the hired men have enough food to spare, and here I am dying of hunger! I will go home to my father and say, "Father, I have sinned against both heaven and you, and I'm no longer worthy of being called your son. Please take me on as a hired man."

So, he returned home to his father. And while he was still a long distance away, his father saw him coming. Filled with love and compassion, he ran to his son, embraced him, and kissed him. His son said to him, "Father, I have sinned against both heaven and you, and I'm no longer worthy of being called your son."

But his father said to the servants, "Quick! Bring the finest robe of the house and put it on him. Get the ring for his finger, and sandals for his feet. And kill the calf they have been fattening in the pen. We must celebrate with a feast, for this son of mine was dead and is now returned to life. For he was lost, but now he was found." So, the party began."

Luke 15:11-24

If you're running, know what and who you're running to or running from.

As for me, I have quit running and now stand in strength.

CHAPTER 8

EARLY MISTAKES

SAYING "I DO" AGAIN

1997. I was 34. Looking back at old bridges I've crossed is hard—harder still to forgive myself and others.

I failed myself again. I saw what I wanted, ignored what I didn't, and after one bad marriage, rushed into another. Enter partner #2—the one I never saw coming. He seemed like a savior when I was most vulnerable. I loved him, hoped he'd love me back, and never considered that I couldn't love enough for both of us. I tried. I failed. I wanted to trust him—but I couldn't.

He played me like a fiddle. Love bomber. Pain. Humiliation. Accolades. Praise. Put-downs. Dismissal. Pride. Cheerleader. Encourager. Ridicule. Hatred. He was every contradiction wrapped in a charming package, feeding me just enough love to keep me hooked, then yanking it away to watch me scramble. The would-haves, could-haves, and should-haves still haunt me.

He was five years younger, never married, and swept me off my feet. His nickname was Tattoo because he stood barely over 5 feet tall. He talked about dreams and family and played the part of a perfect partner, but he was running from a loan shark and living with roommates scrambling for rent. I had my own home, a daycare, and stability. He had none of it—but he had me convinced he was my future.

The moment he hooked me? A road trip with my boys. We stopped at a gas station and saw a Jeep full of rowdy guys, laughing, living wild and free. I told him, "I don't blame you if you'd rather be with them." He didn't miss a beat: "I thanked God I'm here with you and the boys." Just like that, I was his. He knew exactly what to say, exactly how to make me feel safe, wanted, and chosen.

I ignored warnings from friends. I set firm boundaries. And yet, within months, we were engaged. Divorced in April, married in June. He and his dogs moved into my home, my life, my world.

Our first year was fun. Then, the truth unraveled. He was a thief. First, his best friend accused him

A father's love

of stealing. Then, bringing home a stolen trailer, welding off its serial numbers, and boldly using it for work—until the rightful owner spotted it. His crime made the local paper. He swore innocence. I wanted to believe him, so I did. But I knew better. I knew the truth. And still, I stayed. I just wanted him to love me, so I loved him all the more.

With his reputation wrecked, he ran to Spokane, WA for work. I stayed, building my banking career. He visited on weekends, then took a job in Texas. Again, I had a choice: stay and divorce or follow him.

I followed. I didn't want to start over. I was afraid of being by myself.

ISM's: Image. Used. Stupid. Deceived. Shame.

IDOLATRY

I am 37. Bright lights, rubber floors, the smell of sweat, sounds of deep, guttural exhales, and the sweet sound of iron clinking together. Ahh. The weight room. What a rush.

I enter, smiling and bubbly. My baseball cap is on backwards and my perfect floppy blonde hair bounces as I strut. I'm wearing black tights with a strategic V in the front to highlight my six-pack abs, my perfectly sculpted back, and my arms, which show every cut of every muscle group budding nicely. I've got a yellow cotton spandex sports bra that amply covers my newly enhanced breasts.

The message is clear: Look at me. Envy me. Lust for me. The feeling of pride, masculinity, strength, and sexuality is all-encompassing. My body is as perfect as it can be. I've pushed myself to perfection and my dedication is now being rewarded with an expose of my training by our local TV station.

And yet, I secretly know I'm not the fittest in the room—that title belongs to a friend of mine who has made bodybuilding their sport. I'm here because of manic determination and a desperate need to belong to something. I've arrived at this level with the help of a very expensive personal trainer, a regimented diet, and verbal praise from my partner. I've finally gained his respect, his approval, and bragging rights. I set out to gain a healthy perspective on exercise and body image. Once again, I've crossed the line and used the sport as a path to self-destruction.

2002 was the last time I picked up a weight. Why would I again? I'd already won in my mind.

> ISMs: Ego. Food. Gluttony. Self-punishment.
> Perfectionism. Control.

CHAPTER 9

EARLY WORK PATH

RESILIENCE

It was 1996, and my divorce had left me with no formal education, no recognized skills, and no financial support—other than my babysitting income. Looking back now, I see that I began using my greatest natural advantage without even realizing it: I could relate to people easily and earn their trust.

As a first step forward, I took a job in a call center doing mindless data entry. It offered one crucial benefit: an opportunity to use a computer for the first time. During the interview, they asked if there was any reason I might not be a good fit. I remember blurting out, "Because I'm divorced." The interview team fell over themselves trying to reassure me that divorce was not a crime. At that moment, I realized how deeply ingrained the shame of divorce was within me. Overcoming that internalized failure complex would take years.

After about seven months of working outside the home, I made my next move. I walked into a downtown travel agency and told the manager I wanted to be a travel agent. I explained that I had no experience—neither good nor bad—and was essentially a ball of clay ready to be molded. Emphasizing my willingness to learn her way, I was hired on the spot and began my journey as a travel agent in my small Montana town.

Yet early lessons came hard: in the third month, my paycheck bounced. The fourth month, it happened again, incurring numerous bank fees that neither the owner nor I could afford. Realizing the instability, I reached out to another agent friend, Kim, and asked her for a job. I quickly noticed my phone didn't ring as often as the other agents', so I asked if I could go out and deliver my cards and travel brochures to surrounding businesses. At the time, I didn't know this was called cold calling. I just knew I was having fun meeting people and introducing myself.

I see sales as solving a puzzle. It makes sense. All the steps work like connected gears. I watched my dad making gears when I was young—bit by bit, one groove after another. It's not a process that can be rushed. Understand and improve the steps to make

First corporate photo

your work productivity better, faster, and easier. See all aspects of a solid outcome. Analyze everything. Whatever you need that outcome to be, work through the plan to make it happen. Perhaps it's a backwards puzzle. I see the outcome before the task has begun. This upsets others who are incapable of seeing things this way. It's not embraced. Or sometimes, thankfully, it is, and that's where I found success.

Six months later, I had brought in 60 new accounts. Soon I was having lunch with "the boss," who had driven 100 miles to meet me. Anticipating a raise, I was shocked when I received just a $.05 hourly increase. Disappointed but not deterred, I left that lunch and walked into a local global Original Equipment Manufacturer (OEM) distributor's shop specializing in water technology equipment. I knew the owner from Gold's Gym, and she had mentioned I should come sell for her. Despite knowing nothing about water treatment, she assured me they would teach me. I started the very next day, straight commission with a small draw. It was a significant leap, but since I had been making only $7.71 an hour—about $1,000 a month—the risk seemed worth taking. This would be a pivotal test of my resilience, as I was now 100% responsible for prospecting, identifying solutions, coordinating installations, and encouraging maintenance contracts. All on my own initiative.

At the travel agency, my former boss was shocked when I quit. She couldn't understand why I'd leave just as I was doing well. In a twist of fate, as I climbed the sales ladder in corporate, I eventually became one of her best clients for the next 10 years—traveling extensively and bringing her plenty of business. Full circle.

Working straight commission with three small boys at home forced me to grow up fast. I remember the desperate feeling settling in my chest as each day passed without a sale. I knocked on doors, phoned reluctant prospects, and prowled new neighborhoods, trying to sell water treatment equipment to homeowners rushing to finish construction. Initially, going door-to-door felt uncomfortable, but my boss, Perry, offered priceless advice: "When they open the door, imagine 100,000 other team members standing behind you. You are not alone. They'll remember the trustworthy, knowledgeable woman at their door, and they will buy from you." Visualizing that strength, I found the courage I needed.

My straightforward, honest delivery and newfound confidence soon paid off. My first paycheck surpassed two months' income from the travel agency. This marked the start of a remarkable trajectory in sales. As I expanded my network, a bank president offered me a position as a private banker. "I know nothing about banking," I told him. He replied that he could teach me banking, but he valued my sales talent and connections. I accepted the job and loved it, studying commercial lending, passing bank tests, and mastering industry jargon. It confirmed what I'd begun to suspect: it didn't matter what I sold—if I understood the sales cycle, I could succeed.

CHAPTER 10

NEW HORIZONS

By 2002, I was in Dallas, job-hunting. I wanted a role with a large territory, heavy travel, the ability to work from home, and generous pay. Simple goals, right? A stroke of luck came when I found a newspaper ad: "Heating, Ventilation, Air-conditioning, Refrigerant (HVAC-R) service sales, no experience needed."

On interview day, I wore my best suit. Waiting for my turn, I watched a nervous young man exit his interview looking defeated. When my turn came, I repeated my tried-and-true pitch: "I know nothing about the industry, but I'm ready to learn from scratch. You can teach me your way."

I felt confident. On the way out, I saw another eager interviewee sitting in the exact spot I had been one hour prior. Without thinking, I reached out my hand, shook his hand, and said, "Hi, I'm Joanne. Good luck in there."

I was later told that the poor boy couldn't muster one complete sentence during his interview. That was the moment I knew I could succeed in this high-pressure industry.

The HVAC job clicked immediately. I devoured equipment courses and sales books, leveraging my love of chemistry and physics to understand the cooling cycle—gas to liquid, pressure to volume. I learned each space needed properly sized equipment, and I didn't shy away from cold-calling businesses. I surveyed rooftops in dress clothes on 100-degree days, unbothered by the strange looks from old-timers who'd never seen a woman in their mechanical rooms. I learned fast: in HVAC and beyond, landing large accounts was more profitable than one-offs. I targeted a restaurant management company with 100 locations, secured them as a client, and joined networking groups to grow my contacts. No airplanes yet, but I felt like I was flying high.

And then it happened: I stumbled upon the largest sale of my life—the Whale.

Beside gaining a career, my time in Dallas also opened my life to unthinkable excesses.

I was open and excited to live a larger life than I had in Montana. I was making money and had a new lease on life. I was open to anything—and my partner was full of suggestions.

FAKE IT 'TILL YOU MAKE IT!
....

When I was offered my first corporate job, I was ecstatic. Then I learned there was a hair follicle drug test on entry to acceptance.

I had been smoking weed regularly the past year to enhance my bodybuilding focus. I was doing workouts at 5:30 a.m., training at lunch, and then back in the gym each evening to cut fat. Cannabis charged my brain, kept me super focused, and tremendously helped manage such a grueling schedule. I did this in secret from my family. I counted backward, and since moving I had not had any weed in over two months. But a hair follicle test goes back much further—it can be more than 180 days. I felt pretty stupid. I confessed to my partner that I may not get this great job as expected. He was surprised but offered me encouragement to try to pass anyway.

I went in and had my hair cut short and bleached platinum blonde. I ordered a special shampoo to try and negate the hair follicle test. Basically, I fried the hell out of what little hair I had left.

I passed and was working the next week. I wasn't sure if I had really passed, and each day just waited for my boss to tell me I had to go. After eight weeks of working at my desk, my boss finally asked if I was ever going to move anything personal into my cubicle. I had been prepared for the day my boss asked me to leave because they found out I faked my drug test; I would only have to pick up my purse and leave without incident. The only reason I passed is I was less than 8% body fat and the drug had nowhere to store itself in my super lean body. Oh, and the high possibility of the grace of God.

ISMs: Dishonesty. Worry. Secrecy. Shame.

MY FIRST WHALE

....

I had been in my position selling HVAC service contracts for three months. I had befriended a kind older sales professional who was helping me carve out my way. I knew nothing about my new trade. All I knew was that the clients needed someone to sell to them, educate them, assure them we had it under control, show them we had heard what they wanted, and then deliver on that promise. At the end of the day, you just had to have accountability.

Let's just say I knew enough to be dangerous.

One day, the service manager dropped a sales lead request that had come from a popular telecommunications provider. It must have made the rounds to all the other salesmen and been rejected as a waste of time before it got to me. I was still very green, so it made sense.

I called the name on the request form and set up a meeting.

I arrived early at what appeared to be an old warehouse. The door was locked, so I sat there buzzing for what seemed an eternity. Finally, a big, boot-wearing, pressed and starched jeans Texan opened the door. He took one look at me—from head to high heels—and let me in. I was in a baby blue suit and a matching cotton dress shirt with delicate flowers. I was smiling and seemingly very anxious to speak with him. He eyed me suspiciously.

He told me what he was looking for and asked if we could deliver. I already knew we could do the work but wondered if my boss would feel the same way. He had 554+ shelter sites in the Dallas area that needed a maintenance contract. Each site was miles from the other either in distance or traffic. Many needed extra security to enter. Our technicians would have to be radio frequency interference (RFI) certified—and they needed water on their trucks to wash coils. His schedule was tight, and the demand was critical.

He expected spare parts for quick repairs and demanded two-hour response times for emergencies. He also said he wanted someone with a brain to anticipate needs and be accountable. On top of all that, he had one of the coyest smiles to go along with his seasoned gruffness. It made me want to work hard for him.

I shared the opportunity in our next sales meeting. I had worked with my old salt dog salesman, and we had created a good price to get the contract while making a profit. I had gotten a list of expected spare parts, and we priced out each truck's needs. On top of that, we'd mapped out a basic maintenance route to show that the job was possible. I worked with the client to truly understand what he needed and wanted. With two service trucks, we estimated we could perform the work in less than three months and then get more tactical on the second and third round of quarterly scheduled visits each year. The number on the contract was almost half a million.

My boss wasn't all that impressed. Lower-paying five-ton unit contracts (also called small equipment—which is what I was hired to sell) were not as profitable as chillers or air handling units (larger equipment and much more complex), which often had more wiggle room than a two-hour response. They wanted me to look for bigger rooftop units than this. Basically, they were saying, "Good work looking into it—but we're not sure we want the work."

I asked my boss to meet the client and then decide.

My client played right into my boss's hand. He told him what was needed and felt we would do a good job. He said, "In fact, I'd like to move forward with formalizing a contract. Yes, Joanne did explain the process. Yes, she did cover that. Yes, that is what I said and how I want the contract written."

"I'd like to meet at a site tomorrow with a few technicians to go over expectations," he said. "Yes, Joanne was straight in setting expectations for two-hour response times and expectations on spare parts. We have already made some adjustments for difficult sites. Yes, I feel she is a good account manager. Yes, I know she just started. She has told me her story."

By this point, my boss figured he had to start selling. He committed to the client on the truck stock and even fibbed and said we would make parts onsite if we needed to. Something about cutting down fan blades? He committed to the training and having water available at each site. He shook the client's hand and skipped out the door.

Within the first month, we were replacing units and fixing exhausted equipment. We were stretching our service techs and leaving some other clients to service this new one. But the money was rolling in. The hotter it got, the more it rolled.

Two months into the contract, I got a call from my client's peer in New Orleans. He wanted the same deal in his region. He had 785+ sites. They were in worse shape than the ones in Dallas because of the saltwater environment. He wanted me on the next plane to discuss. He had heard we were doing a good job.

I went to my boss and told him of the opportunity and asked him for a plane ticket. He looked me directly in the eye and said, "What does the New Orleans branch have to do with the Dallas branch? You work for the Dallas branch."

I wanted to say: "Well, we are a global company with hubs in all major cities and resources to service the entire country. Within two months, we have already made the entire year's contract price in service calls. And we have a high margin. Oh, and we are already considering hiring two more technicians full-time just to service the Dallas account." But I didn't. Instead, I said, "Okay, I understand."

And then I walked to my desk and placed a phone call to a stranger (who is now one of my lifelong friends) and asked for help within our national strategic accounts organization (SAO). I explained to Bob how I had secured the Dallas account. I told him about the margins thus far. I discussed the truck stock and the expectations and then did some rough math on what the Louisiana region would be worth to us. I told him about my district manager's denial and asked him for help. I told him that in the southwest region alone, there were about 3,000+ more sites, and in the U.S. market, there were over 44,000 sites and growing. He asked if he could call me back in 15 minutes because he needed to talk to his boss, Jon—the vice president of strategic accounts. Fifteen minutes later, he called back and said he had booked me an airplane ticket and he would be going with me to the meeting. He advised me to tell my boss I was working outside the office that day. Finally, he said he would see me in New Orleans tomorrow.

We arrived at the airport from our prospective cities, and in the rental car we made our plan. The meeting went well. The new client in the New Orleans region pulled out a white piece of paper and wrote down his expectations, the number of sites we would service, and the expectation of cost. Then he signed it and pushed the paper back to us.

I boarded that plane beaming—not only because we had signed a new deal, but because I felt that, for once, my opinion had been valued. In the days that followed, I stewed over the potential fallout, fully expecting my boss to find out what I had done.

Sure enough, a few days later I got a call from the SAO (Strategic Accounts Organization) VP. He asked me about the strength of the national telecommunications client, the scope of the opportunity, and the structure of the client's regional and senior leadership decision-making. I knew all the answers. At the end of that call, he told me he'd be in Dallas in two days to interview me for his team.

Predictably, my boss was livid. How could I defy him? What gave me the right? In his words, I didn't know a thing about this industry. Who was I to make that call to SAO? That was his call to make, not mine. I was "just" a maintenance salesperson, apparently not worthy of stepping beyond my station. It made for a very frosty atmosphere until my upcoming interview.

When the day of the interview arrived, I stood in the front office next to my furious boss as two VPs walked through the door. I'd prepared for this moment, wearing my best suit: a newly acquired Garfield & Marks marked down to $328 at the Dallas Galleria. It had a six-button vest, cuffed pants, and a single-button, double-breasted jacket—blue and white striped silk-linen blend that screamed corporate professionalism. I paired it with $600,

3 1/2-inch Bally heels—affectionately termed my "bowling shoes." They had patent leather tips and heels in navy blue, soft white kitten leather with dark blue rivets, blue laces with tassels. 1940s flair and modern chic.

Did I have $1,000 to spend on an interview outfit? Yes, I did. By then, I was making more money than I'd ever imagined. My very first corporate salary of $38,000 had once seemed astronomical, and now here I was, able to purchase professional attire with ease. I'd always known how to dress well in Missoula while paying my bills, and I still shopped within my budget—just with more zeros attached.

Having already spoken with Jon, the VP of SAO, I felt relatively comfortable as the meeting began. We started with pleasantries, then the questioning turned to my boss, the district manager, to confirm the profitability and progress of the account. This was his chance to shine, to show our accomplishments. Instead, he couldn't contain his anger. He told the VPs that I didn't know what I was doing, that I was full of myself, uncontrollable, and unworthy of promotion—or even ongoing employment. He claimed I'd lied about my intentions and disobeyed his directives.

I sat there, recalling how just weeks before I had been his golden child, the pride of his district. He had bragged about me and my account to his district and regional peers. Now, he tried to tear me down. Yet I didn't shrink; I sat taller, calmer. That's when it happened. Jon, towering at six feet, stood up and slowly pulled his wallet from his back pocket. He took out a business card, slid it across the table with a single finger, and reintroduced himself to my district manager. He made it clear he was the executive

VP of SAO, overseeing 67% of the company's profits. He stated he believed I was valuable and articulate, and that this opportunity was worth SAO's time—even if my boss and district didn't think so. Then he thanked my boss for his time and dismissed him from the room. Bam! That felt great. Wow.

I started in SAO as soon as the paperwork cleared. But there were some objections to my promotion; one group president and a director had heated discussions and tried to block the transfer. They insisted they had "found" me first, and SAO had no right to poach me. But in the end, SAO won, and I received the largest raise in the company's history. My move from a maintenance service sales specialist in a branch to a national strategic account manager was monumental.

As the New Orleans region went live, we added five more states in the southwest. Within a few years, the entire eastern region joined. In total, about 27,000 additional sites were brought under contract. The company rolled out specially outfitted factory trucks with real water tanks and 200-foot pressure hoses. We had over 900 technicians, branches, and service leaders, and I had seven full-time SAO account management members supporting this one account from the Charlotte headquarters.

During one national sales meeting convention, I discovered an entire 20x40 services display featuring the trucks specially designed for my telecommunication account. I walked past them unsuspectingly, then realized: my vision had been brought to life. Over a thousand of these trucks had been deployed nationwide—all because of the account I had championed.

And who ended up managing my account for the national service organization? My first boss from Dallas. Ironic, to say the least. He never acknowledged all I had accomplished. But I knew the truth: this account, and those trucks, those men and women working existed thanks to my relationships and knack for client magic and pushing. Now I was in a separate corporate division with equal say in the accounts management, owning the client's trust and reaping the benefits. He had doubted me—and I had sold the ultimate whale right under his nose. Well done, dude. You couldn't keep me down.

WORKAHOLIC'S HANDBOOK

Continuing to expand, I targeted their retail stores and began meeting their needs for general maintenance. In a casual conversation with senior client leaders, I learned their biggest headache was that vendors had to travel to each site for everything—HVAC, fire extinguishers, eyewash kits, landscaping, safety lights, you name it. A light bulb switched on in my head.

Admittedly, my specialized technicians grumbled at handling general maintenance, but I didn't care. Work is work, and margins tell all. Thousands of men and women were paid because of this account, and for the next two years, the general maintenance contract produced an insane margin. We were already onsite for HVAC; spending an extra 45 minutes doing general maintenance was pure profit.

Later, after a merger with another large telecommunications company, I landed all the chillers and data centers under contract, further boosting the scope and complexity of our involvement.

When I first joined the strategic accounts group, I felt like a minor league ball player alongside seasoned pros. Jon's team, however, was magical—helpful, supportive, and nurturing of this new service account. I was the sole female SAO manager, the greenest, and the only one with just a high school degree. My new VP was thrilled by the account's growth.

Make no mistake, servicing this contract wasn't easy. In New England, our teams had to use snowmobiles in winter. Muddy springs plagued remote sites where trucks got stuck. Client regional managers wouldn't tolerate even one unserved site, and our teams had to maintain water tanks, spare parts, and meet strict standards. If they failed, the client complained to me, and I passed it down the line.

My toughest critics were district managers. They had little influence on strategic accounts yet had to follow SAO's lead. They knew what I had done in Dallas and felt disrespected. Many tried to bully or intimidate me, accusing me of catering to unrealistic client demands. They claimed I didn't know what I was doing—pure nonsense. I had access to their margins and productivity data. I optimized routes and tech efficiencies, turning their complaints into dust. Their lambasting never lasted long. The accounts' revenue, margins, and growth spoke for themselves, and I kept hustling year after year.

Within six months, my commissions soared. My first commission check hit $17,000, the next quarter was

$37,000, and my year-end bonus dwarfed any amount I'd ever dreamed of earning back in Montana. I traveled constantly—85% of the time—across North America, staying in beautiful hotels, enjoying fine dining, wielding an expense account as needed. The first five years rushed by in a blur of client dinners, executive meetings, corporate retreats, and unforgettable boondoggles.

I remember my first trip to New York City. Strolling down a crowded street in my business suit, computer case in hand, I couldn't stop smiling. Just a few years prior, I'd been running a daycare out of my home in Missoula, Montana.

To keep the account thriving, I organized an eastern seaboard rollout for RFI training. It was summer, and I took my two younger sons with me for a 30-day trip spanning from Rhode Island to Williamsburg, VA. I calculated that staying on the East Coast and renting a car would be cheaper and faster than flying back and forth. Training had to be done before the contract started, and the client was eager to proceed. A private car would pick me up each morning and bring me to the office, where over 30 technicians and telecommunication managers waited for my guidance.

Teaching felt natural. I'd always wanted to be a teacher, and now I was doing it on a grand scale. Every hotel knew I was traveling with my sons and helped arrange tours for them while I worked half-days. Evenings were filled with fabulous dinners, concerts, sports events, a Fourth of July celebration in Philadelphia, visits to historic sites like Gettysburg and other colonial towns, and even comedy clubs in New York. Some thought my sons were too young, but they loved it. They got to "live large" while I got my work done. My boss thanked me for my prudence and asked if my boys had enjoyed themselves.

After seven years, my tenure at this great company ended. A competitor bought us, and the old and new leaders assured us nothing would change—then announced we'd have to re-interview for our jobs. My account was worth millions each year, generating new growth, yet I had to prove myself *again*? The interviews felt like a sham. They offered me a customer service manager position instead of the strategic business development director role I'd held for seven years. A newcomer would fill my spot. It turned out the same president and director who had tried to block my career seven years ago were now in charge—and they wanted a new direction.

I fought back with everything I had. They eventually relented, offering me the senior role I deserved, but I refused. I informed them that accepting their offer would only delay the inevitable—another attempt to push me out through a witch-hunt. No thanks.

In the end, the account I left behind had been an impressive multi-million-dollar annual earner with sky-high margins, year after year. Within a few years of my departure, the account collapsed.

Replacing trust and vision doesn't always yield success.

THE LORD'S PRAYER

For five years, I had built my life in the corporate world without a single thought of my mother. Our last conversation before I left Missoula had been a blowout, and I never said goodbye. If I called home and she answered, I would ask for my dad. It felt freeing to be beyond her influence during this season of growth. Even when I returned to Montana to tend to my rental house, I stayed with friends.

Then, in a moment of deep weariness, I found myself reading my devotional, meditating on The Lord's Prayer:

> *"Our Father in heaven, may your name be honored. May your Kingdom come soon. May your will be done here on earth just as in heaven. Give us our food for today, and forgive us our sins, just as we have forgiven those who have sinned against us. And don't let us lead to temptation, but deliver us from the evil one."*
>
> **Matthew 6:9-13**

The words I had recited countless times suddenly became piercing. "Forgive us our sins, just as we have forgiven those who have sinned against us." It hit me like a weight dropping into my chest. I had to forgive my mother. Not because she asked, not because she deserved it, but because God spoke it into my heart.

Forgiveness wasn't about her. It was about obedience. It was about freedom for myself.

So I booked a flight to Missoula that day.

Early the next morning, I walked through the back door of my parents' house. The first time in five years. My mother sat at the kitchen table in her robe, sipping coffee, reading the newspaper—just as she had done every day for decades. Everything was exactly the same, except for one thing. Me.

She looked up, startled. Maybe it was the red hair, but I think it was more than that. I was different. Confident. Secure. Strong. Convicted.

I sat down across from her, reached for her hands, and said, "I forgive you."

She blinked, confused. "What on earth for?"

I squeezed her hands, then let go. "For exactly that response."

Then I patted her shoulder, kissed her forehead, and left it at that.

After that morning, I was welcome in the house again. My mother admired my career, my salary, the way I carried myself. She told me she had always known I needed a backbone—never once considering that I needed it with her.

We never talked about the years of separation until much later. When we did, she brushed it off as my misunderstanding. I asked for forgiveness again—not because I had wronged her, but because I refused to fight.

Forgiveness is the greatest gift you can give yourself. It doesn't erase the past, nor does it demand reconciliation, but it releases you from the weight of resentment. Christ has already forgiven you—who are you to withhold that same grace from others?

We clutch unforgiveness like a weapon, believing it punishes those who wronged us. But the truth is, it only keeps us bound. The moment I let go, I wasn't proving anything to my mother—I was freeing myself from the pain and listening to God.

Grace is not about fairness. It's about freedom.

And I chose to be free.

Heavenly Virtue: Faith

CHAPTER 11
GLUTTONY

"And now I will lift your skirts so all the earth will see your nakedness and shame. I will cover you with filth and show the world how vile you really are."

Nahum 3:5

Gluttony is overindulgence of something you desire—with a limitless appetite for more. You're just not overindulging to live, but rather living to overindulge.

My next 11 years were filled trying to satisfy my gluttony. Desire for something seeps into your mind, convincing you that you always need more and more and more. When you fill the hole—whether it be too much food, too much shopping, workaholic actions, lustful desires, or vanity—another hole opens that needs to be filled with *more* excess. Gluttony is hard to break free from because it doesn't just take hold of your habits—it takes hold of your heart. It distorts your sense of need, making you a slave to your desires rather than a steward of your soul.

Evil knows how to use our gluttony to its advantage as it watches you. It learns from you. It whispers in your head notions of neediness and stirs up anxiety. You actually feel pain if you do not stuff yourself full of your desires. You convince yourself that you lack, that you are missing something essential; but in truth, you are feeding a hunger that was never meant to be satisfied with things of this world. The more you indulge, the emptier you feel, and that is the deception—because sin will always promise fulfillment while delivering only decay.

I've had my dogs now for four years. They have learned by watching me. They know when I'm ready to get up, when I'm getting ready to go to bed. They know when I'm going out for the day. They know how I lay on the couch and watch TV, how I do yard work, and how I sit at my desk in silence. They also know when the treats come out. Every movement I make, they focus on me. They have become accustomed to my behaviors by watching me and studying me. Treat time is pretty habitual because now they let me know when something is missing. They interrupt my work when I've been ignoring a treat for too long. They call me to action and remind me that I've broken a normal habit. And they always look for more treats. They may not get them, but they test me every day.

Sam I Am got impatient waiting for his treat and sneakily pulled an entire box of milk bones into the backyard. He ate himself sick back there, hiding while he gorged. He started getting sick and then began eating his vomit. Eating the same thing, again and again, made him sick. He had no restraint. No sense of enough. He kept consuming what was destroying him.

This is how sin works. Sin knows your daily routines, desires, and resistance to things we know we should not be stuffing ourselves with. When we are fat and happy and just going along with every desire that we think we need, we feel pretty accomplished. We feel pretty proud of ourselves—whether what we're doing is broadcast for everyone to see, or whether we're keeping it a secret. But it's no secret. The Father above knows your every move, as does Satan. Both of them have been watching you for years.

The question is, who will you serve?

> *"Come to me, all who labor and are heavy laden, and I will give you rest. Take my yoke upon you, and learn from me, for I am gentle and lowly in heart, and you will find rest for your souls. For my yoke is easy, and my burden is light."*
> **Matthew 11:28-30**

I took my independence as a sign to live to my heart's content—taking anything I desired.

CHAPTER 12

LIVING IN BLINDNESS

Trauma has a way of making a home inside you. It rewires the way you think, feel, and crave. It teaches you that survival is about filling the void—quickly, recklessly, and without question. I wasn't chasing joy. I was outrunning pain.

> "Trauma has a way of making a home inside you. It rewires the way you think, feel, and crave. It teaches you that survival is about filling the void— quickly, recklessly, and without question. I wasn't chasing joy. I was outrunning pain."

There's a fine line between indulgence and self-destruction, and I crossed it so many times the edges blurred. I drowned in the temporary highs—sex, shopping, plastic surgery, work—each a different drug, each promising relief, none delivering redemption. But gluttony doesn't satisfy; it devours. It feeds the hunger, never silencing it.

The world might call it excess; I call it proof. Proof that I had wounds too deep for moderation, proof that I would rather numb than feel, proof that I believed—deep down—I was unworthy of real peace. And so, I lived in extremes.

This is not a confession. This is not regret. This is the truth of what happens when trauma teaches you to feast on anything that keeps the past at bay. The confusion of the mind games that sin uses to its advantage.

And the past? It never stops chasing until you stand up and expose it.

ROCK BOTTOM

I've hit rock bottom (or so I think).

View from the floor. Cold, white marble. Very cold, in fact. Very hard as well, but the bruises won't show for a few more days. My eyes and mind are wide open, but my body is frozen in a heap where I fell. Collapsed, more like it—but who's to know but me? I've vomited by the toilet the remains of a very nice steak and more than a few glasses of wine. I spot my pair of Bally's in the corner and am relieved to see that no red-stained vomit hit the shoes.

The room is spinning again. I'm going to be sick. My mind says get up, get some help, but my body is unresponsive. I have never felt so sick. I have never felt so weak or afraid. It hits me like a ton of bricks. I've done it this time, I think. I could very well be dying on this beautiful, albeit vomit-ridden bathroom floor in Miami due to a drug overdose given to me by the handsome Turkish soldier in the bedroom.

It will be my 40th birthday in three hours. Memories of my boys run through my mind. My dad and mom's reaction to hearing of my death in such a manner shames me. My partner is flying in tomorrow to celebrate my successful year. I try to move again, which only results in retching out what is left of my dinner; the remnants oozing down my chin. Shakar (the Turkish boy) yells, "Come on out, Jo. I'm missing your smile!"

ISMs: Business. Spending. Drugs. Alcohol. Sex.
Soul destruction.

MY SECRET KEEPER IS DEAD

I'm packed for the Masters. I'm very excited about this trip as it will be my first time, and I have some very important clients attending as my guests.

But then the phone rings at 2:00 a.m. It's my youngest son. He tells me my best friend Lisa has died. Disbelief and hysterical sobs explode from my broken heart. I just spoke to her six hours ago. We're going to see Sting in a few weeks. We just made plans for an East Coast trip. This can't be real.

I call her in-laws, not caring about the time difference or their own grief. I'm relieved they answer. I'm so upset, all I can say is, "Please tell me it's not true." I'm begging now, please tell me it's not true.

It's true. My childhood secret keeper is dead. I am alone in this world without her. She was my girl. She was my messed-up rock. And now she is gone.

When it happened, I knew my life would forever hold open a void she had once occupied.

My 6:00 a.m. flight to Atlanta just became a death march to Missoula. Suck it up. Be strong. Plan a funeral. Buy food, arrange a reception, and order a cake. Learn her family didn't know her birth date. Write a eulogy and speak of her life. Hug her children. Bury my best friend.

Fly to Myrtle Beach directly after the funeral to drink for four days.

> ISMs: Abandonment. Emotional distress. Dissociation. Self-harm.

SHOPPING

Piano softly playing, fresh flowers, champagne, and the exquisite smell of an upscale boutique. I professionally browse through racks of Escada, St. John, Ellen, Zelda, Ralph, Elle, Tocca, and all the rest of the beautiful "girls and boys." Money is no object. Business suits, silks, wools, shoes, outer coats ... ahhh, ALL of it! Fabric, taper, fit, and flair is all that matters to the two salesclerks whose days I'm about to make. I'm very, very good at this sport. I can spot a perfect piece the second I see it. I can call out an overenthusiastic clerk who thinks she's dealing with an unconfident female or work an experienced one into a fun frenzy of "show me your best." I'll try on the entire store if I so please, and I have no remorse if I simply walk away without buying a thing if my interest suddenly shifts. My figure is hourglass—perfect for good cuts. The thrill as the "yes" pile of precious goods gets bigger and bigger is intense. Nothing, however, can compare to the rush of the final bill, which has become a personal game to me. I liked to "beat that bill" each time I shopped.

>ISMs: Ego. Spending. Control. Adrenaline. Power. Numbing.

Envy takes many forms. It can come as a form of jealousy for another, or envy for self-identity.

When it comes out in the form of jealousy of another, it really sheds light on how you think about yourself. It has nothing to do with the other person—it's all within you. How you feel about yourself when you are around others, or how you compare yourself to others' achievements, is a trap.

My envy of myself had no bounds. I felt pride that I could buy or not buy anything I wanted. I just needed more and more to feel accomplished. I can't recall ever feeling the twinge of jealousy toward another besides Sue's grocery basket. I've never felt jealous of another. If I wanted something, I would accomplish it myself.

QUICK FIX

....

Sitting in a hot bath up to my waist, crying in pain. My first bath in six days. I've had seven Vicodin over the course of the day and three shots of Grey Goose. My body has deep black and red bruises stretching from my stomach to my knees. My eyes are swollen from tears and hidden stitches—ones promising a youthful appearance. My face, neck, and chest are on fire from a deep Obagi blue chemical peel. I have seven perfectly administered holes in my stomach, hips, buttocks, and thighs that serve as a small stainless-steel straw (cannula), which pulls six quarts of body fat from my body. My body used to be perfect, I slipped so far—liposuction is not for the weak. I'm in such pain; I can barely move. Walking is excruciating, sleeping is impossible, thinking about anything but the pain is useless. I heard my partner come home. I am relieved I may get some comfort. Some empathy. Some compassion. He walks into the bathroom, looks at me like I am pitiful (which I am), and scolds me for my intolerance. He tells me to "Toughen up. You were the one that chose this, after all you used to be a bodybuilder, you're used to pain." He leaves me sobbing like a baby in the tub.

My body used to be perfect—he used to be so proud of me.

I felt so alone. So rejected. So devastated. He said yes. He said I should do it. He encouraged me. He brought me to the surgery and stayed like a devoted hubby afterwards in the hospital. He brought me home. And then he abandoned me.

I had traded his pride in my appearance for nothing at all. He liked a version of me that was unattainable. When I drained the tub, the water was pink.

ISMs: Image. Conceit. Ego. Need for perfection. Self-mutilation. Abandoned.

CHAPTER 13

LUST

CONTENT WARNING:
SEXUAL CONTENT, DESPAIR,
AND REDEMPTION

This chapter contains frank depictions of sexual experiences, substance use, emotional despair, and the consequences of living through deep betrayal and brokenness. These stories are told with raw honesty—not to shock, but to reveal the truth of wounded choices and the ache for healing.

You may find parts of this chapter difficult to read. Please approach with care. Step away if needed. Pray for discernment. Return when your spirit feels ready.

This is not a story of shame.

It is a testimony of what God's grace can reach—even in the darkest places.

*L*ust isn't just about sex. It's hunger—raw, desperate, and insatiable. It's the gnawing void left by trauma, a beast that shape-shifts to fit the craving of the moment. It promises power, validation, escape. It wears the faces of desire, obsession, and addiction.

For a trauma survivor, lust is rarely about pleasure. It's about control—taking back what was stolen, proving worth through conquest, mistaking attention for love. It's the high of being wanted, the temporary relief of surrender, the illusion of safety in someone else's arms, hands, and eyes. But no matter how much is taken, given, or chased, it's never enough.

Lust seeps into every corner. It's in the way we seek admiration, the way we dress, the way we throw ourselves into work, ambition, power—anything that lets us feel something other than empty. It's sex, yes. But it's also addiction to the chase, the fantasy, the idea that maybe this time, this person, this moment, will be the one that makes us whole.

But it never is. The aftermath is always the same—shame, disillusionment, the sinking realization that we were never in control at all. Lust tricks us into believing we're the predator when, all along, we were the prey.

This isn't just a story of indulgence. It's a reckoning. A brutal look at what happens when trauma twists desire into something darker—something that consumes rather than fulfills.

And the cost? It always comes due.

GATEWAY DRUG

My partner and I had always shared a very sexual bond. In hindsight, that intimacy is what drove me towards him. Ideas of the sexual depravity of swinging were introduced. My mind grew more and more tantalized by the day. We spoke about it nightly. I entered into a new secret. Every fantasy became fair game.

HEDONISM

View from the balcony: low lights, velvet drapes hanging from 40-foot ceilings, provocative art, a smoky haze, and techno music common in all swinger's clubs. I'm the hostess with the mostest tonight in my girlfriend's club. I took careful care dressing in a provocative little number, one that leaves very little to the imagination. My "job" for the night is to give tours to the newbies, make them feel welcome, and introduce them to others. Loaded on my vices of choice—weed and Grey Goose—I am certainly up for the job. Shades of Grey has nothing on me. I've lived it, learned from it, and I've crossed more lines than anyone could think of. Walking up the stairs in my thigh-high boots and short skirt, I know the view the new bait is getting. (After all, I'm a planner.) In this space, seeking pleasure is currency, and boundaries are made to be crossed.

Every male is fair game, and they are happy to oblige. Like a kid in a candy store, I brazenly approach two men sitting at a table chatting while their partners are gathering drinks. I ask them to follow me, and they scramble to keep up.

> ISMs: Used up. Reckless abandon of my soul. Body sacrifice. Drugs. Alcohol. Empty.

COMPLACENCY

I have proof that my partner has been stealing and cheating. Printed-out, undeniable proof. I thought it would be different this time. This abandonment of trust is the last straw. His mocking attitude, put-downs, and emotional rejection was not enough, I guess, so I sat him down with the new rules: bank accounts are separate from a common house account. I've already set up my direct deposit into a different bank, adjusted my 401K contributions, purchased a whole life policy and transferred funds accordingly. He asks, "Are we getting a divorce?" and I say "No, but I won't be that stupid bitch that wasn't prepared."

That was it. I stayed five more years. I could well afford to go out on my own, but I was afraid. I had never been on my own. I pushed down all the pain, put a smile on my face, and did my own thing. I actively stayed in an abusive relationship. I thought I still loved him. I still had hope in us.

> ISMs: Greed. Gluttony. Work. Not giving a shit. Self-hatred. Complacent. Shame of divorce.
>
> Heavenly Virtue: Prudence.

DEBAUCHERY

Low-mood lights, booze, cigars, strippers, and leather captain chairs surrounded by thick red velvet drapes and ropes that lead to dark plush corners. I'm the only non-stripping woman in this sea of male peers, bosses, reps, suppliers, and senior executives. It's national account meeting time, which is code for gross misconduct and huge expenses. The men, who are pure dogs, are quick to pull out $20s from off-premises ATMs. That way, they can hide from both expenses and spouses and head directly to the corners. Many just expense the experience.

As the drinks get poured heavier and the trash talk enters teenage prompting, soon all the corners are full of waiting lines and voyeur delights. I'm in the mix, accepting lap dances from the girls. And my dances will never quit, for this is the favorite fantasy of men. At least 90% pull out their wallets and 5% openly barter with the girls to come back to their rooms. I can name only two men I never saw accept a dance in a memory bank covering more than 10 years of this particular mayhem. Two out of hundreds—

No, I never slept with a teammate during any of this—I wasn't the target. I was the provoker and prodder. The power I had to make men lower their walls was a high.

ISMs: Power. Lust. Perversion. Stealing.

SEX

....

View from the floor of a black stretch limousine as it swiftly cuts through New York bridges and travels into the city. Ice bucket full of alcohol, and Jerry beside me—my millionaire drug of choice at the moment. I have on a black skirt with tulle underneath the lining to appease corporate sophistication or instantly flirty and fun. Red pageboy suit jacket and black patent four-inch ankle boots. I've just closed a large equipment project, and Jerry has flown into the city to spend a few nights with me while his wife is home in Dallas. Under my suit is a beautiful La Perla ensemble, which I can't wait to show off and he can't wait to take off. We joke about hidden cameras rumored to be in limousines, and I play it up all the more. Forty-five minutes later, as two top-hat-wearing valets open the door, two radiant, beautifully dressed, successful individuals get out looking like they own the Plaza.

> ISMs: Pure Satan-inspired lust. Utter soul destruction. Power. Uneventful. Hollow.

VIEW FROM THE WEB

....

Ahh, perfect. Just perfect. My mirror never lies.

I am unattainable. I am untouchable. I am stunning.

I am out of everyone's league. I know it—and they know it.

I'm that woman you would never see coming—but you can't quit gazing at.

Perfectly tailored suit, light wool cashmere blend for the feel and the movement. Business blue, cut perfectly at the waist, tapered just enough to enhance my breasts. Silk shirt, closed at the second button. I like the feel of silk as he wraps his hands around my waist and kisses my neck.

Boots tonight are Prada. Black patent leather—four inches to increase my presence, to keep my back straight and my figure undeniable.

Overcoat is camel, straight lined, sleek, buttoned to the top with a colorful silk scarf wrapped gracefully around the collar.

Pearl drop diamond earrings, no necklace—I want no distractions. Diamond Rolex, complete with my wedding ring.

But that's not the best part—it's what's underneath that's fun. It adds to the allure. Men are so visual—it's rewarding for my ego.

Extensions are in, hair is fun and fresh. Nails are not too long, not too short—French, of course. Eyelashes are staying in nicely. Makeup is tasteful. One last look—bright red lipstick against pearl white teeth. Brilliant.

I am captivating.

Room key—check. Phone—check. Bottega clutch in hand—check.

Perfect.

Oh so perfect for hunting. He won't know what hit him.

I am a predator.

I hunt when I choose. When I need filling.

I seek whatever I fancy. I take whatever appeals to me. I can spot my victims a mile away. I seek affirmation and a hit of adrenaline. Sex is fun, but it's the control I crave. The absolute power of my enchantment—that is the ultimate drug, the power of self-satisfaction.

My prey is typically businessmen. Important in their own minds—big smiles, confidence oozing out of them, quick and witty or quiet and complex. Intelligent. I like intelligence. Married or not. My needs will be met.

Slide in next to him, order a drink, open a tab. Smile.

I'm a pro at playful banter, flattery, and smooth conversation. I'm a pro at bringing out deep and personal thoughts and offering wise, heartfelt replies. But ultimately, I'm a successful businesswoman with a trove of great stories. I can relate to men as their peer. I'm amongst a sea of men who haven't been mentally provoked in a very long time—or ever. Such easy pickings. Simpletons.

Whether he's with a group or alone in the city, it doesn't matter. He's mine if I want him. I never miss my mark. It's a game.

I let him think he is the pursuer. I let him think he is the most fascinating man on earth. Drink, food, laughter, then his hand swipes my knee. Game, set, match. Few have escaped my web. I always paid the tab regardless of cost. I owned them. I was in complete control. My terms, my choice.

My favorite moment is when they see what's underneath the buttoned-up coat. It's laughable how easy it is to charm a snake.

> ISMs: Wrath. Sex. Gluttony. Soul extinction.
> Despair. Numb. Starving inside.

REPENTANCE

This was me a period of years ago. My secret.

This was how I saw myself. This was my other life. This was my drug of choice at the time. I was trying to fill a void I've felt my entire life. I was living in a million-dollar house, owned fancy cars, went on elaborate vacations, and was a dutiful wife and corporate-America-businesswoman making more in a month than I'd ever thought I would make in a year. I was respected in my field and trusted by clients and coworkers. I had a beautiful family, good friends, great sons, and a smile that never left my face.

But under that glossy image, I was utterly broken and morally bankrupt. I was feeding myself with anything I could find to drive out feelings of loneliness, unworthiness, rejection, and self-loathing. I was living in a grave of despair. Utter darkness.

As for me, I was driven to such lewd behavior because I felt rejected. Unloved. Not just rejected from my partner, but rejected from feeling accomplished at work, rejected because of my gender, intelligence, and fortitude. Rejected from feeling like I wasn't a good enough mother, daughter, sister, friend, or worker—rejected from any feeling at all because I wasn't enough in any situation. No matter how hard I tried, my tank was always empty. I was broken to the point of shattered glass—and I was constantly seeking…

Perhaps you're thinking "oh my!" I have done some of the things you mentioned, but I'm not that bad. I'm better than that. I'm good. I don't seek what I need like that.

I was good too. At hiding. Like my abusers were. At hiding my true intentions in plain sight to the prey. A shiny star. A challenge and a conquest. I was phenomenal at multitasking and plotting to get my fix—whatever that fix may have been. At believing things would get better, just one more time. And just one more time after that. Just one more intentional cut to my underbelly. If others in my life would just fill me up instead of tearing me down, I wouldn't feel the need to fill that bottomless void within me. Insatiable.

FOLLY

There is a story in Proverbs 7 about immoral, adulterous women. (I wouldn't limit this warning to just women, as men very often play this game without thought, shame, or ridicule.) This story goes like so:

> *"I was looking out the window of my house the other day and saw a simple-minded young man who lacked common sense. He was crossing the street near the end of the house of the immoral woman. He was strolling down the path by her house at twilight, as the day was fading, and the dark of night set in. The woman approached him, dressed seductively and sly of heart. She was a brash, rebellious type who never stays at home. She's often seen in the streets and market soliciting at every corner. She threw her arms around him and kissed him, and with a brazen look she said, "I've offered my sacrifices, and just finished my vows. It's you I was looking for! I came out to find you, and here you are! My bed is spread with colored sheets of the finest linen imported from Egypt. I've perfumed my bed with myrrh, aloe and cinnamon. Come, let's drink our fill of love until*

morning. Let's enjoy each other's caresses, for my husband is not home. He's away on a long trip. He has taken a full wallet of money with him, and he won't return until later in the month." So she seduced him with her pretty speech. With her flattery, she enticed him. He followed her at once, like an ox going to slaughter, or like a trapped stag awaiting the arrow that would pierce his heart. He was like a bird flying into a snare, little knowing it would cost him his life. Listen to me, my sons, and pay attention to my words. Don't let your heart stray away towards her. Don't wander down her wayward path for she has been the ruin of many, numerous men have been her victims. Her house is the road to the grave. Her bedroom is the den of death."

Proverbs 7:6-27

How about this one?

"The woman named Folly is loud and brash. She is ignorant and doesn't even know it. She sits in her doorway on the heights overlooking the city. She calls out to men going by who are minding their own business. "Come home with me," she urges the simple. To those without good judgment, she says, "Stolen water is refreshing, food eaten in secret tastes the best!" But the men didn't realize that her former guests were now in the grave."

Proverbs 9:13-17

As you can see, what I was doing was certainly nothing new. What I was doing, and seeking, became a reality well before any of us were born. What I was doing has been here since the beginning of time and will be here until the end of it. If my sexual abuse of my body exposed some feelings or actions you have in your life, those aren't new either.

Lust must have its way. Godly love is patient. Lust doesn't care about another; it only cares to have its desires filled. Lust drives you to extreme promiscuity. The desire is urgent—it must be *now*. It is a spell. A web of deceit. Worse yet, it's just a game. Who cares if you win or lose? Sin always wins by hitting the bullseye.

I hold a deep sadness for the men that met me during this time. I didn't care about them. I didn't even know them. They were pawns in my sick little game of power. They should have ran away screaming. But instead, they were flattered.

I was blinded by my own gaze. I was naïve in my belief that I was in control. After all, I could stop anytime I wanted—right? Not a chance.

When I read these scriptures for the first time, I sobbed and sobbed, repenting my actions. I was so shameful admitting to Christ what I had done and who I had become. The pain I felt for the men I lured to my bed was immense. When I *understood* the scripture for the first time, I sobbed in gratefulness of Christ's love, for He had offered me mercy. Undeserved grace. No works here to boast about.

I was Folly. That woman was me.

> *"God saved you by his special favor when you believed. And you can't take credit for this, it is a gift from God. Salvation is not a reward for the good things we have done, so none of us can boast about it. For we are God's masterpiece. He created us anew in Christ Jesus, so that we can do the good things he planned for us long ago."*
>
> **Ephesians 2:8-10**

It's time to get real. Time to dig deep. Time to face yourself and shed any shame. If any of this is true for you, it's time to be content with your accused shame and move toward the truth of your situation. Time to make some changes. Ask for help. I sure wish I would have.

CHAPTER 14

WRATH

CONTENT WARNING:
ABORTION, DESPAIR,
AND REDEMPTION

The following chapter contains a raw and honest discussion about abortion, including its emotional, spiritual, and personal impact. This chapter is not intended to judge or condemn, but to wrestle with the weight of this experience and the journey of healing that follows.

I recognize that this topic is deeply sensitive and may be painful for some readers. Please read with care, and if at any point it becomes overwhelming, I encourage you to pause, pray, and return when you feel ready.

Above all, this is a story of truth, grace, and the redemption that only God can bring.

UNNAMED

....

2007. I am 44 and pregnant. Unbelievable. Five pregnancy tests, all torn apart in some hotel in Kansas City. All positive within seconds. Stunned. Flabbergasted, really. Between us we hadn't used birth control religiously in years. Not because we were trying for a child, but because after years of being casual about birth control, we assumed he shot blanks. Guess the joke was on me.

That night, I met an old colleague to catch up. I was dying inside but couldn't—wouldn't—share. Not that he wouldn't have accepted me.

I was afraid. Prideful. In shock. In denial.

I called my partner and told him. He asked how it happened. Lack of birth control, bud. Elimination of suspects. Nothing else. No one else. Yours. Mine. Not ours.

By this time, our marriage was just a show. Smoke and mirrors. Happy looking, successful, beautiful couple. What a farce. What a shame. Not happening. Empty. Dead.

I recall praying. I recall crying. I recall the decision to call the clinic and make an appointment to terminate the pregnancy. I called my mom and gained her support. I distinctly recall it was my choice. I did not consult my partner on the topic at all. Some regrets live on, and some don't. This was one that didn't. I simply was not going to get myself into any situation that would force me to be dependent on or intertwined with his. I couldn't trust him with anything. I certainly could not depend on him to be a father, and I was not going to do it myself. I did not feel connected to this child.

As I walked into the clinic in Dallas, an anti-abortion rally was being held outside its doors. I saw they were approaching the young, scared, pregnant women entering and engaging them in persuasive conversation. Not me. I stood tall, dressed in my business clothes, and walked through that crowd like I was going on a sales call. Confident, scared to the root of my soul, ashamed, assured my decision was accurate. I'm pretty certain none of them expected a 44-year-old client.

Once inside, I was at peace. The waiting room was full of such young, scared girls—some with boyfriends, others with mothers or sisters, and some alone, just like me. I realized as we sat there waiting for our names to be called that we all had such different paths and stories that had led us to the exact same point. I somehow found peace in that. Maybe it was the birds of a feather thing.

"Joanne," my name was called, and I slipped into my gown. All the nurses were so kind, gentle, and soft-spoken. The furniture, beds, and the clinic itself were threadbare and reminiscent of the 1960s. But to me, it felt like a comfortable old blanket. Like grandma's house. Not fancy, but spotless and full of love and peace. I felt comfortable, safe, and unjudged. The realization of seeing the tiny heartbeat and having the nurse assure me that I was, in fact, six weeks along was surreal. I could identify the night of conception. Oddly, I recalled thinking that night that we should use birth control. I had let my guard down.

Next the doctor came in. He was in his 60s and looked like he was tired of fighting the daily fight to perform procedures that were firmly protected by our constitution in 2007. He asked me why I was thinking about an abortion. I clearly explained that I did not have a spouse who gave two cents about me, how much I loved my career, and how I could not afford to give my job up to raise this child. I told him I had three beautiful adult sons, and that I was done with child rearing. I told him I had based my decision on logic and knowledge, not fear.

While recuperating in a warm, dark, soft, music-playing wardroom, I felt at absolute peace. Nestled into my blankies alone with my thoughts, I knew I had made the right decision. Six hours later, I got up, dressed, and walked out the door into the same crowd I'd walked past seven hours earlier. They now knew. I knew they knew. Again I strode past them, my head high, my eyes raised, confident that I had taken control of the rights women own over their own bodies and minds.

ISMs: Self-hatred. Broken. Pride. Desperation. Murder.

Heavenly Virtue: Faith

> "Thou shalt not Kill."
>
> **Exodus 20:13**

ABORTION

....

Undeserved grace and reverence for Christ. Even now, recalling that afternoon that changed two lives, I do not live in regret of my choice. What I regret is the way I was living and the mindset I once held. At the time of my abortion, I was encased in sin but did not recognize it. I thought I was in charge, morally sovereign over my fate. That was the truth of my situation at the time. Fear was my driver; ignorance was my shame.

Later, I found release from shame and regret by reading the Word and understanding Christ's ways. Scripture helped me comprehend my former choices. This was not an act of free will; it was an act in defiance of Christ's will. Overwhelmed by Christ's love and the sacrifices He made for my arrogance and ignorance, I wept. The Holy Spirit forced me to examine myself honestly.

Our Lord took many whips and beatings to finally be brought to the cross. Once there, He endured pain that is inhuman to finally die to this world.

The weight of that realization broke me. It wasn't just an acknowledgment of wrongdoing; it was a moment of profound understanding. I clearly saw my choices, the suffering I had caused, and the immense love Christ had for me despite my rebellion. This truth was a gift. I saw it clearly.

I sobbed knowing how many whips I had caused my Christ. All of my wrong-doings—everything I did before was a cut, a whip, a spear, a thorn, or an accusation and mockery right into His Holy Body. The way I had been living had caused Him so much pain. But He took it for me.

Through reading the Bible, I discovered a roadmap for faithful living, even for someone who had been a wretch. The more I read, the more I learned to respect Christ. "Fear of Christ" and "Respect of Christ" mean the same thing: to stand in awe of His power and His authority to grant grace or discipline. He is a jealous God demanding full allegiance. Utter respect is due for His endurance on the cross to bring His chosen children home. He leaves the 99 sheep to find the one lost sheep—that is how involved He is in your destiny. We should indeed fear Christ, knowing He alone decides our salvation.

Looking back, I realize the magnitude of Christ's mercy in my life. I was not just a person making a poor decision; I was a sinner living apart from God, blind to His truth. Yet, even then, He did not abandon me. His love, patience, and forgiveness were waiting for me to turn to Him. It is humbling to think that the Creator of the universe cared enough to pursue me, even in my darkest moments.

I do not regret my decision to abort my child. And I do not have time for regrets from the time I was dead to Christ. The Lord knew I would face the decision before I was born. That doesn't mean it was His desired path for me, but He knew I'd choose it, as He is omnipresent and all-knowing. He understood every aspect of my life from my mother's womb to this very moment. He granted me undeserved mercy.

This is my story of abortion. My story of murder. This is my truth in finding resolve and healing.

I'm comfortable standing alone in my story of grace and giving praise—but many aren't so comfortable exposing their truth.

"To deny a woman's feelings is to deny her humanity and the uniqueness of her journey to salvation."

To deny a woman's feelings is to deny her humanity and the uniqueness of her journey to salvation.

CHAPTER 15

GREED

THE PRICE OF WANTING MORE

Greed isn't just about money. It's about never feeling like enough—never having enough, never being enough. It's the hunger for validation, the desperation for status, the need to prove to the world—and to ourselves—that we matter. Trauma plants that seed early. It whispers that survival depends on having more, on being more. And so, we chase.

> "Greed isn't just about money. It's about never feeling like enough—never having enough, never being enough. It's the hunger for validation, the desperation for status, the need to prove to the world—and to ourselves—that we matter. Trauma plants that seed early. It whispers that survival depends on having more, on being more. And so, we chase."

Idolatry creeps in quietly. It's in the things we worship—success, beauty, power, people—anything that promises to give us the worth we were denied. We shape-shift, mold ourselves into whatever the moment demands, wearing masks so perfectly fitted that we forget what's underneath. We play the roles—devoted spouse, overachiever, the one who always has it together—because if people saw the truth and the cracks, we might lose everything.

> "No title, no lover, no bank account balance will ever be enough to outrun the voice inside whispering: If they really knew you, they wouldn't stay."

But the more we chase, the emptier we become. No title, no lover, no bank account balance will ever be enough to outrun the voice inside whispering: If they really knew you, they wouldn't stay.

So, we hide. We perform. We gather things, people, and admiration hoping they will finally quiet the storm inside. But they don't. They can't. Because greed and idolatry don't fill the void; they deepen it. The masks grow heavier. The lies become harder to keep straight.

And then one day, we look in the mirror and don't recognize the person staring back.

This is the cost of wanting more. The illusion of control, the slow erosion of self. And in the end, the only question that remains is: When everything is stripped away, when the masks fall, who are we really?

GLASS HOUSES

Looking for houses in Denver. Or rather: looking for a house to rent in Denver. Between us, we make close to $400K, but we don't have a pot to piss in together and I don't feel like sharing. This one's too small. That one's not a home. I don't want a bachelor pad, especially when I'm the one paying the rent. This one is perfect. Grand staircase. Three stories. Windows everywhere. Settled deep in the mountains of Golden, Colorado. Gourmet kitchen. Sauna. Steam room. Complete bar. Fireplaces everywhere. Four acres of beauty. Private drive. Million-dollar price tag. I can rent the home of my dreams for $3,400. I make $16K net a month. Sold. No waiting, no saving, no patience, no diligence to have my dream house. No commitment with my partner.

I know this is smoke and mirrors, a stage set for a role I've been rehearsing. I know my motives are tangled—part pride, part ego, part raw hunger to be seen as successful. But right now, none of that matters. I'll settle into this illusion, become the lord and lady of a manner that isn't mine, and pretend that everything we lack can be replaced with space, luxury, and the sweet lie of perfect appearances.

ISMs: Greed. Pride. Ego. Image. Money. Identity. Idolatry.

WORK, WORK, WORK

My career continued to excel within the walls of the Fortune 100 OEMs. My next roles were similar—they included relationship building and influencing the mechanical and technology offerings to global clients.

Mostly I just got to be me. See the solution, map out a plan, and offer it up to the client. No matter what I was selling, I saw the path.

In one role, the new boss was assigning vertical markets to the new team. He made up circular placards of all the verticals and was having a great time holding up each sign and asking the team who felt what vertical would fit them best. He looked at me and threw me the hospitality vertical. "This one is yours," he said. I had assumed he would put me in the telecommunications or the data center role, but he felt I would be perfectly suited to hospitality—especially with my personality and the fact that I was always hospitable and smiley.

This role was exciting. For the first time, I was selling large gear: 1,000-ton chillers, controls, massive air handling units, thousands of RTUs, and a new product they were bringing to market called variable refrigerant volume (VRV) systems. I even got to explore projects with geothermal and diesel generators.

Also very exciting was that I had to forge new relationships with new clients and company manufacturing reps. One of my favorite parts of selling has always been building relationships based on trust. I started contacting all the brand executives, ownership groups, respected engineering groups, and design firms. I dug in and quickly came to understand how this vertical buys, requests bids, and releases awards. I visited as many cities as I could to work with our manufacturers' reps' principles to gain their support for the vertical. I wasn't just selling services—I was selling all the offerings we manufactured. Huge return-on-investment (ROI) mechanical projects were my specialty. In these global companies, the structures are the new salespeople, and the service groups fight like cats and dogs because they are all pitted against each other on how their separate books of business hit the bottom line.

I didn't care. New sales were now teamed with service on all jobs. It made no sense to me to sell chillers and not have my company service team install them. At first, the squabbling was a lot, because the service department thought I was telling them how to run their business, and the new sales folks were not used to the service folks being in client meetings and having opinions.

But after the first two successful projects, everyone got on the same page. A tremendous team, all working together and supporting our clients, had been forged.

We started crushing it. One global hospitality brand in particular loved the new approach. I had executives sending me all their property improvement plan (PIP) lists that needed new chillers or large mechanical upgrades. I had successfully cut out the general contractor middleman, which allowed brands and owners to purchase directly from the manufacturer rep. I had grown tired of large construction companies buying our chillers at a good price and marking them up 20% just because it was "standard" practice.

I was able to get the brands to accept new equipment into their brand standards so our new equipment could be sold in the Americas. I set up large maintenance contracts and put together numerous platforms that would save money for our clients, reduce frustration on their end, and allow our equipment and services to make decent profits.

I was having a blast.

The new boss had indeed put together a magical team. I wasn't the only woman—there was one other—but she didn't last long in the overseas culture. Something to do with the way she dressed, as I heard it. We were all friends on this team, and we covered each other's backs and offered support happily. The new boss, it turned out, was a rip-roaring drunk at the time. Work hard, play hard—that was his motto. I found myself right back in the same role I'd had for seven years. Once again, I had an unlimited expense account and nearly unlimited authority to manage my vertical exactly as I chose, with 100% autonomy. For me, these were perfect working conditions to be successful.

Plus, the team was a family. We were all friends in and out of work engagements. We golfed together. Invited each other to our homes to share adventures. Taught each other to ski. And often called each other to shoot the breeze. True greatness was created.

THE FISH-A-ROO

One work boondoggle proved to be a game changer for me as a woman. For years before I'd started, the company held an annual outing called the "Fish-a-Roo" at Lake Winnibigoshish in Minnesota. It was a three-day event where some of the top salesmen could invite their clients to go fishing. When the registration came out, I was sure to get my clients and myself a spot early.

Weeks passed without me hearing any of the details of the trip, meaning I couldn't get back to my clients. So, I started inquiring. Marketing didn't seem to have any answers, so I asked my vice president. About 10 days later, I got a call from the new boss asking me how bad I wanted to attend the event. I told him my clients were planning on it, and I would certainly make myself available. And then I heard the frustration and exhaustion in his voice as he told me, "It's going to prove difficult." I said, "Why would it be difficult? I'm from Montana and I certainly know how to fish." He said a woman had never attended the camp. He also mentioned that the cabins housed three to four individuals apiece, my being in a cabin with men would cause an issue, and there were not enough cabins for me to have one by myself. I immediately told him that if neither my husband nor my father had an issue with me sleeping in a private room in a cabin with other men, then he, the company, marketing, and HR shouldn't either.

I hadn't realized it, but for weeks HR, marketing, and leadership had been stewing about my registration. Even the CEO and chairman knew about the request. When my new boss called and told them my response, there were fireworks. It was relayed to me later by the executive vice president of HR that they said it would not be allowed. "Tell her no." The executive HR was also a woman. She told me she looked at them and said, "If you don't let this girl go fishing, you can write the zeros on the check." She also told them that I was a water walker and that they would not want the issues I would bring down upon them if they didn't allow me to go. It was pure sexual and gender discrimination. And six months later, that female HR leader was gone.

I went on that little Fish-a-Roo. I brought an impressive client and a rep, and we all had a wonderful time. I even caught the largest fish for the award, which the leader of the Fish-a-Roo, who had objected to my attendance, told me I should give it to my client. And I did, happily.

Don't tell a Montana girl she can't fish. Don't tell me I can't go somewhere men are invited—but I'm not—because I am a woman.

The HR lead was correct. I would not have sat by and taken that answer without a fight—even if it meant losing my job.

My first year there, I had a quota of $2 million that I crushed. To get commissions, you had to earn nearly double your quota on this new pay structure. The second year, they raised my quota to $4 million because that was what I'd sold my first year. The third year, I had to sell over $8 million to make a decent commission. This continued year after year—them raising my quota just for me to make the same amount of money as I had the first few years in commissions.

When I realized that new salesmen entering our group were being put at the same $2 million quota and making just as much (or more) than I was now at my much higher multimillion quota, I spoke up. My boss told me I was lucky to have a job. I started job searching the next day, and within a month I had accepted a new role. The Americas CEO called me at home once he heard I had resigned and asked me to stay. I told him I appreciated the call, but given the company culture and how it viewed women in leadership roles, the flat commission pay structure, and the fact that there was no other role for me to go into within the organization, I felt it was best to leave. He had nothing up his sleeve to sway my decision. I'm pretty certain the overseas leadership didn't know he was placing the call.

It was a sad farewell. I really liked that job and my teammates. Magic like that doesn't happen very often.

CHAPTER 16

ESCAPE

CONTENT WARNING:
DOMESTIC ABUSE, SUICIDAL
IDEATION AND DESPAIR

The following chapter contains a raw and unfiltered account of domestic abuse, including emotional, verbal, and/or physical harm. It explores the deep wounds left by such experiences and the journey toward healing and restoration.

If you have experienced abuse or are sensitive to this subject, please read with care. If at any point it becomes too overwhelming, I encourage you to step away, seek support, and return when you feel ready.

This is not just a story of suffering—it is a testimony of resilience, faith, and the unshakable hope that light can break through in even the darkest places.

TAKING THE DOCTOR'S ADVICE

He beat at my door for what seemed like hours. I begged him to quit and leave me alone. The banging continued. So did the threats.

My chest seized up, and I collapsed to the floor. I couldn't breathe without pain. I had been crying for hours and couldn't catch my breath. I opened the door and crawled out, telling him I had to go to the hospital. I had his sister on speaker phone in my hand. At the hospital, they immediately started working to get my blood pressure down and my breathing under control. Many morphine doses got me steady. My body was jerking around spontaneously. I couldn't control my limbs. I was in a dream state. The devoted hubby sat and held my hand, stroked my hair, and said sweet things about me being alright when the doctors were examining me. I moved his hand away from mine, turned my head, and tuned out his presence. A very astute emergency room doctor told him to leave the room, to which he loudly objected. Finally, guards came and escorted him out. I was so relieved.

The doctor pulled up a chair and told me the facts. I'd been lucky this time that they could pull me out of this severe panic attack. I was in a desperate state when I walked in. Next time, I could be facing worse consequences. If I continued to live the same way, the outcome may not turn out so good for me.

He looked me in the eyes and said, "I don't know what's going on in your home, but I recognize what's going on with that man. You need to get out. Now." A wave of relief washed over me, followed by a wave of safety. He understood. He saw my pain.

They made my husband leave the hospital so I could spend the next few hours regaining my strength and being watched.

When they checked me out of the hospital around nine the next morning, I drove to the Jefferson County Courthouse. I spoke with very kind women in the domestic abuse division, and within an hour, I had a court order of protection for 180 days. It seemed the emergency room doctor had already made a report and submitted it. By the time I got home, there were two deputy cars parked above my driveway, waiting for him to come home. When he did get home, the officers closed in on him, followed him down the drive, handed him the protection order, and told him he had 20 minutes to pack. Then, of course, he turned to gaslighting the officers—he said I had been threatening to shoot myself, that I was crazy, and that I needed protection from myself. The officers didn't buy a word of what he was saying, and took his guns away which caused him to go ape-shit. Guess that lie cost him. Out the door he went. Finally.

ISMs: Ill health. Depression. Used. Broken.
Manipulated. Fear. Trapped.

Heavenly Virtue: Justice

OUT ON A LIMB

Along the way, I started working for a private equity firm out of Manhattan. I was the VP of sales for a niche HVAC manufacturing company. I took the job because I felt I wasn't getting paid enough in my last role—or recognized enough.

My directive was to hire seven+ new sales professionals, design the newbie training, set the national sales/marketing strategy, and work with HR, manufacturing, and operations to put some numbers up on the board. I should have seen this one coming. It was a shamble of a product and a hornet's nest of dysfunction, with the founders still in charge and the private equity firm breathing down their neck.

Why didn't I see this one? My last job was a bottleneck. There was nowhere to rise up to. I wanted some free rein. I was bored. This opportunity popped up like a shiny penny and I got caught in the brilliance of my need for more validation.

I cherry-picked my new national team from past peer relationships. The strategy worked, and we had six large pilots going with national retailers like big box electronics, department stores, grocery chains, fast food, and a national bank. The equipment worked well in the warmest states. When it worked, retailers could save close to 40% on their HVAC energy bills. Okay—not so bad. I led the charge to institute Salesforce into our little team to accurately determine the pipeline. Eleven months later, the new sales team had a solid $20M+ in the committed pipeline and counting. The caveat was that each opportunity was only valued at $1 until it turned into a committed sale of equipment. To say I had no fluff in my projections and actual sales would be an understatement.

The CEO was an arrogant banker. He didn't understand a thing about the industry or relationship sales and resented my knowledge and industry connections. When an insecure controlling man hires a confident female to justify his paycheck, things rarely go well.

> "When an insecure controlling man hires a confident female to justify his paycheck, things rarely go well."

The top brass from the private equity firm flew in to discuss my Q3–4 sales results and projections. I was excited to show my team's results. We had a great deal of momentum in the retail market and true team spirit.

But he wasn't pleased. In fact, he was rather disappointed. He indicated the pipeline didn't accurately show the value of the accounts we had working with us. He noticed I only had six of a certain department store chain opportunities and wanted to know why we didn't have all 1900+ of their sites listed. I told him the six we listed were actively in the pilot stage and that we had the equipment installed there. We had to successfully pass the pilot with the criteria we had put together with the client's engineering teams to get to the next gate of selling. We still had four months to go collecting metered data. Also, out of the 1900+ stores, only about 20% would be ideal for our solution.

He disagreed with everything I said. He went row by row through all the giant retailers and told me that all their sites needed to be identified and placed in the pipeline. The story for all the other pilots was the same. We had to successfully prove our claims of energy savings during phase one to roll out more in phase two. He absolutely did not agree. He said the pipeline of $20M+ needed to be well over $440M+. He said he had figured out that number based on total stores and wanted it listed that way in my report.

I had fiduciary responsibility. Legally, I had to sign my name to that bogus amount. And I said no. Everything in me said no. My dad's business ethics said no. My reputation said no. My personal integrity said no. No. No. No.

Seventeen days later I was out. So was 79% of the staff, my entire sales team, and the lousy CEO.

I was proud of my team. I was proud of our momentum. We had a mission and a directive, and we were all delivering as a team. They never let me call my sales team—they called them blind and just fired them. That is where my pain lies: I brought individuals that I respected and revered into this company based on my relationship and respect of their abilities. They were my friends. Sure, they knew the stories of PEs—but I had led them there to be slaughtered.

The private equity team had thought I'd be a pushover. They thought perhaps they could fudge the sales reports, split the stock, and make lots of money. I was indignant when I said no. Nice try. I wasn't going to jeopardize my freedom by signing a false report. It wouldn't have been him going to prison if they got caught—it would've been me. No way.

ISMs: Pride. Work. Worry. Deceived. Used. Angry.

Contrary Virtue: Diligence

UNEMPLOYMENT

....

I had never been fired. I'd always had something up my sleeve and had always been the one walking away—never the one abandoned and turned out. The feeling was denial and shame.

I had never lost a job so fast or in such an unexpected fashion before. One moment, I was sitting at the top of my career, confident in my strategy, my reputation, and my ability to navigate any corporate minefield; the next, I was out.

I knew it was risky working for a private equity firm—I'd heard all the stories. But ego is a dangerous thing, and mine demanded I try. I wanted to be the one who cracked the code, the one who played in the world of sharks and walked away unscathed. Instead, I got a four-year degree in brutality in 11 months and 17 days. Never again.

The ground beneath me was shaky.

At the same time, I've been divorced for almost a year and was still living in my mountaintop home. The walls came crashing down, and the mask I had carefully constructed started to slip. I had built my entire identity on being untouchable, invincible, and in control. But now, stripped of everything that had defined me—my job, my marriage, my financial security—I stood face to face with something I had never truly confronted: myself.

Though I was in a deep depression, I found ways to force myself to move. I skied that season like my life depended on it. I had an Epic Pass and was on the slopes every chance I got. I didn't have insurance, so I took it easy, but I was methodological. I practiced form, carved my turns perfectly, and built my lung capacity. I had never been physically stronger or mentally weaker.

And yet, I was drowning.

SLOTH

Get up and pee. Go downstairs and find some food. I should shower because I stink. I should brush my teeth before they fall out. My hair has been in a knot on my head for 21 days straight. Agh—I'll do it tomorrow. Grab my cigarettes and go cry on the front porch, looking at my beautiful garden. Smoke 12 before I grab some weed and try to clear my mind. Crawl up the staircase back to bed. My thoughts are full of disbelief, uselessness, doubt, worry, injustices, and anger. Three weeks ago, I was at the top of my game. I was beautiful, smiling, and powerful. Today I'm nothing. Today I'm broken. Tomorrow will be the same.

> ISMs: Depression. Ego death. Broken. Lost. Unemployed.

DREAMING OF ANGELS

CONTENT WARNING: SUICIDAL IDEATION & EMOTIONAL DISTRESS

The following chapter contains honest and unfiltered discussions of suicide, deep emotional distress, and the weight of despair. These experiences are shared with raw truth—not to glorify pain, but to shed light on the reality of suffering and the journey toward hope and healing.

If you are struggling or have been affected by these topics, please read with care. If at any point it becomes too heavy, I encourage you to step away, seek support, and return when you feel ready.

You are not alone. There is hope. There is help. And there is a God who sees you, loves you, and is with you in even the darkest moments.

If you or someone you know is in crisis, help is available:

📞 National Suicide Prevention Lifeline: 988 (U.S.)

📞 Crisis Text Line: Text HOME to 741741

Your life matters. ♥

Rocking back and forth on the heated wood floor in front of my stone fireplace in my beautiful mountaintop home. I'm stoned out of my mind, numbed out on Grey Goose, and snapping whippet after whippet out of brightly colored balloons, sucking out the sweet nectar of nitrous oxide. Tears are streaming down my face, my body wrecked by sobs. I'm naked except for a long wool shawl. Sarah is singing about angels and I'm dreaming about death. Thoughts of pure shame and pure grief encompass my every thought. I'd just pulled myself out of the bathtub, where the ice and razorblade were waiting. The thought of complete escape brings peace. But suddenly, my mind is filled with the overwhelming feel of Love. I feel my dad holding me. I hear the words, "This too shall pass. You are loved." I wake up 12 hours later, sunlight streaming through the wooden blinds, the fire roaring, birds chirping, my head screaming. I am alive. I'm glad morning came. I am thankful—as I will be many times to come—that I have been spared from myself.

ISMs: Wrath. Broken. Suicidal idealization.

Heavenly Virtue: Hope.

FINDING STRENGTH

I started to turn to my Women's Devotional Bible. It had been given to me before I left Missoula, but I never used it more than a spiritual painkiller. When life was smooth, it sat untouched. When life hit hard, I cracked it open like a lifeline.

Devotionals made it easy. They gave me bite-sized truths, small enough to digest but powerful enough to pull me out of my own head. I stayed mostly in the New Testament. The Old Testament felt too heavy. But the New Testament—especially Matthew—made sense.

I related to Matthew. He knew exactly what he was. A fraud. A schemer. A man who positioned himself among the powerful, leveraging his skills for personal gain. He knew how to put on the charm and when to be ruthless. His world was built around people like him—tax collectors, professionals, sinners who thrived within the system.

And yet, Christ called him.

I'd grown to think of myself in Matthew's profession. Not a tax collector, but something close. Money had become my world. I craved validation and influence. I was always chasing the next title, the next big deal, the next strategy to prove I belonged at the table.

And then, in an instant, it was gone.

But it wasn't just the paycheck—it was the loss of purpose.

With the job, I had a title. I had the travel, the clothes, the dinners. I had strategy meetings, growth plans, and objectives. I had an identity. Without it, I felt like a ghost in my own life. I spent so much time proving myself in my career that I had forgotten to live.

And now, standing in the wreckage, I experienced what some call ego death.

It wasn't just about losing a job. It was about losing the illusion of control.

It was about realizing that all my achievements, all my power moves, and all my professional wins had been amassed covering something fragile underneath.

And I did not like what I saw.

I remember staring at these words in Matthew and feeling like they had been written directly to me:

> "Your heavenly Father already knows your needs, and he will give you all you need from day-to-day if you live for him and make the Kingdom of God your primary concern. So don't worry about tomorrow, for tomorrow will bring its own worries. Today's trouble is enough for today."
>
> **Matthew 6:32-34**

God already knew my needs.

He already saw my struggle.

And yet, he wasn't asking me to fix it. He was asking me to trust Him.

That realization shook me. What if I didn't have to fight for every inch of ground? What if I didn't have to scheme my way forward?

What if I just let go?

I wanted that kind of love that Matthew had from the Father. I wanted that kind of peace.

But surrender was not in my nature. I spent a lifetime surviving, fighting, and proving my worth. I didn't know how to just accept grace.

So I did what I always did. I skated off. Got another job. Rebuilt my confidence. Stopped reading the Bible. Made more money.

I convinced myself that this was just another phase, just a temporary crisis that I had to push through. But now, looking back, I know the truth. That moment—that verse, that ego death, that invitation from Christ—was my way out.

And I walked right past it. Not because I didn't believe it.

But because I didn't yet know how to stop running

> *"So now I hate life because everything done here under the sun is so irrational. Everything is meaningless, like chasing the wind. I am disgusted that I must leave the fruits of my hard work to others. And who can tell whether my successors will be wise or foolish? And yet they will control everything I have gained by my skill and hard work. How meaningless!"*
>
> **Ecclesiastes 3:17-20**

THE MOVE

It is 2012. I am still pretending to live in a beautiful Mountain Home. Alone. The pretense has worn thin, stretched over the surface of a life that no longer fits. I sit in the silence of that grand house, with its sweeping views of the mountains, and feel nothing but the weight of my own despair. The house, once a dream, has become a cavernous reminder of all that is missing. My youngest is in the dorms most of the time, and I am left alone, rattling around in rooms too big for one person, in a life that feels just as empty.

One morning, the realization hits like a sharp gust of wind—I have no one and nothing in Denver who is invested in me. The people I once leaned on have either drifted away or were never really mine to begin with. My second grandson is almost due, and my first grandson is in Dallas with my oldest and his wife. That thought pulls at something deep inside me. I am missing everything that matters. Move now. Pack up and jump ship.

And so, I do.

Packing up 4,000 square feet of furnishings is both a physical and emotional labor. Every object has a story, a tie to a past version of myself. I sift through rooms, deciding what will come with me, what will be stored, and what will be left behind. It's the first time I am making this decision for myself, without anyone else's input or approval. And yet, despite the exhaustion, there's something liberating about it.

I take a three-bedroom apartment in Dallas, something manageable, something that belongs entirely to me. I fill one container with what I need for the 1,700 square feet that will be my new home. The rest—memories, excess, remnants of a life I no longer fit into—go into two garages I rent on the property. My brother/uncle, Tom, owns the complex, so my rent is discounted. A huge blessing, and one I accept with gratitude.

I have never lived in an apartment by myself. I have never been on my own. Every move before this was dictated by someone else—a husband, a job, a set of circumstances that demanded I adjust. But this time, it is different. For the first time, I am choosing where I will land. And I love it.

There is a simplicity in this new space. A lightness. No more heavy burdens of homeownership. No more empty hallways echoing with what used to be. There is a church across the street. I take note of it, unsure of what it means yet, but comforted by its presence.

Within a few months, I have a new national role and am traveling again. There is relief in closing the door behind me, knowing that I have nothing to maintain and nothing to fix. My life is my own now. And for the first time, that realization doesn't terrify me. It frees me.

YOU GET WHAT YOU ASK FOR

On the golf course in typical form. Only woman on the scramble team. Drink in one hand, cigar in the other.

Today, however, I notice my cigar is a wet mess and I keep getting my lips stuck in my teeth when I talk. Odd. Think it's a dry cigar, so I put it out and forget about it.

Six hours later I take a bath and brush my teeth. The brushing part was fine, but flossing was another story. Every time I open my mouth to floss; my upper lip falls over my teeth. Have to hold my lip up to floss—what the heck? Concerned. Now I do a few experiments. Smile wide, and my impressive smile lights up. But as I hold my smile I watch in horror as my face muscles melt and the smile slides down into a frown. Suddenly I look like the Joker. Three times I do this trick, and each time my smile falls faster and deeper. My bottom teeth are now what show when I smile—I kind of look like a bulldog. Am I having a stroke? I place a call to a horribly unsupportive friend, and she calls me stupid. I must be exaggerating, she says.

Sister, you can't exaggerate this shit.

Then it occurred to me that seven days ago I got Botox. Is that the issue? I call my doctor off hours and ask. Realization sets in. Yes, it appears my zygomaticus major muscles have been impacted by a wrongly placed shot of Botox in my crow's feet. I'm perfectly wrong on both sides, evenly frozen. Well done. What's the cure? Smile, talk, exercise your jaw muscles with exaggerated A, E, I, O, and U motions eight times a day for the next few months until my smile comes back. The doctor tells me it will come back, but it will take time. Have a good night. It's not a stroke. It's the price of vanity.

I explore my options. Curl up in a ball for however long it takes for the Botox to move through me. Or I can continue to be me. I look at myself in the morning. It's truly horrible. I look like I've had a stroke. My entire face from forehead to chin is smooth and placid like putty. Under my eyes is a gap that hangs low. It's no longer supported by my cheek muscles, which are now on vacation. My eyes weep constantly. I have round and low jowls around my jawline. I chew on my inner cheeks with almost every bite. The dimple on my left cheek, which I've had since birth, is gone. Erased like it was never there. Pronounced smile lines are gone. Cheek bones eradicated. I look horrendous.

I decide to ignore it. Work, travel, talk, eat, play, smile, be me. Lie. Say it is Bell's palsy. I've had it before on the left side, so it's a good cover because it looks exactly the same. My boys never discussed it. My ex, of course, told me people would assume I had a stroke and were just being nice by not mentioning it. Friends offered encouragement—enemies were cruel.

Had a toxic co-worker call and tell me he's missing my smile. One month earlier, I told him, "The next time he wanted to say something about me, he was to pull out his balls and say it to my face instead of going to my co-workers." I Shook his hand and walked away. Guess face to face wasn't his jive. Shame me over a phone call? You low life.

Losing my smile when it's one of the things I valued most was very hard. Having the courage to just ignore the situation and move on was a gift. I can't recall shedding a single tear for myself on this issue. I owned it. My smile came back 100% in eight and a half months. Funny, you get Botox and love the results, and it only lasts three months. Rotten results last much longer.

ISMs: Gluttony. Ego. Image. Identity. Vanity. Pride.

Contrary Virtue: Humility.

PRIDE

....

Pride is the root of all sin. Pride takes many forms to trick you up. Couple it with a skewed mindset, and it gets to control your every thought. Our appearance is the first thing people notice. In time, they may see what's underneath and begin to love you, but outward impressions usually rule first impressions. I knew I was empty inside but built a wall of defense surrounding my outward form. Need to impress. Need to appear perfect. Need to look accomplished and beautiful. Pride—its power is very persuasive and destructive.

> *"Look at the lilies and how they grow. They don't work or make their clothing, yet Solomon in all his glory was not dressed as beautifully as they are. And if God cares so wonderfully for flowers that are here today and gone tomorrow, wouldn't he more surely care for you? You have so little faith! And don't worry about food or what to eat and drink. Don't worry whether God will provide it for you. These things dominate the thoughts of most people, but your Father already knows your needs. He will give you all you need from day-to-day if you make the Kingdom of God your primary concern.*
>
> *So don't be afraid, little flock. For it gives your Father great happiness to give you the Kingdom."*
> **Luke 12:27-32**

I had great peace with the acceptance of my face during this time. I celebrated small successes each day as my smile returned. When others gave me sympathy while

I stood under the lie of "Bell's palsy," I felt like a fraud. I felt I deserved these results and now I had to hide.

But over time, something happened. My priorities began to shift. At first, I thought about my face constantly, measuring the tiniest changes, aching for normalcy. But then the obsession faded. My worth wasn't in my cheekbones or my ability to dazzle with a smile. I had lost something I once equated with power—but it didn't stop me from being me.

I went back to my 30-year reunion with my joker smile. One memory I have is of a photographer taking a small group photo where I was in front. He kept taking the photo, looking at the picture, and then taking another. I finally went to him and told him the photo was fine—it was just my face.

Then I realized that my shame and embarrassment had lost its grip on me. I had found peace in the ashes of trials.

Contrary Virtue: Humility

Act 2

CHAPTER 17

FAITH OF A CHILD

SOWING OF THE SEED

I had a quarterly business review in Vegas with a client. Going to Vegas was nothing new, as it was a common meeting site. What was unique was that I had texted my friend Robin while on the airplane to meet me for dinner. She quickly responded "Yes!" so we planned to meet at Caesars Palace. Robin was a friend from Missoula. A former policeman's wife and one of the few remnants of friends I had left from my young marriage. She has always been a bright light in my life, encouraging me. She has known me for so long that there has never been any need to pretend to be anything but myself with her. Robby threw me baby showers, taught me how to smoke a cigar, and to dance like no one was watching.

She's a nurturer and a true ray of light in this world. Robin has a servant's heart for Christ, as did her husband,

Bill. I'd known this about them for 36 years of a close friendship.

I landed in Vegas, met with my team, had our meeting, and soon Robin arrived for dinner.

At first, we stayed at Caesars for a beer. Then we went to TAO for dinner. I remember getting in the cab for dinner—nothing else. The last picture in my head is of my hand on the door handle.

I woke with a start. I was in my hotel room, alone. Jammies on, hair in a knot. The room was orderly. No headache. A sweet little note dispelled my fears and told me I was safe that night. The note, which was by my bedside, had sweet little hearts and musical notes on it. It was from Robin. She told me what a wonderful time she'd had last night, said she wished we'd had more time together, and invited me to stay at her house anytime. Then she wished me God's blessings.

Confusion doesn't even describe how I felt. I had passed out more times in the past than I could count, but I always had some fragmented recollection of the night before. This morning, my mind was a blank canvas. All I knew was that I had to gather my stuff and get to the airport to catch a flight. I was going home to Montana for my 49th birthday and a winter stay with mom. I was frazzled.

I arrived at the airport 15 minutes late for my flight and was refused a seat. I thought: No worries, I'll catch the next one. But then the agent told me the next flight was Monday. It was Friday. I needed a plan quick. Instantly, I called Robin and asked to stay the weekend.

I had been a guest in Robin and Bill's house many times when they lived in Montana. Their house is always the same: comfortable, loving, peaceful, and inviting. Their new home in Vegas had the same feeling. I settled in and started a journey I'm still on today.

I was worn out, worn down, and very burdened at this point. I had just moved back to Dallas, had been working my new job for four months, traveling 80% again, and was still deeply wounded from my divorce. I had been reaching for my Devotional more and more, and I shared that with Robin. We sat for hours talking about our lives. I saw the impact Christ had on her life. Her peace was undeniable, and her faith was all-encompassing. Tears spilled out as I told her how low I was, what a wretch I had become, and how I had no hope of anything getting better. She seemed to understand everything I said.

We spent hours on her back porch talking, crying, laughing, and reminiscing. She mentioned our talks at dinner and how she knew I was ready to make a change. When I told her, my head hung in shame, that I had no recollection of the night after hailing the taxi to TAO, she looked at me, baffled. I asked her if I'd had too much to drink. She assured me I was fine; we only had a few beers. I asked her if someone could have put something in my drink? Was I talking fine? Was I walking straight? How could I have been fine if I couldn't remember a thing? I told her how relieved I'd been to see her note the next morning—to hear now that I'd been safe with her all night.

What she told me next will never leave me. She said, "We spoke of Jesus all night." She said I asked tons of questions, and she answered them all to the best of her abilities. She said at one point two men sitting nearby approached us. They were acting friendly and wanted to engage in conversation, but I shooed them away forcefully so we could continue talking. Now, this action wasn't unique to me; I've dismissed many men. But I usually laugh about it the next day with friends!

She spoke of my actions and our conversation in a very animated way. She assured me I'd been cognitive, engaged, and present. She said that after dinner we went back to my hotel and gabbed the night away at the pool and atop queen beds like two teenagers until the wee hours, when she left to go home.

Regardless of her assurance of my safety the night before, it left me scared to death. What would've happened to me if I wasn't in such safe company? Looking back now and reflecting on that consciously unconscious night, I know a seed was planted. It was the supernatural love of Christ to perform the Father's Will and the Holy Spirit engaging. The Trinity at work.

At the time I met Robin, I was fully immersed in darkness. I was broken to a point of shattered glass. I was lost, trying to improve by unknowingly feeding sins of pride, lust, worry, and gluttony. I felt fear and doubt every day. I was at rock bottom, searching for something to fill the massive hole within me. I believe the Holy Spirit took over my body, pushed out the evil, and allowed Robin to help fill my soul with Christ's word deep in my heart. Simply put, I think the devil tried to snatch the word from me—but the Lord had other plans.

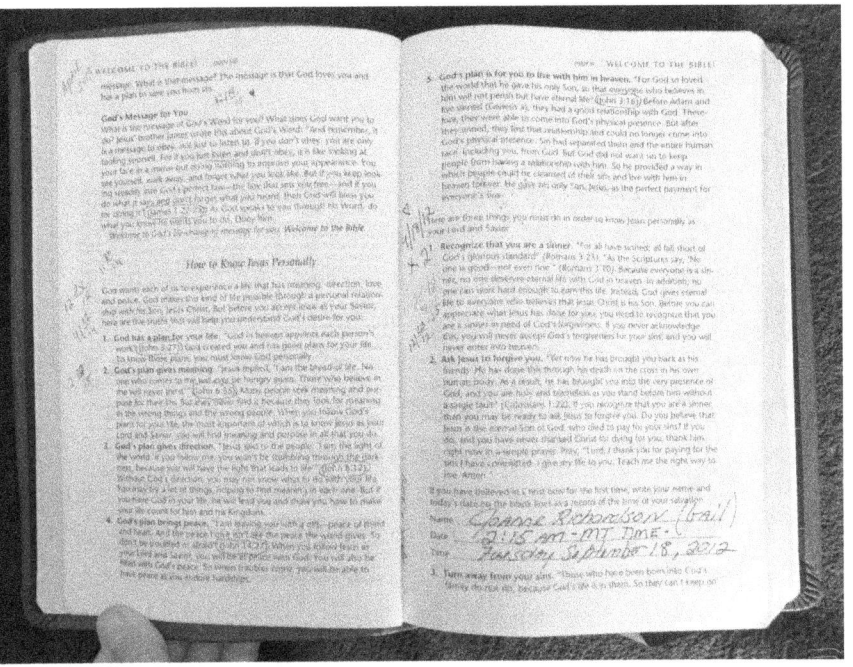

"A farmer went out to plant some seed. As he scattered it across the field, some seeds fell on the footpath, and the birds came and ate them. Other seeds fell on shallow soil with underlying rock. The plants sprang up quickly, but they soon wilted beneath the hot sun and died because the roots had no nourishment in the shallow soil. Other seeds fell among the thorns that shot up and choked out the tender blades. And some seeds fell on fertile soil and produced a crop that was 30, 60, and even 100 times as much as had been planted. Anyone who is willing to hear should listen and understand!!"

Matthew 13:4-9

> *"Now here is the explanation of the story I told about the farmer sowing grain. The seed that fell on the hard path represents those who hear the good news about the Kingdom but don't understand it. Then the evil one comes and snatches the seed away from their hearts. The rocky soil represents those who hear the message and receive it with joy. But like young plants in such soil, their roots don't go very deep. At first, they get along fine, but they will wilt as soon as they have problems or are persecuted because they believe in the world. The thorny ground represents those who hear and accept the Good News, but all too quickly the message is crowded out by the cares of this life and the lure of wealth, so no crop is produced. The good soil represents the hearts of those who truly accept God's message and produce a huge harvest—30, 60, or even 100 times as much has been planted."*
>
> **Matthew 13-18-23**

TESTIMONY OF CHRIST

....

Later that afternoon, we spoke about Christ again, and Robin Wicks testified to me.

Do you believe Jesus Christ died for our sins? Yes.

Do you believe you are a sinner? Yes.

Have you asked the Lord to forgive you?

Gasp. Ask Him to forgive me for what I had done? All those terrible moments of self-abandonment? Who I had become? How I was living? All my secrets? All my shame and disgrace?

In utter humility, I asked Him to forgive me. I had never asked for forgiveness.

Do you ask Jesus into your heart? Yes.

Do you agree to turn away from your sins? Yes.

The words and sobs that were released from my body when I answered yes to all those questions shook my core like an earthquake. The power and strength of total release felt like an explosion. I felt so light—like someone had lifted me up and made me weightless. Joy and shame-ridden tears poured out of me. I felt hope enter my body. I felt my entire body become hot. I felt a release of pressure hit me like a wave—and then another wave of the rawest pain I've ever felt hit me, too. This wave contained all the self-loathing acts I had committed. My body was heaving with sobs, but my mind was crystal clear. Releasing all the negative emotions and deep feelings of shame from a lifetime filled with regrets feels like you are being turned inside out. It feels like you're having new skin exposed. The sins literally shed off you the minute you ask for the Lord, and then He grabs you. It is like a car collision. You know how time slows down and your mind can recall every second of the crash in deep detail? Being re-born into Christ is like that. We have no control over our natural birth, as so it is with our re-birth in Christ. Surrendering to Christ is like a lightbulb going off in your body. You can see. It's the feeling of love that hits first. You feel like a child who has been scooped up into your Father's arms. You feel a tight hold. You feel acceptance and understanding. You feel a comfort in your soul knowing that you are safe. Loved. Home.

I heard Satan screaming in my head. He reminded me of all the negative things I'd done, making me doubt that

I could change. He told me that "Christ was fake, and you are unworthy of His love." He told me, "You will never change."

But then I heard Christ's reassuring voice. "I am with you. This is real. You are loved. I am expecting you—come to me." He was calling me to Him. So comforting. I've known His voice—I've always known his voice.

Again, I heard Satan's threats: "You will not be free. This feeling is fake. You are being deceived into believing."

"I am here—come to me"

"This is a lie. He is not real. You are being deceived into thinking you can be free."

"Come to me—take my hand"

It seemed to go on and on in my mind. Back and forth. But then, in a sudden flurry, a choice was demanded. Choose. Choose now! Yes or no.

I committed completely to Christ. Everything within me exploded YES. Yes, yes, a thousand times yes. And then I believed. I understood the truth. I saw. I had been given grace at exactly the time it had been predetermined by God before I was even born. I did nothing to work for this, as you've read. No worldly works can assure salvation. In an instant, I understood God's instruction and calling on my life. It was the classic battle of good and evil. I heard Satan's screams. I felt sin flee from me. I actually felt a release of power that is unworldly. I felt all the chains and claws of evil release. I felt the presence of Christ filling me with the Holy Spirit, and surrounding me with love and acceptance that I had never felt in my life. A wanting that has been answered. A filling of such abundance that it took my breath away. Alive.

I felt totally exposed. Totally cleansed and purified. My entire body was racked in fits of deep, guttural sobs. My muscles were shaking. I could hardly breathe or talk. My Spirit was on fire!

But then there came complete peace and total understanding. My mind went quiet. Truth. Knowing. Appreciation. Humility. Thankfulness for such mercy. Understanding the depth of the commitment I had made with Christ. I was free. I was pure. I am new. Supernatural love of Christ. I was always His—another wave of understanding how far I'd run. Relief. Praise. Welcome home. In my Father's arms.

I slept for four hours after accepting Christ as my savior. My Spirit waged a forceful attack, scattering all that was feeding off me.

> *"God saved you by his special favor when you believed. And you can't take credit for this; it is a gift from God. Salvation is not a reward for the good things we have done, so none of us can boast about it. For we are God's masterpiece. He has created us anew in Christ Jesus, so that we can do the things he planned for us long ago."*
>
> **Ephesians 2:8-10**

THE WORD

As I packed up to fly to Missoula, Robin presented me with a new Holy Bible. She said the Women's Devotional Bible I had been reading was good, but that the Holy Bible would better feed my growth. She said I needed God's words to stay strong and suggested I start with John. I hugged her, put the Bible in my suitcase, and went on my way.

I made it to Missoula, saw mom, settled in ... you know, all the normal travel day stuff. And then late that night, around 11 p.m., I finally unpacked and pulled my new Bible out. I felt the cover and let the thin onion skin paper with its gold edges glide along my fingertips. This kind of Bible had always been intimidating to me. I said the Lord's Prayer, feeling every word I spoke. I invited the Holy Spirit to help me read and understand the words. I asked for God's guidance and opened John. As I read, I felt like I was in the Bible, experiencing every word. I wept with a total understanding of what love is.

After I read the Book of John, I again held the Bible in my hands. I kissed the cover and turned to the first page. Robin had inscribed: "Reach out your hand and He will grab hold and never let go." Another wave of tears overcame me, as I knew those words to be true.

Then, moving to the preface in the Bible, I learned how to properly use the Bible, its purpose in my life, and how to enact the Spirit for wisdom. This reading also led me to personally commit and offer a testimony of my surrender to Christ. Reading through the commitments again, which Robin had led me through earlier, this time alone, was one of the most powerful personal experiences I've ever had. The waves of emotions this time were streaming tears of gratitude, thankfulness, love, and acceptance. Being alone in my childhood bedroom, safe at home with mom—feeling raw, exposed, and fragile, much like I assume a baby does—I was at total peace. I felt myself in the presence of the Lord. I felt his breath, his comfort, his pleasure, and his love.

After you read the preface in the Bible, the next page is for your signature. Wow! I had no idea. Not only do you go through a shedding, but you must commit. As I filled out the signature page, it asked the date and time. It was 2:15 a.m., September 18, 2012. My 49th birthday.

The Lord has a great sense of humor. I had been given the biggest gift of my life. Reborn on my birthday through a domino effect of circumstances that were clearly outside of my control. Now I could take my place with the Lord. Yep, I control nothing. I am merely a conduit of His will from now on.

In your face, hit you over the head with a skillet—smack! That is how I felt the Lord had come after me. I know He owns my path. He knew the condition He would reclaim me in, but He also knew it would take a swift kick in the head and heart to scatter the demons that had been driving, empowering, and feeding off me for years. He simply didn't mess around. My thinking changed. I understood the end of the story. Christ wins. Complete surrender is believing your war is over as Christ is in control of your destiny. My identity intertwined with Christ when He called me. So peaceful. I understood all of it. Nothing hidden from me about the Kingdom of God. Nothing hidden from me in the Word of the Bible. Truth. It was like my mind had been swept clean and only pure thoughts of love and peace were present. I felt the forgiveness of my entire past flow through my veins. I understood that I was not going to hell and that I had been stripped out of the devil's possession. I understood

I had been chosen as a son by The Almighty King. I had total trust in the Lord. Two days into my new Christian path, and I could feel the fire inside! Incredible. The Father knows who His children are and the plans He has for them. I felt ecstatic and gratitude that Christ was leading. I was exhausted—it was rejuvenating to have someone else lead. Such relief.

The next morning, I got up, went into the kitchen, took mom's hand, and told her I had committed myself to Christ. She looked at me unfazed, nonjudgmental, and replied, "Well you've been looking for something for quite some time." Boy was she right.

"I am the way, the truth, and the life. No one can come to the Father except through me."

John 14:6

ENGAGING AND FOLLOWING THE SPIRIT
....

Let's just say not everyone understood.

"What did you just say? Christ? Have you been drinking? Are you okay? Who are you? Where's Joanne? What did you just say, Joanne?"

I could have knocked half my friends over like dominos when I told them I had surrendered to Christ. It wasn't just what I said—it was the passion and absoluteness in the way I recanted it. You could not walk away from me without clearly understanding that I had just gone through a life-altering experience. What was more frightening to some, I think, was that I believed and knew the oath I had taken was real. I had an absoluteness to me that was unbending. The sheer force with which I told and retold my birth to anyone who would listen was impressive. The good news was pouring out of me.

I started devouring the Bible at night. I took time out of my workday, climbed Lolo Peak, and found a nice field to read in for hours on end. I called friends in Missoula, who I knew were rooted in Christ, and asked if I could come by and talk about the Lord. Being in Missoula after surrendering really allowed the seed to grow. Missoula was a safe place. No need to be splashy or charming. No need to impress or repress. Who cared if my old friends thought I was crazy? Heck, they probably already thought that! The feeling that surprised me was how exposed I felt. It was as if I was being watched. I felt expectant. I felt cautious, like at any moment I could be pulled back. I felt His love—but also felt another force. How do I express that being with Christ felt like I had sea legs? Daily inklings of doubt would pop into my head, and I would feel as if I was a fraud. When I expressed how exposed I felt to Christians, they all echoed the same warning. Watch out, they said. Be careful. The devil wants you back. He will set traps. He looks to foul you up. Stay close to the Lord. Be vigilant. Watch your step. You are now of the Lord and the devil can't have you back, but he will mess with you. Satan will still tempt and distract you, and he will use adversity and emotions against you to keep you small and ineffective in spreading the word of God. Not only am I walking around feeling exposed, but now I realize I'd made a powerful enemy. Great.

But the relief and peace were so encompassing, consuming all my thoughts. As I look back on it now, I realize how peaceful and empowering my spiritual growth was.

It had been my plan to work out of Montana from September through January. I was winding down my fourth quarter travel at work and looked forward to a slower pace. Did you catch that first sentence? It had been my plan.

One month after accepting Christ, I was released from my job. Oddly enough, it was the exact date I'd lost my job a year prior. Ouch.

I knew I was very fragile. I was angry. I was stunned. I also knew I now had my Bible. I had my faith. And God willing, I now had the right words, instincts, and clarity to follow His directions in what felt like a black haze. I went home to Dallas. I made this decision mainly for my personal growth and the space I knew I needed. I also did it for my mom. She was concerned for me and carried the weight of the situation on her shoulders. I hugged her when I left and assured her everything would work out according to God's plan. It was enough for her, and it was enough for me. I had faith it would be fine.

Upon returning home I found my church family next door. Valley View Christian Church.

CHAPTER 18

HOPE

WATERING THE MUSTARD SEED

Returning to Dallas unemployed, devastated, with my career upside-down, and unsure of my future was a hard reality. I remember arriving home and going to bed for a week. I was a train wreck. What a shot it was to a fragile disposition. I had pitiful savings, barely replenished from my divorce and from being unemployed for eight months prior to this five-month gig. On top of that, I felt fearful. A week of sleeping, reading my Bible, and considering my options forced me to reflect on past choices. I crashed. I experienced what I believe to be ego dissolution. I saw things clearer than I ever had. I put aside all alcohol, weed, and Tylenol PM—everything but cigarettes. I was pulling myself together in slow motion.

I slept, ate, read the Bible, joined the church across the street, attended Bible studies, and cried. I slept, ate, read the Bible, went to church, attended bible studies, and cried. I simply could not concentrate on anything but my Bible.

It was the only thing that interested me. I isolated myself from friends and all social activities except church and watching my grandchildren a few days a week. Christmas was approaching. I was alone, low on money, had no job prospects, and was still emotionally numb but spiritually alive. I wrote my children letters instead of gifting them gross amounts of Christmas gifts. I expressed my love and gratitude. I never sent my mother flowers, which she questioned, and I told the truth: "I'm broke." But I had hope. I wasn't worried about finding a job. I wasn't worried about money. I wasn't worried about myself. Others were. My friends were concerned. My family was concerned. But I wasn't. I was reading my Bible close to nine hours a day. Just pouring through the pages, learning the stories of David and Goliath, Samson and Delilah, and David and Joseph. Bible stories I should have learned in Sunday school. I couldn't get enough. And I started praying. A lot. Praying for continued love, continued forgiveness, continued support. I prayed every day for the Lord to hold me close, hold me tight, and protect me from evil. Then He answered one of my prayers on His timetable.

WOMAN IN WHITE

December 21, 2012. I was in Mineral Springs, Texas, with a girlfriend. We were staying at her brother's house, making big bonfires, catching frogs, and shooting guns during the day. On December 23, I was awoken early with a strong feeling that I had to go to church. I got dressed and came out of the bedroom. My friend was surprised.

She asked me where I was going, and I told her to church. She laughed and said, "Are you just going to drive up and down the countryside to find a church?"

"Yes," I said.

I went into the small town and looked for steeples. I found one on the hill and went in. I was late for the start of the service. The sermon was a typical Christmas message. They passed the offering plate, and I realized that in my haste to get out of the house I had forgotten my wallet. I dug into the bottom of my bag to pull out some coins.

As I headed back, I noticed a lot of cars turning left. I followed them. They were going to another church, and I went in with them. This time I was early. I took a place in the back pews. A stunning older woman in a silk white suit with white hair walked down the aisle. I saw her pause and slowly turn back to me. She approached me then. She told me she was praying for me. She told me tomorrow would be spectacular, touched my shoulder, and went on.

The sermon was about Mary. It was unique, as it focused entirely on Mary's strength. It spoke of Mary as a strong, independent woman who understood sacrifices. It told of her bravery. It told of when Mary had paid her debt to the household she served and could be free, she stayed in servitude. She enjoyed her life and worked because she desired to serve the Lord. Mary was not some meek woman who had no say in her life. She was fearless. This story resonated deep within me. I saw myself.

When the offering plate was being passed around again, I panicked. I forgot I had no money. I dug out two pennies. At that exact moment, the pastor was telling the story about the poor widow offering two copper coins into the collection box. He said not to think of the offering plate as small. Believe when you give your offer that your entire being is going into the plate. He said this just as I dropped my pennies in.

> *"While Jesus was in the temple, he watched the rich people putting their gifts in the collection box. Then a poor widow came by and dropped in two copper coins. 'I assure you,' he said, 'this poor widow has given more than all the rest of them. For they have given a tiny part of their surplus, but she, poor as she is, has given everything she has."*
>
> **Luke 21:1-3**

What I didn't understand at the time about this scripture is all the people giving money at the temple that day were actually giving to esteem themselves in front of others, or deceived they could buy a blessing from the Lord. This poor woman, gave her pennies to a false religion that public display of faith (works) can bring salvation. The Lord saw her heart and granted her grace.

I gave myself in that offering. I knew I had been saved by grace. I no longer had to hope and wonder.

I drove back to the farmstead and told my friend and her daughter we were leaving early. She was confused, as we had plans for the day. I told her this couldn't wait—we needed to go. Then I dropped her off and pulled into an old Salvation Army parking lot in the south side of town and called my pastor. I asked to be baptized on Christmas Eve. He said they don't normally do baptisms at that service. I told him it wasn't me who was asking.

During my motherhood, we would go to services on Christmas Eve. We planned the dinner around the service we attended. I would sit with both husbands and openly cry while singing "Silent Night" and lighting candles. I would sit in the pew knowing how miserable I was and praying for peace and love. I felt like the weight of the world was on my shoulders in these instances. The Lord was knocking, and I hadn't slowed down to recognize it.

On December 24, 2012, during a candlelit service, just after singing "Silent Night," I was baptized at Valley View Christian Church. Before I hit the water, I asked my pastor to ensure every hair was totally submerged. Never being baptized as a baby made this moment all the more powerful. I knew once again that my Father knew what I needed, knew the innermost yearnings of my heart, and had taken charge.

To be baptized on Christmas Eve, rising out of the water feeling pure peace and love, after so many years of struggling, was the best gift ever! I had found salvation on my birthday and publicly professed my love and faith in Jesus Christ on His birth. It was such a Gift.

No family. No celebration with loved ones. I was alone—but whole.

> *"And the Holy Spirit helps us in our distress. For we don't even know what we would pray for, nor how we should pray. But the Holy Spirit prays for us with groanings that cannot be expressed with words. And the Father who knows all hearts knows what the Spirit is saying, for the Spirit pleads for us believers in harmony with God's own will."*
>
> **Romans 8:26-27**

Heavenly Virtue: Faith

TURING ON A DIME

Being a wretch and turning on a dime is both confusing and enlightening. Trust me on this. It's as though all your old thoughts and ways have been literally threshed out of you. You are not the same person you once were. Your every thought is filled with honest evaluation. Is this the right thing to do? Your human nature is so used to thinking in the worldly view of what's expected, and then bam. Christ grabs you and takes hold and you know in your heart of hearts that you are being led down His path for you. It's very mind-blowing on a spiritual level. Outwardly, you look the same and sound the same. You have the same car, job, clothes, hair color, eye color, and speech patterns. But inwardly, you are now alive, awake, and purposeful. You now radiate on a different wavelength. And anyone who interacts with you can feel it. Friends will say, "Have you lost weight? Changed your hair? Met someone? Because you are glowing." It's frightening to others. They can't comprehend how much stronger you've become since surrendering all control.

After being saved, the fear of the old "known feelings" woke me up at night. When you've been bad for so long, it's hard to appreciate how things have changed. It causes me to pause from time to time and think hard. I wonder: Have I broken God's law and ultimately failed myself? Of course I have! I am sinful by nature and must accept that. Have I held true to my convictions and held myself in honor at all times? Of course not! I am human, and no one can be as perfect as Christ. I strive daily to deny unneeded temptations. For the first few years after accepting Christ,

I would literally count back to the last time I'd had sex, stretched the truth, indulged myself with materialistic pleasure, drank in excess, smoked weed, or said or did something I was disappointed in. Moments of doubt would slip into my thoughts and a rush of shame and guilt would rise in my throat. I'm not good enough. Who am I kidding? Sin has had me at its whim for decades.

That terrifying thought keeps me alert to schemes—and yet I still fall into them every now and then. As far as I've come, I still know it's a slippery slope. So, I purposely walk straight, talk straight, and keep my eyes up and my head down and focused. I actively push out thoughts that tell me to let loose, be the old Jo, go back to who I was. The truth is, I beat myself up for not being good enough and then realized that the Lord doesn't put these defeatist thoughts in our mind. It alas is just another ploy of sin to lower my defenses and loosen my resolve. As I've gained more wisdom and time has passed, I can clearly see others as encased by sin as I was. I see they are riddled with worry, negative self-speech, and self-degrading attitudes. They wear their demons like heavy cloaks, just as I did. They live in fear of failure, ridicule, and of never reaching their goals. Many are frozen in a time when life was better. They are overwhelmed by life in the present and terrified of the future. Most empower image and worry as their master and do not recognize the need for Christ. Most cannot see out of their own darkness—just like I used to be. But I see the warfare clearly now.

I find I can raise them out of these feelings by offering support and building up their value. I can speak about the Lord and what He has done in my life and ask them to unburden their life. Nine out of ten times the next day they are back in the same dark hole, armed with hundreds of reasons for why today isn't a good day to change. Don't get me wrong—these are all good-hearted, intelligent, successful men and women. They are intellectually capable of formulating plans and taking positive steps. But they don't. I do not know why some can be brought to the light while others decide to stay in darkness. And truthfully, it's not my worry. All I am instructed to do is throw kindling on the fire bound by Christ's words and let Him take over.

During the time of my sanctification and growing daily in Christ's word, I let many of my old friends go. Very few of them liked or appreciated my new way of living and thinking. Even fewer had any interest in learning about Christ or the changes occurring in my life. Doubt and ridicule became their only defense to sway me off my path. But I held strong in the storm.

I had an old lifestyle friend express concern for me that I was too involved in church with weekly commitments of Sunday service, nursery teaching, and Bible study. She didn't think it was healthy to focus so heavily on religion. I asked her where her concern was when I was out drinking and whoring myself three nights a week while traveling. No response.

My family, children, and most of my friends never wanted to hear my testimony then—or now. They never ask about my faith or my heart for Christ. No interest.

But I wish they would. Because the love and redemption I have found are not just for me. They are for everyone, including those who doubt, those who mock, and those who think they don't need saving. If you have ever felt lost, if you have ever woken up wondering if there is more to life than this endless chase of success, money, or pleasure—there is. Christ changed me in ways I never imagined possible. And He can change you, too.

I believe those who have great faith have no fear. I am not afraid to alienate anyone with the truth of The Word and Christ's teachings. I am not afraid to fail myself and prove your justification for your scorn when I submit to worldly desires that you deem hypocritical. I was released of rejection once I believed; yours holds no power with me. But if you ever wonder—if even for a second—that there might be something to this faith, I invite you to ask. You don't have to take my word for it. Seek Him yourself. See what happens when you let go of control. Because I promise you, turning on a dime may be confusing and terrifying, but it is the greatest freedom you will ever know.

ACQUIRING THE TRUTH

> *"Obviously, I'm not trying to be a people pleaser! No, I am trying to please God. If I were still trying to please people, I would not be Christ's servant."*
>
> **Galatians 1:10**

I was given life in Christ—hope, peace, and belonging poured into me. But I didn't know I was dead. Though I had done nothing to deserve the Lord's grace, He felt otherwise. The fact that I received mercy was all Christ's doing; it is the free gift of God.

I lived 49 years of my life in darkness but believed I was in the light. I couldn't see my actions and reactions past my own nose. I thought I was a Christian. The Bible calls this being blind—and yes, I was. But I believed I could see. I was told lies by my own mindset, lulled into thinking I was going to heaven when I died or not giving it a second thought. I thought I was free, independent, successful, and had righteous qualities. Not worse than others, but not as "good" as some either. And yet, I certainly didn't think I was evil.

That misconception is the Devil's way of keeping you in your place—complacent, ignorant, and unconcerned.

> Isaiah 29:13 says, *"These people come near to me with their mouth and honor me with their lips, but their hearts are far from me."*

Thinking you are "good enough" is nonsense. It is a lie wrapped in pride, keeping you in chains. Evil thrives on these lies—the ones we tell ourselves and the ones we tell others. It keeps us small, ineffective, and blind.

A DEEPER LOOK—
AN UNCOMFORTABLE TRUTH

What is good? The Bible is clear—there is no such thing as a "good" person apart from Christ. The only ones who will enter the kingdom of God are those supernaturally called and reborn of the Spirit. Christ is the only way to enter the Kingdom.

As John 3:5 states, *"Truly, truly, I say to you, unless one is born of water and the Spirit, he cannot enter the kingdom of God."*

This is not a man-made process. No human being—no pastor, no priest, no pope, no prophet—can lay hands on you and "give" you salvation. No one can "give" you the Holy Spirit. That is ridiculous. That is the world's false religion keeping you blind to God's redeeming power. That kind of thinking is pride—the same arrogance that makes people believe they can control who is saved and who is not. No religious leader, no ritual, no ceremony, and no church membership guarantees salvation. It is the work of Christ alone.

Your name was written in the Lamb's Book of Life before the world was created. You did nothing to deserve this gift. Grace is not something you earn—it is a free gift of God that not all will receive. The Holy Spirit searches the depths of a man's heart and convicts him of Christ. The road is narrow, and few will find it. It doesn't matter how you've lived or how you were raised. Christ chooses, as He already knows who is going to accept His hand. I have heard this mystery explained as being two parallel truths: God elects, and man is called to believe.

Yet, the call to salvation is open to all. It is not for us to assume we are saved because we were raised in a Christian home or attended church. Being baptized as a baby doesn't secure your eternity. Attending church five times a week doesn't mean Christ lives in your heart. Singing worship songs and taking communion will not save you.

Salvation Is Not a Feeling, Not a Ritual, But a Transformation.

From my experience, the Lord delights in us when we are filled with the Holy Spirit! Heaven cheers when a soul is reborn! The moment you are truly saved, you will know. Why? Because the Lord does not hold back His joy. He wouldn't make you wonder, "Am I really saved?" No! He makes it clear. When Christ saves you, you are changed. You don't just feel different—you are different. The weight of deception is lifted, and the truth sets you free.

This is not about emotion. This is not about some spiritual high from an altar call. This is not about signing a card, passing a class, or deciding you'll "try" to be a "better person." This is not about thinking you're "good enough."

This is real. It is personal. It is empowering. Life changing.

The only ones needed in the room when you are reborn are you, the Father, the Son, and the Holy Spirit. And when it happens, you won't have to guess. It will be like getting hit square in the nose with truth.

So don't be deceived. Don't let your pride keep you in the dark.

Be curious. Stay curious. Seek the truth—before it's too late.

Jesus wasn't crucified for being agreeable. He was crucified for saying the truth.

MY IMPOSTER

I had an odd dream right before I accepted Christ.

I awoke in my dream to realize I was in my childhood home, in my mother's bed, with her sleeping peacefully on my right side. Through her bedroom door frame I could see into the lighted hall from the darkened bedroom. In the doorway, I saw myself standing in the hallway. 'She" had on one of my favorite outfits—right down to the jewelry and purse. Her hair was long, sleek, and beautiful, and her smile was so bright. Everything about her was a spark—*my spark*. She didn't talk but instead beckoned me to get up and follow her. I didn't want to. She persuaded harder using all my smiles, hand gestures, humor, and charm to get me to follow her. I didn't want to and instead moved closer to my mother for safety and tucked deeper into her comfort. When "she" realized I wouldn't follow her, I felt fury as she was dismissed from the doorway. I felt afraid of her.

I woke from the dream with a start feeling very eerily afraid in my own bed.

The dream was so profound it bothered me for weeks. I found it as disturbing then as I do now. I believe I experienced my own imposter doppelganger evil. I also believe this dream was the foretelling of my salvation a few months later.

I was afraid of who I had become.

IMPOSTER SYNDROME

I have examined my life as a whole and came to terms with my trauma and addictive nature. I have a better understanding of what pushed me astray.

I was born into sin. I was born having no identity in Christ. I was born without the Holy Spirit indwelling me. I was born to slavery.

Never feeling good enough about myself aided my anorexia, excessive exercise, social alcoholism, spending sprees, dangerous risk-taking, sexual recklessness, despair, shame, guilt, and deep, suicidal depression. I am a sinner of the worst kind. I knowingly took my gifts to inspire others and destroy myself.

Do you have any idea what it's like to live without self-worth? To feel fraudulent and ugly without all the glam on? Feeling like you live a lie every day eats you alive. Never knowing that someone is interested in what you have to say wears on your soul. Knowing you're far from independent, and far from being perfect. Do you know how hard it is to work every day in play and life to simply be understood and liked? Daily inklings about acceptance, respect, and worth. But I had lived so long being "lucky" that I began to believe it.

Who was I to feel so grand? Who was I to succeed? Who was I to do well? Who was I to be smart? Who was I to look totally put together? Who was I to do well on my own? Who was I to make such money? Real money? Seriously. I'm just a simple girl. Unimportant. At a young age, I learned to take what I could.

But suddenly it was me that was creating a spark. It was me finally getting the attention I craved so very much. I knew all I had to do was set my sights, sail my course, be honest and true, and excel at being myself. Why I'd suddenly become afraid of myself was a mystery. I didn't feel part of my own skin. True, I dressed it, styled it, and played it up, but it was just like playing dress-up in the basement. I was someone else. An imposter. This imposter was respected. This imposter was smart, cunning in business, and a force to be reckoned with. But it was all smoke and mirrors. I knew what I saw. Everyone else saw what I believed and yearned for. Or they instantly hated what I exuded outwardly.

If you haven't figured it out by now, during these times (and sometimes even today), I feel like a fraud. I worry about getting too close to others for fear they will discover or uncover the real me, whom they will then find repugnant. I've hidden and protected myself for so long that it's a habit to keep my sword up.

With grace, understanding, and a great deal of therapy, I have been able to shake off my imposter syndrome. I now know that my identity goes much deeper than others' acceptance.

Even still, I put on the armor of God every day to keep me safe and my ego identity healthy. I work every day in play and life to simply be better than I was yesterday. I no longer count anything I have done as good or bad; all are nothing more than dirty rags to Christ.

Sure, I have inklings about acceptance, respect, and worth. When I do I open my Bible.

But to be clear, I'm afraid every day that I might slip down the slope again. So, I watch myself closely and let others in help me walk a straight line.

So I return to the truth when doubt comes knocking. Not the mirror. Not the memory. The Word.

> *"For I was born a sinner—yes, from the moment my mother conceived me. But you desire honesty from the heart, so you can teach me to be wise in my innermost being. Purify me from my sins, and I will be clean; wash me, and I will be whiter than snow. Oh, give me back my joy again; you have broken me. Now, let me rejoice. Don't keep looking at*

my sins. Remove the stain of my guilt. Create in me a clean heart. Oh God, renew a right spirit within me."

Psalm 51:5-10

CHAPTER 19

TIME OF TRIALS

> *"Consider it pure joy, my brothers and sisters, whenever you face trials of many kinds, because you know that the testing of your faith produces perseverance"*
>
> **James 1:2-3**

Trials are not signs of God's absence—they are proof of His refining work. Scripture tells us that suffering is not meaningless; it is a process, a fire that burns away the false securities we cling to and draws us closer to Him.

Pain strips us bare, exposing the idols we once relied on—control, success, approval, and even our own strength. When the storms rage and everything crumbles, we are left with one truth: God is enough.

> *"My grace is sufficient for you, for my power is made perfect in weakness"*
>
> **2 Corinthians 12:9**

The enemy wants trials to shake our faith, to make us doubt God's goodness. But suffering is not the absence of His love—it is the very place where His love meets us most profoundly.

> *"Though He slay me, yet will I hope in Him"*
> **Job 13:15**

The breaking is not the end of our story; it is the beginning of deeper faith, of unshakable trust, of surrender that leads to peace. God never promised an easy road, but He promised Himself. And in the fire, in the storm, in the waiting—He is there. Always.

> *"When you pass through the waters, I will be with you; and when you pass through the rivers, they will not sweep over you. When you walk through the fire, you will not be burned; the flames will not set you ablaze"*
> **Isaiah 43:2**

This is the testing ground of faith. The question is—will we trust Him in the fire?

SUCKED BACK IN

I had been divorced for one year.

He called me on a chilly Chicago day, where I happened to be for work at the time. He said he had just been forcibly removed from the company he had ⅓ ownership of, and that a sheriff had delivered legal papers and escorted him out. His partners took his laptop and office keys, and then they booted him out the door with the promise of a day in court.

Seems he got caught stealing again.

He was despondent, upset, and afraid.

I shouldn't have taken the call. I shouldn't have taken the bait. He needed a computer to find a lawyer and get his affairs in order. He was sobbing, and I had compassion. I'd once been let go and had my laptop taken abruptly, so I knew all too well how he felt. I told him I had a spare one he could use. I gave him the passkey to my home and allowed him entry. So stupid. I had misplaced empathy. Patsy.

An hour later, he called and said that he had transferred $1M+ to my bank account from the business. He was the CFO and had backdoor access to all accounts. After all, the business was his, he said. I lost my shit. I told him I didn't want to be involved in his schemes and crookedness and that I was going to call the sheriff myself. He must have heard me—because he reversed the transaction.

What I didn't know but later found out from a kind FBI Cyber Division agent, months later, was that my ex-husband had actually used a combination of my name, my social security number, and my address to set up a new bank account at Chase Bank. Why? So he could transfer stolen money on my laptop and from my IP address. And they were making an arrest.

I was a pawn in his scheme. We were divorced and I had moved on, yet he continued taking from me. He felt entitled to use me for his gain. He felt confident I'd go along with his lies, and he had no empathy for me at all. The investigators had looked up my record and seen the domestic restraining order I had taken out against him a year earlier, so they quickly brought me into their protection. I worked with the Colorado and federal legal system to testify against him.

It seems cybercrime is a very serious offense. It is also punishable for intent to commit a crime. His canceling the transaction was just as punishable as not repenting. The "smart" con man finally got caught in his own snare.

The state of Colorado flew me in from Dallas for the court appearance to testify on my behalf. I exposed the truth of the corruption. I saw one of the partners passing as I was being escorted into court. I always liked him. He shot me a glance that said, "I'm sorry."

As I no longer lived in Denver, I stayed with my youngest son and his roommates during this trial. It was one of the best few days of my life.

My youngest didn't understand what was going on, as he loves my ex. he didn't want to hear much. I shared with him some of the details and he was comforting. He just knew his mom was really upset.

I got to the courthouse early that day. I had on my favorite wool brown sweater and jeans and boots. I found a spot by the window heater and read my Bible for hours before testifying in court.

> *"Wherever your treasure is there, your heart and your thoughts will also be."*
> **Matthew 6:27**

This passage stuck in my mind. My heart was light and full of love. I didn't feel anger, rage, injustice, or revenge. I was there to clear my name. I was full of joy and peace. Sure, I didn't appreciate that I was wrapped up in this, but the few days with the kids were great. Let's just say I felt my cup was running over.

But the abuse (and the thievery and lies) didn't stop.

WRITING ON THE WALL

May 25, 2014. The corruption is still unfolding.

I had just returned to Dallas after watching my youngest graduate from Johnson and Wales University in Denver. Both my exes attended the graduation; one was sulking and angry, whereas the other acted like he was running for mayor. Mom, the boys, and I had a great time.

There was a summons from the court on my door when I arrived home.

It was from an insurance company stating that my ex and his elevator company—his partners and their wives—had defaulted on two large construction surety bonds signed in 2009. A surety bond, sometimes referred to as bonding insurance, is a guarantee to your clients and customers that your business will fulfill the terms of the contract. It is insured by a surety, a business that underwrites the bonds. It seemed my ex and his partners' elevator company had defaulted. Now the insurance company wanted the money—1M+ from those bonds—back. And they wanted it from anyone they could find.

I began looking through the paperwork. Sure enough, there was my name. Not my signature, but a bad fake. The bond was signed when he was still living under my roof, just weeks before the protection order. His signature, plus signatures from his two partners, their wives, and my bad fake, was complete with a notarized state seal. WTF? It was time to find a good lawyer and go to battle.

My lawyer fought hard to free me from the web. Insurance companies don't want to let anyone out of a noose like this. They are relentless when it comes to getting their money back from people with deep pockets. The notary, who was the company's secretary, provided my lawyer with a deposition claiming my husband had brought the paperwork in with my signature and bullied her into notarizing it. She testified he'd harassed her, demeaned her so much that she was afraid of him because he was volatile. He insisted that I knew about, signed, and supported the bond paperwork, even though I was traveling at the time and couldn't attend. The other partners went along with the lie—or they simply didn't care—as they needed it signed. But here's the thing: It is illegal to notarize anything without the person in the room. The room was full—six witnesses, each one present, each one seeing the truth. I wasn't there when the document was signed, and they knew it. That was not enough to release me from the lawsuit.

To be released and clear myself, I had to submit over a dozen documents with my real signature on them. These documents needed to be official, and had to have been signed within 90 days of the false signature, and they could not come in the form of bank checks. Well, for a girl who saves nothing, I sure had the goods!

I had a Hertz rental car contract, Hennepin County Hospital signatures for ambulance transfers, and police reports resulting from a two-party crash in downtown Minneapolis. On top of that, I had the signature of the emergency doctor's release from Red Rocks Medical

Center—back from when I went in for a severe panic attack. I had the order of protection from a Jefferson County Judge and documents from the Jefferson County Woman Advocacy Division testifying I had been in duress during the months he'd forged my signature. I also had the emergency doctor's report, which showed that my health was struggling severely as a result of my home life. Finally, I had several legally binding company expense reports. The bonus was the unexpected crash in Minneapolis, just before the Fish-A-Roo, which had occurred around the same time the bond was notarized.

After submitting all these documents, I was released from the insurer's web. And his and the partners. It was $15,000 well spent.

What really frosted me was that I had just seen him at graduation weekend. I was with mom, and it was a great celebration. He was all nice and chatty, wanting to spend time with my boys and me. He brazenly announced "plans" for the night with my boys and assured me his girlfriend wouldn't be participating. In front of my sons, I dismissed him, telling him I wanted a night with my sons, and he could be with his girlfriend. He left quietly.

He never pulled me aside and told me he had been running from his summons for months. A summons that had my name on it. No warning, no guilt. A crime defaulting on a bond would cost me my career. He never gave that a second thought. He needed that bond signed at the time and he didn't care. He knew I would never have signed it. He has been a thief for decades.

I called him the night I got the summons. He told me it was a mistake and that I shouldn't be involved. He told me it would go away—he would take care of it. I told him to call the bondsman who had been trying to serve him and get his paperwork. He said he didn't have time. Screw them. I told him that in the morning I would call his HR division, tell them the true story, email them the paperwork, and use their help to get this legal issue resolved. The next day, the bondsman met him in the Dallas airport to serve him. Me and that bondsman became friends.

He swore to me he would repay the money I spent getting clear of his scheme. He lied about that, too.

ISMs: Deceived. Used. Abused. Stupid.

Contrary Virtue: Diligence.

Given the paperwork proof I presented clearing myself, including the Notary Public deposition of active participation of the crime, my lawyer encouraged me to fight. Take down the notary, call into discovery of every project ever notarized. I was told this was a landmark case of a blatant State Notary Public corruption. I could win this case. Beyond gaining freedom of my neck out of the noose, I would drive needed change.

I declined. I signed away my right to sue. I didn't even sue for legal fees. I set out to get my name cleared and did just that. I won the battle; the additional battles that many might have taken, I was not interested in. To me the fight was already won. I didn't want to be distracted by the nonsense of this scheme to suck my time and energy. I shut the door.

Her name was Cindy, and she was abused by my ex-husband. I wish her well.

> *"She is clothed with strength and dignity;*
> *she can laugh at the days to come.*
>
> *She speaks with wisdom, and faithful instruction is on her tongue. She watches over the affairs of her household and does not eat the bread of idleness."*
>
> **Proverbs 31:25-27**

CHAPTER 20

A HEART FOR GOD

During this time of constant turmoil, I clung to faith. I also became committed to my church community. I was thriving! I told everyone of Christ's grace. Unashamed—I am that girl.

Being so alive as a juvenile in Christ, I was a wildman! I could not read enough scripture; I could not study enough about Christ's direction and will for my life. I was growing every day. I was so thirsty for the truth—I had been starving and suddenly I had milk. I wore out my first pastor and had so much respect for my second. I was on fire, donating time and resources, and witnessing crazy spiritual growth in a community. I didn't stop praying for wisdom in my trials and discernment. I didn't quit praying the prayer of Jabez with true expectation. Bless me indeed!

Professionally, I was enjoying sharing my testimony of faith with clients over a cigar and single neat scotch in the swankiest clubs in all the fabulous cities or over a casual burger or golf swing. I remember every reaction and conversation.

I told everyone the good news. To some I confessed my sexual sin, and they realized I had them in my snare at the time. Boy, I remember those faces as I apologized and asked for forgiveness. They had a lot of truth shoved at them at one time. I was unashamed. They left with their own actions.

I've never met a stranger; I like to talk, and others like to talk back. It's a ride, talking about Christ so honestly. I simply didn't care what anyone thought. I was still Joanne, just a rush like nothing I've ever known. It's a power that elevates you. You never worry if you should have moved left instead of right. The Lord has you right where he wants you.

My best line: eating dinner alone at an upscale hotel. I've done this for decades—I attract men, and they come over. I invited them in. This time just a different agenda.

Chitchat: What do you do? Yada, yada, yada.

In between bites I look them in the eye ask them, "Where are you in your walk with Christ?"

It is a question that demands an answer. I'm aggressive. I probe.

The men were so many that I lost names. But I remember faces and their stories. I inspired hope and collected more emotional sincere hugs than I deserve. As I shared my testimony with my story, so many confessed their darkest secrets—secrets they had never told anyone, least of all themselves. My questioning was like a razor into their thoughts and high walls. I offered vulnerability, and my testimony of Christ was able to reach so many men during this time of my corporate influence. I was walking fearlessly.

The Trinity works to put you in front of others who need to hear Christ's message. Remember, this is Christ's path for you—He does all the leg work to put you in the right place. No fear. Being so free consumes you of the truth and drives out doubt. It's a force that you are protected and expected to proclaim your faith. When I spoke to these men, who approached me for their own reasons, I was a lightning strike. That's what happens when you share your testimony with someone who needs to hear it. Eyes up. Stay the course. Say the truth.

That kind of light from Christ can also attract many others' attention. Desiring connection to other followers of Christ, I reached out to many—family, friends, and those in my church—to help me in my growth. What a fast learning curve of what many believe is the Word of the Bible.

I ultimately repelled many who claimed religious sounding nonsense was the truth. I wasn't willing to bend or misuse the Word of the Lord to fit their religious view of themselves or their churches.

Do not be deceived by religious-sounding nonsense that is not in the Bible's instruction. Don't be deceived by good intentions and unholy thinking. I saw the pride that laid beneath a facade of faith. This knowledge is one of discernment. So much noise in the world today is going on with the truth of scripture. Stay close to your readings and daily prayers to enhance your understanding and discernment to see religious traps or wolves within the flock teaching lies.

> *"Not all people who sound religious are really godly. They may refer to me as Lord, but they still won't enter the Kingdom of Heaven. This decisive issue is whether they obey my Father in heaven. On judgment day, many will tell me, 'Lord, Lord, we prophesy in your name, and cast out demons in your name, and perform many miracles in your name.' But I will reply, 'I never knew you. Go away, the things you did were unauthorized.'"*
>
> **Matthew 7:21-27**

As for me, this scripture is the reason for my peace. I know He knows me. I have confidence in Christ's ability to redeem the dead. (I was one of the dead.) I know He gave me mercy. He cleared my eyes. No doubting. No second guessing. He made Himself known to me. Now it is my turn to work. I am called to grow His Kingdom one conversation at a time.

Harvesting for the Lord delights me as much as stealing flowers used to. To refresh a blank flowerbed and plant new delicate plants and to see the spark ignite is a delight. To be able to speak of Christ to others is a joy. Just like cold-calling, I have no fear. Unashamed. Stolen opportunities.

I'm sowing seeds. I'm planting plants that will grow or shrink. But the outcome is not in my control, as our Lord does all the work.

A MIRROR TO YOUR HEART

So what's with the ISM's at the end of some chapters? – All the odd placements of Virtues? – well now you'll know. Hang with me—I'm about to walk you through the personal chart that became the backbone of my transformation, and the book you're holding.

2013. In the early days of my walk with Christ, I had a thought so vivid I had to act. I was babysitting my grandsons when it struck—so clear. An urgency. I pulled the boys into my office on the mat they were playing on with the Lincoln Logs and Matchbox cars. I grabbed Post-it notes and started placing them on my office mirror, creating a personal guide—I recognized it as a "Mirror to Your Heart."

I started crafting yellow Post-its with one word, placing them on the mirror. I started with the deadly sins.

Just to be clear, the Bible doesn't give us a formal list called the 'seven deadly sins.' That list came from a Christian monk named Evagrius Ponticus, who originally identified eight destructive thoughts. Later, in the 6th century, Pope Gregory I refined it down to the seven we know today. So yes—it's a man-made list. But make no mistake: every one of those sins is clearly warned against in Scripture. Pride, Envy, Wrath, Sloth, Greed, Gluttony, and Lust—these aren't just personality quirks. They're dangerous patterns that pull us away from God, and the Bible tells us to flee from them.

I then named my personal addictions and labeled them ISMs. I put the Post-it note one rung under the sin it correlated with. Under Gluttony, my ISM was Food/Alcohol/Drugs. Under Envy, I listed Shopping. Under Pride, I wrote Image. Under Greed, I identified Work. Under Lust, I simply put Sex. Under Wrath, I printed Self-Hatred. Under Sloth, I identified Depression. I labeled them correctly under the sin that had been driving my past and present actions.

I took it one step further. I called it what it was as I labeled the bottom rung: Satan.

Under the deadly sin of Gluttony, followed by the ISM of Food/Alcohol/Drugs, I identified the bottom rung as Ill Health.

Under the deadly sin of Envy, my ISM was Shopping, and my bottom rung was Empty.

Under Pride, the master of all sins, I listed Image as my ISM, and Desperation as my bottom rung.

Under Greed, which I proudly worked under for years, I labeled the ISM simply Work. The bottom rung was Worry.

Under Lust, which was once so tantalizing, the ISM is Sex. But the bottom rung, I now labeled as Used Up.

Wrath, which is usually pretty self-explanatory, had the ISM of Self-Hatred. The bottom rung, I instantly labeled Suicide.

Sloth, to which my ISM was Depression, the bottom rung, I hurtfully labeled—the blackest times—as Broken. My personal worst bottom rung.

I stepped back and clearly saw what my life had become—the false narratives that drove my past. They were all traps. Each sin had an ISM—how it showed up in my life—and each ISM had a bottom: the consequence I had already lived. It was a ladder all right—but one I had been climbing in reverse, straight down.

My mind saw more—I was no longer a slave to what I put on the mirror or what had been driving me. I was now a Child of Christ. I needed higher ground to see my true self.

Two more rungs appeared—the high ground of excellence in Christ's eyes: Virtues. I did not know how the Heavenly, and Contrary Virtues laid out on top of the sins. I realized I was understanding something profound for my personal walk.

Also, by quickly researching the virtues, I realized that my "new idea" wasn't new at all! I was pleasantly surprised to see how much study and teaching had gone into this very topic. Amen.

When we think of the word *Bushido*, a warrior may come to mind—honor, discipline, and loyalty etched into their very breath. It was their way of living and dying with purpose. For the redeemed, our code is living under Christ's Virtues—not vague morality, but the Spirit-led pursuit of truth, integrity, and humility.

I used the Bushido virtues not as doctrine, but as a ladder. Each one reminded me of what the world calls honorable—but I found the real thing only in Christ. Bushido is not my foundation—Scripture is. I didn't use it because Scripture was lacking. I used it to expose how even the highest human ideals still collapse without God. The ladder helped me recognize what the world admires—so I could see more clearly what only Christ fulfills.

Post-it notes now covered 90% of my mirror. Boys playing trucks at my feet, my mirror told the story of where I once walked with sin and laid out where I was actually walking with Christ. Those bold words on my mirror. The wisdom I received while making this chart helped me understand my personal walk with Christ and the profound mercy He had for me. I locked eyes with myself in a sliver of the mirror that wasn't covered, and it surprised me. My reflection was sharp. I liked what I saw. It took me 30 minutes, with one potty break, to complete what I saw in my mind from start to finish.

I will continue explaining the chart, starting at the sin, but now, moving upwards.

I'll start with Gluttony—the nice Heavenly Virtue right above it is Faith. Just Faith. A simple jump. Above Faith, the Contrary Virtue of Abstinence. Above Abstinence I placed the Bushido of Right Decisions.

Moving to the sin of Envy, one rung up is the Heavenly Virtue of Charity. Above Charity is the Contrary Virtue of Kindness, and then the Bushido is Honesty.

When you look at Pride, the Heavenly Virtue is Fortitude, the Contrary Virtue to Pride is Humility. And the Bushido is Respect.

Greed is slippery. The virtue right above Greed is the Heavenly Virtue of Prudence. Contrary to Greed and being self-obsessed is Liberality, which leads to freedom. And the Bushido is Benevolence—only to give complete respect for the mercy and grace the Lord has granted you.

Probably the most tantalizing sin is Lust. But above that nasty sin is Temperance, which is a Heavenly Virtue. When you are healing from Lust, pray for Temperance. Above Temperance is Chastity. Chastity allows you to understand in your heart of hearts that you serve one Lord, and you believe His directions are for your good. It allows you to keep yourself pure of heart, pure of your temple, and pure from disease—and smart to the world's trickery. It also sets you apart as a child of Christ, protected from within. In my view, Chastity is a person's greatest armor against the world's lies. The Bushido when it comes to Lust is Loyalty. To truly be loyal to another. To have in your heart a desire to serve another, but to serve Christ above all things. To hold your word and stay the course with those you are loyal to, unconditionally, with the Word of the Bible as your template.

Moving to the deadly sin of Wrath, did you realize it's just a simple leap to get to the Heavenly Virtue of Hope? Hope is where all things begin. Hope is where everything great that the Lord can do for you takes root. Above Hope is the Contrary Virtue of Patience. Slow down on your own stubborn timelines. Seize your anger, doubt, worry—and be still. The Bushido to combat Wrath is Honor. To have honor in all things. To know that you are walking in all portions of your life in honor of Christ. It's a privilege that is obtainable but rarely experienced, and something to strive toward.

And finally, the last deadly sin: Sloth. The Heavenly Virtue to Sloth, raising one rung above, is Justice. Get your ducks in a row. Pull your head out of the hole. Be

7 Bushido Virtues	7 Contrary Virtues	7 Heavenly Virtues	7 Deadly	ISM's	Satan
Right Decissions	Absinence	Faith	Gluttony	Food	Ill Health
Honesty	Kindness	Charity	Envy	Alcohol	Empty
Respect	Humilty	Fortitude	Pride	Shopping	Desperation
Benvolence	Liberality	Prudence	Greed	Image	Worry
Loyalty	Chastity	Temperance	Lust	Work	Used Up
Honor	Patience	Hope	Wrath	Sex	Sucide
Valor	Dilligence	Justice	Sloth	Self Hatred Depression	Broken

prepared—don't be slow in mind. Right above Justice, the Contrary Virtue to Sloth is Diligence. Be diligent in the aspects of your life that will provide long-term gratification. And above Diligence, to combat Sloth, is Valor. Few have Valor by worldly standards. Find yours—it is there waiting for you. Wake up!

But when you start living by ISMs—alcoholism, professionalism, perfectionism, materialism, victimism—you've already started slipping. ISMs are not identities; they're leashes. They give language to bondage and call it personality. Virtue builds character. ISMs erode it. One makes you stand. The other keeps you crawling.

Right Decisions	Honesty	Respect	Benevolence	Loyalty	Honor	Valor	7 Bushido Virtues
Abstinence	Kindness	Humility	Liberality	Chastity	Patience	Diligence	7 Contrary Virtues
Faith	Charity	Fortitude	Prudence	Temperance	Hope	Justice	7 Heavenly Virtues
Gluttony	Envy	Pride	Greed	Lust	Wrath	Sloth	7 Deadly Sins
Food/ Alcohol/ Drugs	Shopping	Image	Work	Sex	Self-Hatred	Depression	ISMs
Ill Health	Empty	Desperation	Worry	Used Up	Suicide	Broken	Satan

How to See Your Reflection

1. **Locate Yourself on the Ladder**
   Look at the chart. Be honest. Where are your thoughts, habits, and choices pulling you—up toward virtue or down toward self-abuse. This isn't about perfection. It's about direction. The top rows reflect a life led by the Spirit. The bottom? A life slipping into bondage. You don't need soft language—you need truth. Look yourself in the mirror and face it. God already knows.

2. **Track the Pattern Before It Becomes a Pit**
   ISMs don't show up overnight. They build through repeated choices, hidden justifications, and old wounds that never healed. Catch the drift before you crash. Notice what you keep feeding—and ask why. Confession isn't about shame—it's about stopping the descent before you hit the bottom rung. You need to have some tough conversations with yourself. You have to go there.

3. **Use Virtue as a Weapon**
   Every sin has a virtue that confronts and cancels it. Pride? Practice humility. Wrath? Slow down with patience. Greed? Give generously. These aren't nice ideas—they're spiritual weapons. When triggered, pause. Don't react on impulse. Call on virtue. Speak it. Breathe it. Walk it out.

4. **Be Brutally Honest**
   This chart is worthless if you won't be honest. If you excuse living in excess, you're already slipping. You know the list—too much drinking, too much spending, too much escaping. Porn. Gambling.

Control. Jealousy. Envy. Resentment. You know your list. Call it what it is. Repentance begins with honesty.

5. **Ask Yourself Who's Been Affected**
   Your ISMs don't just impact you. Take a step back and ask: *Who else has paid the price?* Spouses, children, coworkers, friends—your wake is wider than you think. You don't need guilt. You need truth. See the damage, and let that fuel your healing.

6. **Examine What You Protect**
   Ask yourself: *What am I still defending that's actually destroying me?* Some ISMs come wrapped in self-righteousness, spiritual excuses, or wounded pride. Whatever you're unwilling to surrender—that's where the strongest chain usually is.

7. **Look for the Root**
   The behavior is the symptom, not the cause. Dig deeper. *What need were you trying to meet?* Love, control, safety, validation? When you name the root, the lie starts losing its grip.

8. **Compare Who You Are vs. Who You Were**
   Take a hard look. *Is this still who I am?* Some of the Post-its still stuck to your mirror may be lies from an old season. Don't carry a label God already delivered you from.

9. **Let the Holy Spirit Speak**
   This isn't just about self-awareness. Ask: *Holy Spirit, what do You want me to see?* You'll be amazed what He reveals when you stop trying to fix yourself and start listening for truth.

Life consists of many views. Twisted, turned, right, wrong, spiritual, indifferent. Each view derives from specific actions, timeframes, and seasons of life. But when examined with a pure heart, your true position is revealed. Perspective of your current truth of the matter is a gift. It has nothing to do with how you look on paper. Not your wealth, your title, your marriage, your education, your reputation, your good deeds, your social following, or even the story you've told yourself about your past. None of it matters here. Because the mirror doesn't measure status—it reflects truth. And your view? It's as personal as a fingerprint... and as revealing as a lie detector strapped to your soul.

But there's a problem: If you're not honest with yourself, your view is jaded. Compound that with a lack of faith, discernment, and wisdom, and the lines blur fast. Sin loves to play games.

Sin takes deceptive forms. It appears kind, loyal, and charitable. But it's a snake, waiting for an opening. It slithers into your emotions, wraps itself around your thoughts, identity and works on your soul like a slow-growing cancer, assuring you that you are good, while eating away at you.

Evil is tireless. It hunts. It watches for any way to trip you up, to plant ideas, to feed your insecurities. Think how hard virtues must fight to take root in your character. The question is: Who do you want working through you?

As I became more discerning, I saw how deeply I had fallen into sin's traps. I examined my ISMs—the excesses, indulgences, and abuses that controlled my life. I found that once you start feeding these ISMs, you're bound to fall deeper into despair.

Now, it's your turn. Make your own mirror to your heart. Write down the areas where ISM's have taken hold. Then, go one step further—identify your bottom rung.

Right Decisions	Honesty	Respect	Benevolence	Loyalty	Honor	Valor	7 Bushido Virtues
Abstinence	Kindness	Humility	Liberality	Chastity	Patience	Diligence	7 Contrary Virtues
Faith	Charity	Fortitude	Prudence	Temperance	Hope	Justice	7 Heavenly Virtues
Gluttony	Envy	Pride	Greed	Lust	Wrath	Sloth	7 Deadly Sins
							ISMs
							Satan

Look at what you've written. Does your list resemble mine? You might be surprised how much of it overlaps. Sin doesn't need new material—it just recycles the same traps, dressed in different disguises.

I was fortunate to survive the deep claw marks of my past. Grace was given when I didn't deserve it. And even now, I check in with myself daily—not out of guilt, but because I know how easy it is to drift. I self-audit with honesty, asking the Holy Spirit to show me what I can't see on my own.

I once lived in the pit. Now I live on higher ground. But I didn't climb out alone.

There's a reason I share this. Not for shock. Not for pity. But because someone needs to hear it. If that's you—then hear this: Look at your mirror. Look at your heart. Don't flinch. Don't explain it away. The truth won't kill you—but denial might.

Christ's love is greater than whatever you see staring back. You are not your lowest moment.

That mirror was my turning point.

It's where this book began.

This chart, this truth, this confrontation with myself—it became the backbone of everything I've written. I didn't write this book from a stage. I wrote it from the floor.

So start where I did.

Just be honest.

SCARLETT'S SINNER CORNER

During the time I spent reflecting, repenting, and rebuilding, I thought it would be a good exercise to make "the list." It's a long list. Looking back, I can clearly see the self-hatred I had for myself back then. I was abusing my body, taking dangerous risks, and washing it all down with Grey Goose.

I once sought solace in substances, believing they gave me power over my life. Now, I see how they only fed the chaos within me. Through Christ, I have found a new kind of strength—a strength that doesn't come from a bottle or a balloon, but from the quiet assurance that I am loved and redeemed. My scars tell a story—not of defeat, but of resilience. I am not defined by my past addictions, my pain, or my failures. I am defined by His grace, which has taught me to persevere, forgive, and live with purpose.

Binging alcohol and weed were my nemesis. They dull the pain, push aside feelings of insecurities, charge my already zapped brain, and make me very reckless. It's odd—with an addictive personality, I didn't get bitten harder by these "friends." But boy, did I try. I say I didn't get bitten because I felt I had the power to put these drugs back on the shelf when I was done. Still, had I dropped them earlier, I might've stopped the cycle long before I finally stopped it years later. By then, I was already shattered, suicidal, and broken.

I've drank more Grey Goose than the average bear. Weed, my drug of choice. Nitrous was a treat, and the three together made for a perfect recipe for trouble. I knew enough about my personality to stay clear of anything stronger. Cocaine scared the hell out of me because I feared it would love me. The others were too unknown and foreign to me. I wanted nothing to do with them. I liked to think I had the power and felt I could somehow control the effects that large amounts of alcohol had on me.

Goose was the most dangerous and had the biggest impact on my body and soul. The first drink just oiled the pipes. The second, third, and fourth helped me get the crowd going and gave me the attention I so desired. I'm fun, funny, crass, and witty. After drinking six or more, I reached a point of takeoff, and that's when I was game for anything daring. Borrowing golf carts or paddle boats, jumping behind the wheel of a sports car with the willing idiot who owned it, or skinny dipping in the ocean at midnight—you name it. Almost always when I was traveling alone, the Goose train ended in risky, unprotected sex. The pure adrenaline rush of "being in charge" played right into my destructive soul.

The nights I would go down the rabbit hole alone were my darkest. I would prepare all my tools: drink, weed, and NOx ... and then cycle upon cycle would begin. I would ready six balloons of NOx and two additional whippet stainless dispensers loaded with three shots apiece. Meanwhile, I had 600 canisters nearby. The NOx mixed with the weed and Goose allowed me to slip into a wonderful void free of my overactive brain. I had breathing through balloons down to a science.

Essentially, I would cut off oxygen to my brain and replace my blood oxygen levels with nitrous oxide. This is incredibly dangerous to do alone. But secrets are secrets because you are alone.

Alcohol wasn't a factor in my life in Montana. It really kicked in when I went on the road with my first corporate role in 2002. Living on an essentially unrestricted expense report suddenly opened huge doors of excessiveness that I had never experienced. My boss at the time showed me the ropes and led by example. We'd hit the bar of a swanky restaurant after work and board the train, living large and in charge with whole lobsters as appetizers, inch-thick baseball-cut sirloins, and endless mixed drinks. One drank Turkey, the other Glenlivet, and Goose was my choice. Throw in a client or two or two dozen, and we were the party.

One such evening, we had 15 clients and teammates at the Capital Grille in D.C. The food, drinks, and gutter talk reached an all-time high, and the manager interrupted and handed my boss the bill and told him we had to leave. The bill was over $7,000 and growing, but the management cut us short. I remember the laughter when we left the restaurant to find another place to drink. No one in the group was embarrassed or ashamed of our behavior. We couldn't believe they'd kicked us out with the cash that was being thrown around at them like confetti.

Living as a rock star, jetting here and there and everywhere, is indeed a lifestyle choice.

Three more of my jobs had the same vibe. Work hard, play hard—that was our motto. I can't say I didn't have a total blast for more than a decade. The mayhem and success were the icing on the cake. The social alcohol addiction was easy. "Networking dinners" were simply a part of life. Fly in, have an appointment, go to dinner, have a steak, and start drinking. I was sleek, stylish, and usually the only woman in a sea of male clients and peers. All encouraged excess, especially me. Everyone wanted Jo to come in and hold meetings, create laughter, and lead others on a reckless night of abandon and adventure. Problem is, they got to go home and return to normal, whereas I had to fly to another location and indulge another round of clients in the exact same scenario. Looking back, it was one of the most self-destructive excesses I've ever had. Drinking led to reckless behavior, sex with strangers, spending, and self-despair the following day. It was an endless cycle.

When I accepted Christ in 2012, my excessive life of vodka drinking and sexual risk-taking stopped. I no longer had the same desires. But addiction is tricky—it just shifts forms.

Cigarettes are a different story. I have smoked on and off since the age of 12.

I grew up in a smoker's house and never had any negative feelings associated with the habit. Closet smoking for over 40 years has become more an emotional than a physical need. I heard someone say once that a cigarette is your best friend. I can totally relate. A smoke was always there to keep me company. A smoke listens to your thoughts, calms your nerves, and offers peaceful solitude. It's always there, waiting for you to invite its comfort. It also adds to the laughter and adventures with girlfriends or boys who crave its company. Smokers don't feel bad about their choice to sneak off and get their fix. A cigarette doesn't care how you look or smell to others. A cigarette only offers comfort and acceptance. It revels in your dependency and invades your thoughts if you ignore it for too long.

It gets to control your travel as well. Where can I have my last puff before boarding a plane? How quickly can I get off this plane and meet my friend for a 10-minute reunion? Do I have enough? Or do I have to stop into a convenience store to keep up my end of the bargain in this committed friendship? Having a stressful moment? Grab a smoke. Having a great day? Grab a smoke. Crying? Laughing? Golfing? Skiing? Got to have that smoke! Conference calls were my right to sit outside and puff away. Crack a beer? Better have that smoke. Eat a big meal—got to have a smoke.

By the time I went to Sabino, I was smoking close to a pack and a half each day. Wake up in the middle of the night and be comforted. Wake up in the morning and say hello to your friend and confidant. Find a nice, cozy spot in my garden to make the smoke feel comfortable. Make excuses not to go places where you couldn't smoke. Get hotels with balconies so I wouldn't have to sit out front and hide while I enjoyed my smoke.

For now, this craving has been replaced partially by meditation. It's also been stamped out with the help of

Chantix. Smoking while on Chantix is like sucking on a metal spoon. Yuck. Finally, breaking the chains of this habit and rotten friendship is paying off. My cough is gone. My physicality in long hikes or athletics is back. My breath is fresh, and I can actually taste many flavors, like spices, again. However, I will continue to give myself grace if I slip up or purposely indulge. It's a hard habit to kick when it's been in your life so long.

Finally, let's address weed. Like smoking and drinking, weed entered my life at age 12. It was harder to get back then, but thanks to some of my friends' brothers, it wasn't *really* difficult to get.

Uncertain I can ski the bumps without music and weed. Uncertain I can go to a concert without desiring it to add to the mood. Uncertain I could garden all day without it.

When I accepted Christ, I removed this friend from my choices as well. It felt good to have natural dopamine running through my nervous system. But that only lasted so long. I could put it out of my mind and not have it calling to me like the cigarettes, but I willingly welcomed it back into the fold when I realized there aren't many drugs that lessen fibromyalgia and its widespread musculoskeletal pain. I tried expensive CBD oil for six months because I had heard it works great. Not in my case. It tasted bad and offered no relief. It is unsustainable to take Tylenol for the rest of my life. Fibromyalgia is a pain that I simply cannot tolerate for days on end. It seeps into every joint and crevasse in my mind.

I am not ashamed.

Some chains are harder to break than others. But each one brings me closer to freedom.

"For I know that nothing good dwells in me, that is, in my flesh. For I have the desire to do what is right, but not the ability to carry it out. For I do not do the good I want, but the evil I do not want is what I keep on doing. Now if I do what I do not want, it is no longer I who do it, but sin that dwells within me."

"So I find it to be a law that when I want to do right, evil lies close at hand. For I delight in the law of God, in my inner being, but I see in my members another law waging war against the law of my mind and making me captive to the law of sin that dwells in my members."

"Wretched man that I am! Who will deliver me from this body of death?"
Romans 7:18-24

We all fall short of the perfection of Christ. As for me, I no longer strive for perfectionism—I strive for obedience. Perfection was never the goal. Faithfulness is.

CHAPTER 21

ALL THAT GLITTERS IS NOT GOLD

It amazes me the opportunities I've had—some I seized, others I passed on. With me, there's never a lukewarm response when doors appear open or need to be closed.

I was working for another global OEM. The entry was rough.

The first two weeks of any corporate onboarding process are consumed by company policies, ethics, diversity, commerce, and fraud training, each requiring certifications from HR. In the corporate world, this process drains hours each day for the first few weeks. On top of that, I eagerly contacted my clients to inform them of my move while learning the company inside out—like drinking from a firehose—all while meeting new teammates and leadership.

Despite the chaos, I sold my first chiller for the service division in my third week. Of all places, it was installed in Missoula, Montana. A long-standing client I'd sold chillers to for years allowed me and my new company to submit a proposal for the first time in years—and we won. I negotiated the equipment sale and start-up bid through a dealer representative in Spokane, Washington, alongside the brand engineering director and a Seattle engineering firm I had deep connections with. This was the first business meeting in Missoula where I was paid to be there. It felt fantastic.

But quick success breeds resentment.

The new equipment sales VP wasn't pleased. He started calling me "The Pirate" to my equipment sales teammates, unable to fathom how a "service sales" newcomer had brought in early sales with clients his team had been "working" with for years. Instead of embracing my connections, expertise, and efficacy for selling equipment into this vertical, he felt threatened—worried I'd outshine him in front of his peers. My service bosses, however, were thrilled. They loved that I was bringing in clients to both the service and equipment divisions.

The VP's response? He pulled his best salesman from the government team and put him in charge of the hospitality vertical, where I was deeply entrenched. The new guy knew nothing about hospitality, a vertical built on longevity and trust.

The night before a client meeting in Vegas, my new sales teammate and I had a showdown. He informed me that all leads had to go through him for equipment sales—with or without service. I countered, explaining that I could very well sell into this vertical and needed his support. Using his boss's words, he insisted that new sales now controlled this vertical.

Then he asked, "Do you really think you are going to run this vertical?"

I didn't flinch. "Yes, that's what my boss hired me to do."

He leaned in. "Is that what you're being told?"

"Yes," I said flatly. "Our bosses have pitted us against each other."

That moment shifted everything. He sat back, realizing I was right. What followed was an incredibly honest conversation—one where Christ became part of our dialogue. From that night, we built trust, uniting our efforts. We brought in teammates from fire life safety, building automation, VRV, and elevator groups. We called ourselves the Wolfpack.

And we were unstoppable.

Months earlier, I had shaken the North American president's hand, confidently telling him that if our sales methodology shifted, we could move massive market share. It worked. I was offered the role to lead sales efforts for the vertical, overseeing eight global brands under one powerhouse, all promoting hospitality.

My dream job—or so I thought.

I would report directly to the new division and the new boss, with other business groups choosing to work with me. Early buy-in was crucial. But ignorance mixed with pride is a nasty cocktail.

Teammates pulled me aside, questioning if I really wanted to work under the new boss. They warned me about his vastly different style. I shrugged it off, saying I wasn't working for him—I was working for the role's success. I believed I could shift his mindset toward collaboration.

I dove in, reaching out to teammates and clients to gain insights, crafting account structures that prioritized our clients. I kept my new boss informed, engaging him with the established hospitality team. Meanwhile, I juggled my old role and helped recruit my replacement. HR was finalizing my offer.

Then came the cracks.

The new boss wasn't interested in teamwork. He had his own agenda, eroding trust with every team call. In our first face-to-face meeting, I advised against starting with a rigid agenda, urging open dialogue to build trust. He ignored me and opened instead with a stale PowerPoint presentation—one we had already seen and presented at a client meeting the day before.

The room fell silent.

After a full minute, I spoke up. "Thank you for the overview. Now, maybe close your laptop, put the agenda aside, and listen to your team. Let's tighten the strategy we've already started."

The team applauded.

Later, he called me, upset by my "aggressiveness." He said I blindsided him, labeling me arrogant. I told him it wasn't arrogance—it was leadership. I explained the importance of humility, of listening, and that he was naive to think he knew more than the team about hospitality.

Four months later, the offer arrived. For tripling my workload and leading the vertical sales for eight brands, they offered me a $0.36 raise and capped my incentives at

$39K, tied to EBITDA—something I had no control over. In my current role, I had a strong salary, a $180K cap, and full control over my sales and all the relationships with the clients.

I declined. "No, thank you," I told him. "I'll bet on myself."

He was stunned. This was a high-profile role endorsed by the CEO and supported by the board—a fast track up the corporate ladder. But he miscalculated. I wasn't some corporate climber desperate for validation. I was a high-school graduate with unshakable faith in herself.

He tried to justify the offer, claiming I didn't understand the structure. I corrected him, explaining that the last time I worked under a similar offer, I had a $200K base, $100K in stock options, and a bonus tied directly to my EBITDA contributions. I told him I had built a career by defying expectations, and betting on myself was what I did best.

There's no rebuttal to that kind of conviction.

It wasn't about the money. Sure, pride and ego were certainly at play—no doubt. But I felt used and stupid.

It was about the box they tried to put me in—the value they assigned to my worth. The offer didn't encourage me to win—it was a dead-end trap just for glory and prestige.

PRUDENCE

When I got off the phone with him, I prayed for many hours. By all intents and purposes, they had offered me what I had prayed for. Expand my boundaries. Let me make an impact. The Lord delivered his commitment to me ... or did he? The thought of this big job had distracted me for four months. I had lost focus on my day-to-day activities in my old role with my pack. I had mentally made a shift that was morphing my influence toward new areas. Although I had stayed active with my teammates, it was kind of like Elvis had left the building because I was so busy with preparations and a new role.

Worse, I had stopped reading my Bible. I was busy, distracted, and left wondering if the offer was just a shiny ego-driven trap the devil had concocted to distract and limit my influence for Christ's Kingdom. And let me tell you this: When I declined the offer, it was like a cleansing rushed through me. I had complete clarity.

I had not realized how much stress I was under. I constantly needed to be impressive and show them they had made the right decision to offer me the role. I had suckered myself into believing this was what I really wanted because it was a step up. As with everything, my path had already been chosen. The offer was to come, the written offer was to be rejected, and a new path was to be carved.

Within six months, I was gone. Turning down the role offered me no future security with this global company. I believe they chose me, once again, because they thought I'd be pliable. They thought they could use my influence as they needed with internal teams as much as the clients. They knew my relationships were strong and my sales were stronger, and they felt if they offered me the role, I'd stay engaged. I do not think they offered me the role because they wanted me to have any influence over inner company politics—they offered it to me because I hit their radar. To them, I was a pawn. They knew how much I wanted the role. They knew if they hired someone else, that person couldn't compete with my current relationships.

I say this with no imposter syndrome. I had the skills, connections, industry knowledge, and tenacity to handle the role. This was the role I had envisioned since I came into my industry. They hired someone else to lead this group, and within the first month they had ostracized me from all senior client meetings. And within a year, the new group failed. The investment they had poured into assembling, hiring, and marketing this new group had cost them a fortune.

Looking back, I realize there were many traps in that opportunity. I'm so thankful I said no to the big promotion.

PERSISTENCE, RESILIENCE, AND FAITH

Persistence is the quiet voice in your mind whispering, "Try again," when everyone else is shouting, "You need to give up." "Stay down."

Resilience is not about avoiding falls—it's about learning to land more gracefully and rise more powerfully each time.

Faith is the knowing deep inside that you cannot fail. You have already won the war.

Persistence transforms the impossible into the achievable, step by stubborn step.

Resilience is courage in motion—an ongoing process of bending without breaking.

Faith is following His lead and moving forward. With purpose. Trusting. Assurance.

When the world closes a door, persistence drives you to find an open window.

Persistence grants us second chances; resilience teaches us to make the most of them.

Faith says follow me. Trust me. I AM the way.

Resilience is the strength found in scars, each one a story of lessons learned and truth acquired.

Persistence doesn't rely on luck; it relies on grit, patience, and the will to keep going despite all odds.

Faith says this is the path I have planned for you. Be strong, faithful servant. I have you in my path for your mission. You are my beloved.

Resilience is the art of turning setbacks into stepping-stones toward your next success.

With persistence, you shape your future; with resilience, you outlast your fears.

With faith, there is no worry of the future. Your path is firmly in Christ's control and pleasure.

CHAPTER 22

POSTERIOR TIBIAL TENDON DISFUNCTION (PTTD)

YEAR OF THE FOOT

Thanksgiving, age 54, my world changed. I lost the ability to walk without immense pain—a reality that stretched on for 21 months. In one year, I was diagnosed with posterior tibial tendon disfunction (PTTD) and severe fibromyalgia, broke off a romantic engagement, had foot reconstruction surgery, went on long-term disability, and lost my job. It was a time of trial, no doubt, but also a time of self-discovery and Christ's strength.

I originally had a direct flight that got rerouted three times in two cities and became an all-day event. Travel at its worst. I must have walked 20 miles in airports that day in unsupportive Uggs. By the time I arrived, I could barely walk. My right foot was simply not working right. Every step felt like my ankle was breaking. You know the feeling when you're playing volleyball and you come down wrong on your foot? That's what every step felt like. The pain throbs so deep in your foot and body that it wakes you up at night.

I wrapped my foot in an ACE bandage and shoved it in my shoe. Keep moving, I told myself. It will work itself out—after all, I'd done nothing to hurt it. I didn't ski off a cliff, fall, slip, or kick anything that could cause this much pain.

On January 12, 2016, everything became clear when I went to a podiatrist in Dallas. He examined my foot, ran me through walking and balancing tests, and told me I had to try to stand on my tiptoes on my right foot. In my mind, I was telling my foot, "Raise up and go on your tiptoes," and my foot was saying, "No, I'm going to stay flat on this floor." It had never occurred to me to try to raise up on my tiptoes, nor had it occurred to me that when standing only on my bad foot, I could not hold my balance for more than two seconds.

You have stage IV posterior tibial tendonitis dysfunction (PTTD).

What???

I never really thought about my mobility. I never thought about it until my foot quit working.

PTTD is an acquired progressive disease of the foot and the ankle. In one of its most severe stages (stage IV), the deltoid ligament on the inside of the ankle fails, resulting in a deformity of the ankle and a deformity of the foot. Your foot, it turns out, is basically a house of cards. When the foundation goes out because the tendon is no longer supporting you, your arch falls and your foot no longer pronates (back and forth motion). Sometimes this collapse is gradual—other times (in my case), it is sudden. When your tendon goes out, your ankle rolls (side to excruciating side, back and forth, slantways—anyway it wants to, resulting in pure pain). It does this again and again with every step. No support. Essentially, every step you take makes it worse. And it all hurts like hell. Zap, zap, zap.

Progressive? Disease? Like it's going to get worse?! Late stage? Like—is this really happening? I'm an athlete. I ski, I am a road warrior, I scuba dive, I golf. This summer I just hiked the Redwoods for four days with a 26-lb pack. I hiked up a 50-foot waterfall, dammit!

PTTD is also commonly referred to as adult-onset flatfoot. I've had flat feet my whole life, I say. (Denial.) It's a condition caused by gradual or sudden changes in the tendon and its ability to support the arch. The posterior tibialis tendon is a strong cord of tissue. It is one of the most important tendons in your leg. It attaches the posterior tibialis muscle on the back of your calf to the bones on the inside of your foot. Mine had exasperated. The doctor told me, "It's amazing you've made it this far without getting it checked all these years. Didn't your foot hurt?" Sure, my foot/feet hurt, but I've been traveling up to 85% of the time for the past two decades.

In heels.

My doctor prescribed me gabapentin and meloxicam and advised Tylenol for the pain. He gave me a 12-week script for physical therapy, grounded me from travel, provided me a wrap brace, and put me in a walking boot with firm instructions for the next six weeks. I needed to keep my foot raised and iced, walk only when needed, and participate in physical therapy three times a week. The last instruction hit the worst. Because my right foot would be in a boot, I could not legally drive. In fact, I was told I should not drive without my boot because my foot was very weak. And if I got in an accident, I may not have had the strength to brake.

I lived alone. Not only can I barely walk—but I also lost my freedom.

FACING MY PRIDE

After six weeks, there was no improvement. At seven weeks, I got a hard, plastic, custom foot/ankle brace to replace my boot (affectionately known as my Forrest Gump). It had a lightweight plastic custom footbed with arch support that stretched up to my mid-calf. Velcro helped secure it. It helped keep my foot from rolling with each step.

Once I got the custom foot/ankle brace home, I realized I could only wear tennis shoes. The cast didn't even fit into my flat boots. This was where the girl in me really crashed down. My work wardrobe is full of executive suits, trousers, silks, dresses, and skirts that three- or four-inch heels accentuate. I was devastated to give up my shoes. It was one of the hardest changes I'd made—even with all the pain in my foot. I never considered wearing only tennis shoes for the rest of my life. My pride took a severe hit. I experienced denial at its finest and grief at its worst. Yes, beautiful shoes were my master.

An entire weekend of tears went toward realizing that my entire closet consisted of only four pairs of work trousers hemmed short. They were my factory tour pants, which I could wear with flats. Every outfit I tried on made me look short and stumpy without a heel. This stupid foot!

I was prideful. I had Christ's comfort, His acceptance, His love, and all His glory. But I didn't want to sacrifice my comfort to get closer to Him. Especially not my shoes.

I searched all the shoe stores in Dallas to find some sort of professional shoe I could fit my brace into. I started with all the upscale shops, thinking I could find the perfect fit. I tried traditional spots and retail shoe departments. No luck. I tried on a pair of black New Balance tennis shoes to go with black suit pants and cried through the whole experience.

Then, on a random Target shopping spree, I looked in their department and found a pair of plastic patent leather ankle boots. My brace fit in perfect!

RECONSTRUCTION FOOT SURGERY

After months of useless PT to assure the insurance company hoops I wasn't getting better, I made an appointment with a progressive Dallas orthopedic surgeon and went in for my first consultation. He examined my foot and walking, took an MRI and X-rays, and came back with the hard truth: I could either continue using my brace and live in pain, or I could opt for surgery.

I liked him. He didn't pull punches.

"The surgery is complex and will take six to nine months to heal," he said. "You will be non-weight bearing for 12 weeks in a cast. Elevate, ice, and rest 22 hours a day for the first 6 weeks. Physical therapy starts at 12 weeks, three times a week. Plan on being with the PT for three to six months. After the foot heals, the two screws in your heel from the calcaneal osteotomy reconstruction may have to come out."

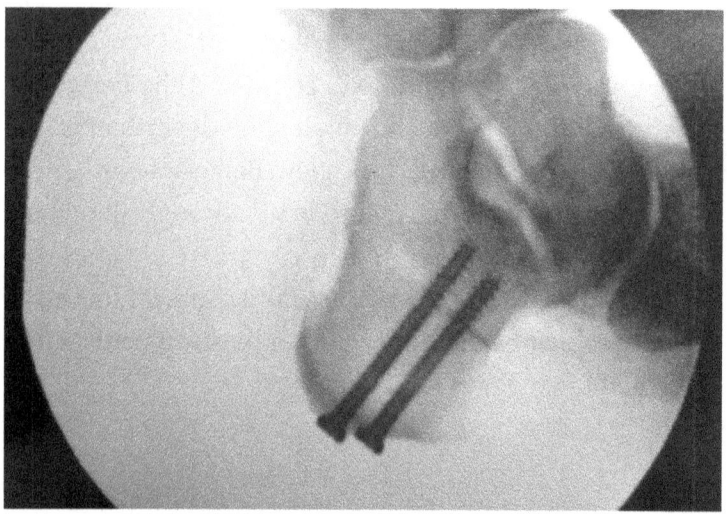

I would, in essence, have two feet that did not walk the same way without extensive physical therapy. I would also most likely walk with a gait in the future. Basically, sports as I knew them were out of the picture for a long time—and possibly forever.

He should have just said: Your foot is a train wreck.

Essentially, replacing the tendon and spring ligament, cutting the heel in half, and readjusting the foot into a new position with two two-inch screws to regain an arch. And as it healed, I would need to carefully understand that

PTTD is a progressive disease, and surgery would only slow the destructive path.

My chiropractor and physical therapy doctor chimed in: "Walking with a limp and putting 80% or more of your weight on your left side also changes your muscular skeletal system. Your muscles and tendons will actually strengthen on the strong side to keep you moving. Meaning they will grow in the exact wrong path of left and right muscles to keep you going at all costs. It's amazing what the body will do. You don't even know it's happening—except for the occasional sore feet or back. After the surgery, once you can walk again, you will need to learn to balance your gait, and keep continual focus on your skeleton, which has been off for years. You will need constant repetitive muscle exercises to get your crazy left side muscles to grow evenly on the right side as well. Your hips will hurt uncontrollably, your knees will ache, and your neck will feel broken because you need to do so much to compensate and stay upright."

I put in for FMLA and long-term disability leave. The insurance company informed me that PTTD potentially qualified me for SSI disability, and I should apply.

Disability? I'm an athlete. I am not out of the game. My foot just stopped working. Don't count me out. It will get better.

PREPARATION

....

I prepared. I dug in.

I formed a medical team centering around my mobility and mental health. I had my podiatrist, surgeon, physical therapist, and the best sports chiropractor in Dallas. I also added a deep musculoskeletal masseuse, who I met with twice a week before the chiropractor. Most importantly, I started seeing Dr. Carolyn Greenleaf, a Christian psychologist. I was grieving—I sought her help to overcome my grief and fear of losing my mobility. The loss of my mobility never crossed my mind—until it did, and it was terrifying.

All this time, my foot was in serious pain, but I had to work until my surgery. Traveling was part of my job description. Every step, brace or not it would freeze up in what felt like a vice that was being tightened and crushing my bones. Pressure from trying to walk would cause explosive nerve pain. Just straightening it out in the morning was torturous. Putting it on the floor felt like thousands of needles were being pushed into it from the bottom. I often had to crawl downstairs because I couldn't walk. Uneven surfaces were excruciating. Because my foot had no support, even with the brace, it would roll back and forth on uneven surfaces in painful sparks, such as public sidewalks. I went to a concert in a farmer's field and felt like I was walking on hot coals with each step. My friends made fun of me. Airports were the worst. I couldn't count on my foot to be strong enough to hold me on an escalator, so finding elevators was my only recourse. So many added steps to the elevators. To combat the pain, Tylenol, ice, and elevation became my best friends. I would travel with breakable ice packs for nights in hotel rooms or for when I needed to break one out and put my foot up on a chair to ice it.

I fought. I prayed.

During this trial, I prayed all the way through. I devoured the scriptures and had great peace. I was reading my Bible daily. I was searching for peace and finding it. I was being pulled through this trail by the Lord. In hindsight, I see that the Lord was bringing me closer to Him and slowing my butt down to pay attention to Him. Odd sort of blessing, but that's exactly what it was.

PAIN

Pain is a snake under your skin. It messes with your head and convinces you that you will never be free of it. It seeps into your dreams until you wake up crying. Minute by minute, it controls your thoughts. It controls your judgment. It prevents your peace. The constant pain is exhausting. Each day, you feel like you've climbed Kilimanjaro in flip-flops. Getting into bed, I'd feel like I was sinking six inches into the mattress. Getting up felt like raising myself out of a coffin. The first hours in the morning were tedious. Can I put my foot down? Nope—better sit back on the bed, give it a minute, and try again. Okay, it's unfrozen now. Let's get up and try to walk out the initial pain until the foot warms up and works a little better.

I'd walk like the tin man because my entire body hurt from foot to head. My hips made it difficult to walk, stand, or sit. My neck was always strained, and my deltoids were up around my ears. And that foot! Every step felt like my ankle was breaking. Foot, foot, foot: That's all my mind wanted to dwell on.

I saw a video of my grandson's seventh birthday party that captured me walking with my back to the camera. There I was, a month away from surgery in my plastic boots, walking across the yard, my entire left arm swinging like I'd had a stroke. Meanwhile, my right arm was curled tight up to my chest. I was horrified. I watched in dismay as I strode faster to greet my grandson, the left arm just hanging and bouncing with each step lifelessly, my hand flopping. I thought: What the heck is going on with that arm? How long has this been going on?

That was when I started searching for a top Dallas rheumatologist.

FIBROMYALGIA

I was diagnosed with severe fibromyalgia. This diagnosis is an elimination of the scary autoimmune tests such as rheumatoid arthritis, Sjogren's, muscular dystrophy, lupus, Crohn's, and Graves' disease. There is no one test for fibromyalgia.

No wonder my body hurt so much. I blamed it all on the foot. Blamed it all on the misalignment of my skeleton and muscles. Suddenly I understood the brain fog I'd had for months. The chronic fatigue. How had all my doctors missed this over the years? Some would say I suffered a double health whammy in one year.

So, I researched my new diagnosis of fibromyalgia and discovered that the causes with women are often linked to emotional trauma and domestic abuse. Fight or flight. Your body simply can't stay on high alert for 54 years without something giving. It was a lifetime in one nasty diagnosis, coupled with a bad foot.

Fibromyalgia is a disorder characterized by widespread musculoskeletal pain accompanied by intense fatigue, sleeplessness, and memory and mood issues. Researchers believe that fibromyalgia amplifies painful sensations by affecting the way your brain and spinal cord process painful and non-painful symptoms. Women are more likely to be afflicted due to prolonged psychological stress. For me, it also presented in the way of temporomandibular joint disorder (TMJ), tension headaches, anxiety, irritable bowel syndrome (IBS), and depression. Like I wasn't depressed enough.

There is no cure for fibromyalgia. There are medications that help relieve the pain, but basically, exercise and Tylenol are your only options. When you have a severe fibromyalgia flare-up, it makes you feel like your entire body has the flu. Your cognitive abilities go out the window with something they refer to as "fibro fog." Fibro fog? I used to think more clearly under a bottle of Grey Goose.

FIBROMYALGIA AND COMPLEX PTSD

Fibromyalgia and complex PTSD (CPTSD) are often intertwined, both rooted in prolonged exposure to stress and trauma. Chronic stress from CPTSD can over activate the body's stress response system, the hypothalamic-pituitary-adrenal (HPA) axis, leading to heightened pain sensitivity and systemic inflammation—key markers of fibromyalgia. Emotional and physical trauma can essentially rewire the brain, increasing its sensitivity to both pain and stress, which helps explain how these conditions often develop side by side. The symptoms overlap significantly: chronic, persistent pain—musculoskeletal in fibromyalgia and often somatic in CPTSD—along with crushing fatigue, sleep disturbances, and cognitive challenges like brain fog or dissociation. Emotional dysregulation, a hallmark of CPTSD, can intensify the physical toll of fibromyalgia, creating a vicious cycle where emotional distress triggers physical pain, and physical pain reawakens emotional trauma. The connection between body and brain is undeniable in both conditions. CPTSD keeps the brain locked in survival mode, fostering hypervigilance and chronic stress, while fibromyalgia amplifies pain signals through the central nervous system, a phenomenon known as central sensitization. This constant feedback loop between mind and body not only erodes physical health but also chips away at one's quality of life, straining relationships, limiting daily activities, and deepening the isolation that often accompanies chronic illness. It's a relentless cycle where trauma fuels pain, pain reignites trauma, and the struggle to break free feels both exhausting and unending.

If Fibromyalgia is part of your story I am sorry. It is a cruel reminder of the past. I have grown to think of it as a thorn in my flesh to remind me every day of Christ's mercy.

"But he said to me, 'My grace is sufficient for you, for my power is made perfect in weakness.' Therefore I will boast all the more gladly of my weaknesses, so that the power of Christ may rest upon me."

"For the sake of Christ, then, I am content with weaknesses, insults, hardships, persecutions, and calamities. For when I am weak, then I am strong."

2 Corinthians 12:9–10

CHAPTER 23

INTO THE STORM

THINKING CLEARLY

During this trial, many discounted me. Perhaps they thought I was embellishing the pain. Perhaps they thought it was not a big deal. Perhaps they were ignorant.

I was very transparent with my clients and co-workers regarding the reason for my absence. I told them all of my determination to heal and return to working for them. Many learned about PTTD because of my story. Many clients told me of friends and family members with the same disability. I knew I wasn't alone, and my clients held me close. I received support from those that trusted me. It meant a lot.

"You walk just fine," a toxic man noted. "I don't know what all the fuss is about." "I heard you were walking just fine in Chicago." "Why don't you just continue to wear those boots and do your job and go about your life?" My friends: "You look cute in those boots, what's the big deal?" "Get up, buck up, it's not such a big deal." I remember defending myself to co-workers and friends about the hours I'd spent in physical therapy, the hours I'd spent with a chiropractor, and my numerous appointments each week. I told them I was walking only because of all those efforts. My foot still needed surgery. Thank you very much.

HEARTBREAK

By this time, my engagement was crumbling. Our entire courtship had centered around fun and sporting activities. We skied, golfed, went scuba diving, hiked, saw the Rolling Stones, attended the Catalina Jazz Fest, backpacked, kayaked, and danced. Each day, I kept him updated about my health. He asked me every day if my foot was feeling better. Each day, I reminded him of the facts and how my mobility had been impacted and my imminent surgery. Again, he asked me if my foot was better. In frustration, I sent him articles on my condition and videos of the surgery needed. Again he asked if my foot was better—he wanted to go skiing and wanted to know if I was in for my half. I broke it off.

It was my fault. I encouraged the relationship. When I met him, I was so lonely. I was actually crying on friends couches because I wasn't in a relationship. He was still the cute and charming boy I had known in high school. I wanted to be in love, and I let myself be. I let him in because I was vulnerable to someone I thought I knew. I lowered my guard.

But I am smarter than this. Joanne, really: How many times?

I felt "we" were different. I was older. Wiser. I had Christ as guide, but I quit listening. I fell back into the trap of wanting to be loved. He knew my testimony of Christ and said he accepted it. Lord knows that's pretty much all I talked about. He said he was different than me—but Christ was in his life. I believed him because I wanted to believe him.

I sacrificed my body. I said yes, I went along with sleeping with him until my Spirit was roaring, imploring me to stop. I prayed. Of course he would understand if "we" abstained for the four months until our wedding. The act was hurting me so much. He replied yes, but soon began to tempt me with lingerie and playful attempts. Old feelings of abandonment—not being heard, being rejected—rose up. I gave myself grace. I forgave myself and asked for forgiveness. I dove into my Bible. I said no.

I knew it was over. I saw clearly that I had been distracted by a shiny new penny promising love. But it was a trap.

...again— *I am smarter than this. Joanne, really: How many times?*

> "*Lead me in the right path, O Lord, or my enemies will conquer me. Tell me clearly what to do and show me which way to turn.*"
>
> **Psalm 5:8**

ASKING FOR HELP

I had asked mom if I could heal in Missoula. I told her what I had been diagnosed with in great detail. She blamed my dad. I then laid out the immediate and long-term plans of my trips back to Dallas for my surgeons' appointments and told her how the next six months would play out. I needed her support. Emotionally, I wanted to be in my childhood home and bedroom as I was healing. She said yes.

The surgery finally arrived.

I had moved out of my second-floor, three-bedroom apartment into a ground-level, 717-square-foot one-bedroom utility apartment in my complex with an attached garage. I had strategically housed more of my furniture in my three storage garages and created a new nest. I'd stockpiled hard goods and prepared for my surgery by working with my clients and suppliers to get them set up for my leave.

My friend Donna flew out to be with me for the day of surgery. She stayed with me for six days post-surgery to get me ready to travel home to Missoula to my mother's house to heal.

During this time, I was reading my Bible up to six hours a day. I thanked the Lord for being with me through this trial and anxiously searched for knowledge. I was in a turmoil of bad circumstances—but in my heart, I was at peace and fully under the Lord's control. I went into surgery praying and came out with the same protective prayer in my head. I went home for three days, then I had to go back to the doctor in Dallas for a check-up. Donna drove the streets of Dallas, which is not an easy feat for most Montana girls, but she did it with gusto and was a great support to me. After they put on a hard cast, I was free to travel home to Montana.

You're probably wondering why I wanted to go to Montana to heal. Mom and I always had long-simmering resentment in our relationship, but I thought we were on a good streak. I wanted to go home to Montana so I could breathe in the mountain air. I wanted to heal in my room and in a house I've known my whole life. I also still had a bevy of friends there and knew that I shouldn't be isolated during this time. I knew I had time and wanted to value every second of it.

PERSPECTIVE
....

I believe Mom was shocked when Donna practically carried me through the door after a grueling day of travel, less than a week after surgery. The journey included 14 wheelchair changes between flights, as American didn't fly direct to Missoula. Donna was a trooper, handling every detail, while I was completely out of it on pain meds. By the time I got home, I was physically and emotionally wrecked—a far cry from the strong, independent woman Mom was used to seeing.

Mom was very kind the next few days. She knew that I was basically committed to dad's La-Z-Boy, with my foot up, except for when I had to scoot to the bathroom or my bed. I continued to read my Bible from dad's chair day after day and go to my new doctors. I feel my convalescence the next five weeks was spent peacefully, intellectually, and observingly of my mother's actions.

But within the first week, the cutting remarks started. "Are you sure you need more toast? How much coffee do you need? Do you really need cream calories? You know all you're doing is sitting there and gaining weight, right?" I tried to tell her, "Yes, mom. But I'm healing, my body needs to heal, I've allowed myself this time to heal. My body needs food, it's healing." But still, she would say, "Well, I'm happy you can manage to be so positive about that." And when I would scoot into the kitchen to make food, she found it insulting because she hadn't offered it.

Christmas was at my brother's house. No, I didn't want to go and have him help me up and down five slippery cement steps. So I told her to please bring me back some dinner. Mom returned with a plate of turkey, some stuffing from Costco, and a bit of mashed potatoes without gravy. I asked her, "Was there no pie?" She looked at me and said, "You don't need it." That same day, I spoke to my middle son. He was incensed that mom would leave me alone on Christmas and that my brother wouldn't bring the food to mom's instead. He was going to his dad's for Christmas, and he promised to bring me over a plate. He came over a little sheepish, holding a plate of 100% meat. His dad would not share any of the food they'd made with me. Only the food that my son had contributed to the holiday meal would be allowed for me.

It was good meat.

Scripture often refers to food as a symbol of God's provision (*"He prepares a table before me in the presence of my enemies"* — *Psalm 23:5*). Despite human cruelty, God's care remains unwavering, and this moment could serve as a reflection on relying on His provision when others fail you.

Food is not just sustenance; it symbolizes care, connection, and community. But it can also be used as a weapon. By denying me access to food from their holiday meal, during such a time of health struggles, my family weaponized one of the most fundamental human needs. This act likely wasn't just an oversight or selfishness—it was a deliberate move to reinforce control over my physical and emotional well-being. Humiliate you by emphasizing your dependency on others. Remind you of your exclusion from what should have been a moment of familial warmth and connection. To me, it was just mean-spirited. All-consuming dismissal—by all.

A light in my life came from an old school friend Bob. He reappeared as a kind angel taking me out and including me into his family on Christmas Eve. He was rooted in Christ and we talked for hours. I will never forget his kindness to me during such a hard time.

ARMOR OF GOD

Two weeks into my recovery, mom's attitude became harsher and harsher. It seemed from the minute my peaceful spirit entered her house, she was on edge. She grew colder by the day. Staying out of her way wasn't that hard, as I could barely move, but my physical weakness seemed to make her meaner. She didn't like me reading my Bible day after day either. She made cutting remarks about my faith.

I decided to fast and pray one day while my mother was at bridge. I moved slowly through the house, praying scripture and asking God to bring peace and truth into every room. Her room was last, and I prayed over it as well.

When she came home, she headed straight to my bedroom. She asked why I hadn't eaten and seemed instantly agitated when I said I wasn't hungry. It was like she could sense I had been with the Lord. She called me ungrateful, useless and accused me of rejecting her as a baby. She brought up things from thirty years ago—told me I always needed my way—and tried to bait me into an argument.

She told me I wasn't as good as I thought I was and that I'd failed at everything. I must have looked weak to her, kneeling on my scooter. But in truth, I felt strong. And that strength angered her more.

I had been reading about spiritual warfare. I had fasted and prayed in a home that wasn't mine, and I believe what was hidden in that house came to the surface. I didn't go in with authority—I went in with obedience. And whatever was stirred up *knew* it wasn't welcome anymore.

My peace of mind and tranquility felt so good. So refreshing and powerful. It was such a change from the battles we'd had before I'd accepted Christ.

She was enraged. Her face was red, twisted, spitting fury—but her words didn't land. I calmly told her I could see how upset she was, but I knew who I was. I had been approved by the Lord Most High, and her words held no authority over me.

That only made her angrier. She raised her hand to slap me—and I blocked it with my Bible. That's when everything changed.

She pointed her finger at the Bible and hissed, *"He is not in charge. He is not in control!"*

I looked her in the eye and said, "Christ dwells in me. HE is in charge. He has full control over my life."

I wasn't scared. I wasn't shaken. I was armored. I was witnessing evil, but it could not touch me.

I packed a tote and called Donna to come pick me up. I left the house that night.

I couch-hopped for five nights, emotionally and physically depleted. My body hurt. The painkillers were wearing off, and I just needed my bed. I called and asked to come home.

When I returned, she said I had abandoned her to punish her. She told me she had done nothing but worry. And still, she hadn't called. She hadn't reached out. She knew where I was. She knew I'd return eventually, before my flight back to Dallas.

We cried. We made up. But the truth stood firm—she had seen something in me that day she couldn't explain. And it terrified her.

> *"Finally be strong in the Lord and in His mighty power. Put on the full armor of God, so that you can take your stand against the devil's schemes. For our struggle is not against flesh and blood, but against the rulers, against the authorities, against the powers of this dark world and against the spiritual forces of evil in the heavenly realms. Therefore put on the full armor of God, so that when the day of evil comes, you may be able to stand your ground, and after you have done everything, to stand. Stand firm then, with the belt of truth buckled around your waist, with the breastplate of righteousness in place, and with*

> *your feet fitted with the readiness that comes from the gospel of peace. In addition to all this, take up the shield of faith, with which you can extinguish all the flaming arrows of the evil one. Take the helmet of salvation and the sword of the Spirit, which is the word of God.*
>
> *And pray in the Spirit on all occasions with all kinds of prayers and requests. With this in mind, be alert and always keep on praying for all the Lord's people."*
>
> **Ephesians 6:10-18**

LIVING IN FAITH

In my mobility trial, I stayed deeply studying my Bible. Through many tears and battles I prayed all the harder—but my Spirit was on fire. My attitude was amazing, and I simply had no fear I would succeed through this dark time. I had joy.

Christ, my first and only love.

Utterly ... all I can think about.

I'm a thankful, hopeful, humble servant. I openly pray to expand my boundaries. I ask Him to let me speak His words. Witness to His loving grace. Begging Him to open the doors to meet others who need to hear the good news. Asking boldly to speak to the witness of Christ and of redemption.

> *"Oh, that you would bless me indeed, and enlarge my territory, that your hand would be with me, and that you would keep me from evil that I may not cause pain."*
>
> **Chronicles 4:10**

The prayer of Jabez is one of my favorites. Boldly ask the Lord to Bless you! Ask over and over again with earnest anticipation. Exclaim to the Lord your desire to serve Him, to increase His Kingdom and to do His bidding. Know that the Lord did not give us his spirit of timidity and fear but one of authority and power. The prayer Jabez is one that I pray all the time for strength, wisdom, and guidance. It's a beautiful prayer. Know that we all should have a bold heart towards Christ so we could ask him unashamedly to bless us! Christ wants us to be strong and unapologetic when talking about his gracious gifts. He wants us to experience love and tenderness and acceptance, and He wants to continue filling us with hope, inspiration, and a longing to bring others to Christ. Christ didn't choose us out of the darkness to not enter into the light and be bold. He chose us to preach his words—to reach into the corners of the earth where people are afraid, deceived, and broken. In our brokenness is when Christ does his best work

Pray that Christ keeps his hand upon you to lead you into new territories and out of distress. Pray that He stays close to you day in and day out and that you continually thirst for the wisdom of scriptures and pour through the words of his direction. Christ is always there, waiting to receive our love and respect, waiting patiently to show His love. He is patient, never oppressive, always longing to be close to us. He is waiting for you exactly where you are.

Do not be afraid to ask for as wide and long and as deep as your imagination can run to serve the Lord's Kingdom. As with anything, when our boundaries expand it is our desire not to cause pain to others as we go through growth and change. Pray that your actions do not bring shame upon the Kingdom but always illuminate and point to the Father in heaven. Do not be deceived by others who would try and steer you off the path that you are on for the Lord. There will be many temptations and traps set for all disciples of Christ to slow or weaken their path. Take heart when you are going through trials as the Lord is drawing you closer to Him.

HEALING AND RECOVERY

In January, my friend Wanda and I flew back for my six-week post-surgery appointment. I navigated the airports on my five-wheeled knee scooter with her trying to keep up. My foot was healing well, and my attitude remained positive. The cast came off, revealing a calf that looked like it belonged to a 10-year-old, covered in dead skin that I eagerly scrubbed away. Then a new cast went on.

We had planned to fly back to Missoula in two days, but I told Wanda I wasn't going. Instead, I'd rely on church friends or Uber to get to my appointments, order food in, and heal in peace. She cried when I told her, saying she was proud of me for choosing myself and making the right decision. Her encouragement meant a lot.

When I called Mom to tell her I wasn't coming home, she was shocked but seemed relieved. She wished me well but insisted I get my clothes out of my room as soon as possible, as if the neatly folded items were somehow taking up too much space in her empty six-bedroom house. It was laughable.

I threw myself into the Word, filling my time with Bible study, creating art with colored pencils, and cooking wholesome meals. I quit all substances—even cigarettes. I read, studied, continued my church activities and attended weekly counseling with my phycologist to address my abandonment issues, pain, mobility challenges, and work crisis. Despite everything, I felt joyful. I was facing this head-on.

The healing process was intense. I've never been overly coordinated, and the sports I excel at rely on decades of muscle memory. Walking in two shoes again felt unnatural, and physical therapy was painful. The pain I'd endured for the past year was gone, but in its place was a new, unfamiliar pain. I had to relearn how to walk. My muscles had atrophied, and every step revealed misalignment I had never noticed before. Bursitis in my thigh and hip brought its own challenges, and my chiropractor worked for weeks just to get my right shoulder moving again after months of overcompensating with my left. My hips were misaligned by two inches even if all I'd done was scoot around the house. My clavicle was tight. It was a frustrating process—one step forward, two steps back—for months.

I fought off depression with faith. Friends came from Montana in sweet two-week shifts, supporting me, meeting my doctors—some of whom they still ask about today. I stuck to my healing plan, attending every therapy appointment, getting massages, seeing my chiropractor, and diligently doing my exercises. I wanted to climb stairs again. I wanted to get over my fear of going downstairs. In physical therapy, we worked both feet, even though insurance pushed back, claiming I didn't need it.

The darkest moments came at night. Doubt crept in: You're never going to heal. This was a waste. You've lost your career. The pain will never go away. My brother's voice echoed: This was useless—we all need to accept growing old. My mother's voice dismissed it all: The doctors are just taking your money. Unsupportive friends said, "You're making too big of a deal out of a sore foot. And then my own thoughts: I'm not strong enough. Even I can't survive this. This is too hard.

But I prayed. I cried my fears away. I let go of unsupportive friends. And I kept going. None of it was a surprise to the Lord.

By the end of eight months I returned to work, feeling triumphant. I could walk without pain. I had accepted tennis shoes into my professional wardrobe—after all, I had fought to regain my ability to walk, and I wasn't going to let footwear get in the way of my progress.

The first few weeks were brutal. Then, eight weeks later, I had to request long-term disability again. The screws in my heel, instead of settling into the bone, had started to push out. You could see the heads of two screws protruding just beneath the skin. It was red, sore, and painful in shoes.

Unemployed again. But I was healing. And I was at peace.

I overcame disappointment with gratitude. I put in the work. Over time, I returned to skiing, walking on the beach, and shore diving with my scuba gear. I hiked again, though I no longer carried heavy packs. I embraced new shoes and regained my mobility. I walked barefoot without pain. My golf game still sucked, but I was grateful for every swing. I lost the weight I had gained during my immobility. I learned to walk with confidence. And I still won't tolerate teasing about my tennis shoes.

If there's one thing I'd pass along from this experience, it's this: Be kind. Even if you don't understand someone's disability, treat them with dignity. Support your loved ones. Don't abandon them when they need you most. Support your daughter and sister when they are broken physically but at peace mentally and morally. Be nice to your teammate who was suffering.

If you've been diagnosed with PTTD, know that there are alternatives to the pain. You can reclaim your mobility. Not being able to move without pain is terrifying—but it can be overcome.

I accomplished my healing with faith. I walked through fire and came out whole. I stayed close to the Word, feeding on His wisdom daily. Christ is the only reason I made it through this season. It was a trial, no doubt, but I thank the Lord for guiding my steps and teaching me wisdom along the way. Not untouched—but refined. Every ache had purpose. Every delay, a divine appointment. What looked like a setback became the sacred ground where my faith found footing.

> *"He makes my feet like the feet of a deer;*
> *He causes me to stand on the heights."*
>
> **Psalm 18:33**

That verse isn't a metaphor to me. It's a testimony.

My body may still carry reminders of the battle, but my spirit runs free.

CHAPTER 24

PRIDE DISGUISED AS LIGHT

EDUCATION

During my medical leave, I had it in my mind to pursue my education and change my path. I worked for a few months on disability on my dissertation application to Dallas Theological Seminary. I went to Newcomer Day's on campus. I soaked it all in. I sat in classes and was enthralled. The speaker, Dr. Charles Swindoll, said, "If you are here because you can't be anywhere else, you are in the right place." My spirit roared.

The master's degree I wished to pursue was in pastoral counseling. Healing from my foot surgery, I had a chance to forge a new life path for myself.

I looked at my finances and realized I could afford it. I knew the lifestyle I'd be living would be a dramatic downshift, but I was fine with all of it and knew the sacrifices I would have to make. I had been thinking about this school for five years, even visiting the campus for the first time in 2013. Now was the time! I planned to get some consulting jobs to stay afloat and strengthen my relationship and knowledge of Christ. Then I would move into a new career of Biblical counseling after completing my three-year degree.

As I had not graduated from college, I studied to pass the Miller Analogies Test (MAT). I took 20 practice tests, studied *MAT For Dummies*, and crammed more factoids into my head than I thought possible.

Passing that test meant I could enroll in any master's course I desired. Essentially, it's the GED equivalent for college. As someone who always felt I'd failed by not graduating from college, the ability to pass this test was a huge personal accomplishment for me. Being a baby boomer, the idea of true success was a college degree. Not having one had bothered me for years—even though I had proven you don't need a degree to get a high-paying career.

I studied and passed the Miller Analogies Test (MAT) on my first attempt at the SMU Cox School of Business. The MAT is an admissions exam used by graduate schools and high-IQ societies across the United States. The MAT measures your capability to recognize relationships between concepts, your grasp of the English language, and your general cross-disciplinary knowledge. The MAT contains 120 partial analogies, and you are given one hour to complete them. One hundred of them will count towards the final score, and 20 are experimental. You don't know which ones will be thrown out.

What are MAT analogies?

The analogies on the MAT are statements that suggest two terms are connected in some way and that two other terms are related to each other in the same way. Mysteries. These analogies are written using the equation form:

A:B::C:D

You would read this as "A is to B as C is to D."

All analogies found on the MAT are partial, meaning one of the terms is missing. For each analogy, you will be asked to fill in the missing term using one of four answers provided.

The MAT covers eight distinct subject areas:

1. Language and Vocabulary
2. Humanities
3. Social Sciences
4. Natural Sciences
5. Mathematics
6. Semantics
7. Association
8. General

TURN OF EVENTS

It took me three weeks to complete my 50,000 word dissertation to DTS. You try articulating your past marriages, reasons for divorcing, and how it affects your witness in under 500 words. (Without the realization of the fact you have complex trauma ...) Ha! The questions were geared to uncover all your past sins and make you explain how you've overcome and surrendered them to Christ.

They were very intimate questions, each with a specific purpose. I was painfully honest and totally transparent about the darkness I had experienced and the servant I'd grown into with Christ's help. I submitted my admission alongside my newly minted MAT certificate, my high school diploma, and my transcript of records from the University of Montana, which showed I needed only 23 more credits to graduate college.

And then I waited. I never once considered I wouldn't be going to school in the spring semester. To me, it was a done deal.

During the admission committee's review, an old friend of mine asked me to consider working on his national team. The role was one I knew well; I respected Brian and knew he'd be a good boss. I could work out of my home with reduced travel and light required hours. I had insurance benefits for my continued foot rehabilitation, and plenty of time to focus on school with a reduced class load. He said, "20 hours of my business development was worth 60 hours of anyone else's."

I thought: I might be able to do it all.

I accepted the phone interview on Monday, and then again Wednesday, then immediately moved on to the face-to-face interview with a plane ticket to Minneapolis on Friday.

I got the letter on Thursday. I wasn't accepted into DTS. It was a nice form letter telling me to continue to build my spiritual gifts and consider re-applying in a year or two. It also indicated that they doubted my ability to get a job once I graduated. Gulp.

I was verbally awarded the new job the following Monday. Seven days that defined my path had come and gone. One door closes, another opens. I was devastated. Did my waver on being a full-time student cause this to happen? Was I being punished for thinking I could take 100% focus off of the Lord? How could the Lord not approve my going to DTS? He's heard my prayers and knows my heart. He knows my desire to pursue him and speak his words. He knows my yearning to be closer to him. Ask and you shall receive—right?

I dropped into the ashes of despair and lamented hard. I tried pleading with Him. Bargaining with Him. Flat out arguing with Him while taking cues from Job. Asking Him over and over, "Why?" But there was no voice from Him. No reply. Zilch. Silence.

I spoke to my pastor and called my friends. They were all shocked and overjoyed at the same time. That Sunday in church, I spoke to the elders in my community group. In tears, I told them of the rejection of going to seminary and of the new role I'd been offered in corporate. They listened to me with caring compassion. One of the older men, Jimmy, looked me in the eye and said, "Joanne, if you cannot accept the door that the Lord has opened and walk through it with confidence, then I don't know what else to tell you." "It's not every day you get such a definite answer of God's will. You've been blessed. He has plans for you and they are not you being tucked away in an environment surrounded by Christians." That really hit me between the eyes. I realized I had made the plan to go to school and for whatever reason the Lord knew better. I started at my new job without looking back.

Through much reflection and prayer, I discovered hidden motives inside my heart: pride.

I had wanted to escape to a Christian environment. I wanted to cut the past off and step completely out of this world as much as I could. I wanted to be the one to decide I was out. I wanted to be the one who decided I was in. I was prideful—I wanted to call the shots. I was stubborn—it was my way or the highway.

But then finally I found humility—He calls the shots. And I was remorseful—back on my knees apologizing and thanking Him for plowing my path. My peace was restored. His voice returned. I submitted willingly—again.

The past year had felt like a relentless season of breaking and rebuilding. From the moment my foot surgery forced me into stillness, I had been in a constant state of waiting—waiting for healing, waiting for direction, waiting for a new life to begin. The pain, both physical and spiritual, had tested me in ways I never anticipated. I had mistaken the open space in my life as an invitation to take control, to dictate the terms of my own transformation. But control was an illusion. The rejection from seminary was just the final, undeniable proof that my story wasn't mine to write—it was His.

Looking back, I saw the pattern: the forced pause, the long months of uncertainty, the doors I tried to pry open only for them to remain shut. And then, just as I was grasping at my own plan, another door—one I hadn't knocked on—swung wide open.

God wasn't punishing me; He was positioning me. He had spent all those months preparing me, stripping away my independence, and forcing me to trust Him when I had no other choice. The foot injury wasn't just a detour; it was an altar. A place where my will had to be laid down so that His could take over.

I had thought healing meant walking again. I now understood healing meant surrender. It meant stepping forward in faith—not into a classroom, but into the world He had called me to, the one I had wanted to leave behind. And as much as I had longed for the safety of theological halls, my battlefield wasn't there. It was here—in the corporate world, in the very place I had tried to escape.

My feet were steady now, not just because they had healed, but because they were finally walking in alignment with His plan.

And this time, I wasn't leading I was following. But I was still prideful of my own accomplishments. Surrender is harder when you thought you were already obedient. But it's often in the *second surrender*—the one that costs your pride—that God aligns your purpose.

ISM: Selfishness. Self-determination. Shoe wear. Pride.

Contrary Virtue: Humility

'Many are the plans in a man's heart, but it is the Lord's purpose that prevails."
Proverbs 19:21

CHAPTER 25

RUNNING

Again, I was on a plane returning from a work event. My hair was in a tousled bun, I wore jeans, tennis shoes, and no makeup—I was totally at peace. I had a new job with a company I knew nothing about, and I was out of pace with the technology I was promoting. Still, I felt optimistic, relaxed, and calm despite the fact that, in the past two weeks, I had looked out at both the Atlantic and Pacific Ocean from my hotel window, all while being fed more information than anyone could possibly retain. My new team was ecstatic. I was on board, and the feeling was mutual.

I hadn't wanted to be there, in corporate America. I had wanted to be tucked inside DTS as a first-time master's student.

I did what I had always done: dug in, learned my way around my new company, contacted my clients, and started with gusto. Seven months passed in a heartbeat. I bought a home, planted roots for the first time alone. I left behind my church and my mission group, barely read my Bible, and my daily talks with Christ were only through tears of disappointment. And once again, I picked up my habit of smoking cigarettes. A dog returns to vomit.

ISMs: Image. Identity. Coping strategies. Stress. Perfectionism. Performance.

JUST BLAKE

Escaping on an airplane. I just buried my brother Blake before his actual death. Left him with a hug and a kiss to die. Two weeks of my life that I wish were my Groundhog Day. Can't I experience the love of my family and best friend again? It would be a great reward.

I witnessed to him about Christ every day for two weeks. He told me he was a believer. Asked a few questions and received knowledge of Christ. We had never spoke about God. Do I know he's saved? Do I know he has assurances of life in heaven? Do I know he is ready to meet The Father? Do I know I love him? Cherish him? Wish I could take his place? Yes. Is this enough to satisfy my worries? Oddly enough, kind of.

I'm uncertain whether I was a good influence. I'm not certain he heard my words of affirmation. My words of sorry. There is a lot unsaid in this relationship to this very day. But Blake and I—we are both survivors.

Truly, I enjoyed being in his presence—in the calm atmosphere of his loving home. It was a dream to have so much time with my brother. Swinging by DQ or KFC on the way every morning if he'd made a request for something he would like. Walking in ready for the day's activities and spending hours on the couch talking. Offering support. Getting to know my beautiful niece Kathryn and re-connecting with June. It was so nice. Meeting all his friends and co-workers and scouting troops was impressive. The sheer number of friends and supporters Blake had was truly amazing; sometimes, he had up to 12 visitors each day. He had a non-confrontational presence and a predictable, painful path to death that he was embracing.

A man who was once robust, certainly obese, and soft-faced is now a pile of withering bones. All in just five months' time. Colon cancer is a snake. It can strike quickly and have no mercy. Get checked. Early.

Going back to my life, forgetting his everyday struggles and his basic needs, which June and hospice is tending to. Forgetting his pain. Being relieved of his sleeping patterns and his quickly diminishing abilities. Not seeing what he does or doesn't keep down, how much he eats, or the bouts of begging him to eat, which surely will come sooner than we think.

Smiles were scarce with Blake since childhood. Mainly because he was mom's target—the fuel for her controlling needs—and a punching bag for the other brothers. As he matured, his obsession with details and escapism into his safe world of clues, paths, and organization was perfect for police detective work and leadership in the scouting organization. It became all he spoke about aside from his family. He had no drive or energy for anything else. Some might've thought he was lazy, but I saw it as his form of self-protection from ridicule. Keep your head down, focus intensely, and complete the task at hand. That's where he found his space and his passion.

Leaving him tears at my heart. So needing and in pain, so afraid, but at the same time in total peace. Furious at my own needs to get on with my life. Terrified of staying and witnessing death's unmerciful dance. Sad to fly away. But I do.

My role as his little sister has been lacking since the day I was born.

Blakey was my favorite. He was nine years older, soft, lovable, and shared the same emotional needs and abuses as me. We were equally ridiculed by mom and tormented by the other brothers. Odd men out, birds of a feather, empaths in a sea of cruel competitors. I was just happy to have a safe zone in a cold, hostile home. Then he left, and I was alone. I was 10, he was 18.

We chose his eulogy together. I opened my Bible next to him for days and we chose the exact scripture. He didn't read my words before I said them, but I know he approved of them. We sat next to each other and went through his old scouting and policeman drawers of memories. I sewed his last patch on his boy-scout uniform, ready for his burial. He meticulously planned his funeral. Does he know how much I care? Does he know how much I love him? Does he know he was a good brother? Does he know he impacted my life? Truth is—probably not.

Seven days after his high school graduation, he boarded a bus to join the Army as a Military Police Officer (MP).

No one told me—they just said we had to get in the car. As the bus was loading and hugs were being distributed, my world was crumbling. You would think someone would have prepared me. I was just a little girl, after all. But why would they think about my feelings? As the bus pulled away, tears streamed down my cheeks. Then he left and I was alone.

The letters came until they didn't. The calls home came until they didn't. The wedding invitation came, and we all got in the car, drove to Denver, and watched. I cried. He married the first woman who treated him nicely. She was domineering, he was weak, and she took over his voice, his thoughts, and his attention. Then he left for good, and I was alone.

Brief visits over the years. Blake sits; June speaks. How are you, Blake? June replies. What's new, Blake? June speaks for him. I think it was just easier for him to sit on the sidelines. It fit his personality to have someone else in charge—especially with mom and our family. June is a strong-minded, good woman. The strongest supporter of my Blake. One of the strongest, fiercest women and most protective mama bears I know. Mom hated June. Hated June for her strength and the way she protected Blake. Left Blake's family out of her will, letting her have the last and final word. Cruelty at its finest—even in death.

Put in for bereavement leave. Arrange and pack for an overseas trip and fly to Billings. Put on a suit. Paint on a strong mask. Don't upset the family. Don't bring up any feelings about the past. Don't upset mom. Don't incite others in conversations to talk about anything real. Don't talk about Christ. Have fun, stay light, and participate in talkative family dinners. Just enjoy each other's company. Be useful and helpful. Deliver his eulogy. Disassociate. I left the Billings Veterans' Cemetery basically after the flag was presented and "Taps" was played. Board a plane to Hong Kong. Get out. Get away. Important engineering meeting I was speaking at. Escape. Run. Numb my pain.

Blake never held a strong place in the family. Not since his birth. He was teased and mocked for many seemingly obvious faults, which others observed often. He was the slowest one in the family—which is very telling. My family is full of highly intellectual, logical, mathematical, engineering, and leadership-oriented folks. We are all leaders in our own right. Very different. And as I found out, most of my family is very ruthless. They acknowledged Blake for his success, but more in a surprised way. He survived off the grid from mom, the brothers, me, and the rest of our family. I respected that.

Blake's trauma response was to freeze. Hyper-observant, detail oriented, a silent processer of peoples patterns and micro-behaviors. He took it all in.

Mom was upset when Blake told her he had no memories of childhood. I understood perfectly. He mercifully shut it all out. I have distinct, visceral memories of events. I also didn't have day-to-day or happy memories in my head. Blake told mom he had none. What a great place to start from.

I have photographs from my childhood with Blake, but I cannot recall many of the memories associated with them. I have many memories of the behind the scenes, but few as an actual member of my family—besides Blake.

His funeral was perfectly planned by him down to the very last detail. I had never seen a police department, or the Boy Scouts of America, honor a man the way they did Blake. I delivered his eulogy after his beautiful daughter, Amanda, poured out her heart and that of his family. Their love for my brother was clear. I spoke with pride of my brother. "Just Blake" was the best man I've ever known. For me, it was easy—because he was my Blakey.

CHAPTER 26

CHASTITY

Chastity. Yes, that's still a word in the English language. The meaning hasn't changed—nor have the boundaries. I get the most complexing look when I use the word. "For real?" people ask, at first somewhat amused. Like ever? What about your needs? Don't you get horny? How do you ever let someone in without sexual intimacy? Does that mean just serious dating and then fooling around is okay? Hah. No. I tried that. It doesn't work for me anymore.

Immediately they assume it's because I'm so "religious." I must be sacrificing myself for my show of faith. I'm holding myself back. The men project sincerity, believing I'm wishful and tempted, just playing hard to get, thinking they just might have a chance if they keep flattering me.

Little do they know I'm repulsed by the thought of sleeping with someone who is encased in darkness so deeply that they try to maneuver their way into me abandoning my devotion to Christ's teachings. Opening my body and allowing a deceived soul to enter me? The thought makes me cringe. It sickens me.

I don't judge them—I was them at one time. I just depart, telling them, "No, thank you. We are not a match."

"Flee from sexual immorality," Paul writes in 1 Corinthians 6:18-19. *"Every other sin a person commits is outside the body, but the sexually immoral person sins against his own body. Or do you not know that your body is a temple of the Holy Spirit within you, whom you have from God?"*

I hold tightly to this truth, which has transformed how I view intimacy.

The man inquiring is usually very nice, handsome, intriguing, sometimes a new or old friend that identifies as a Christian—just "not at my level." He can't believe what he's hearing. Purity in your 60s? He can't wrap his head around the concept. He actually shows pity for me. I guess I'll take his indifference and leave him mystified as to how I could turn him down. They have no shame in asking and prompting more tantalizing temptations. A lot of truth exposed in one honest conversation.

I have long since stopped flirting suggestively and offering my sexuality as the first opening. No more open innuendos to offer intrigue. I became wiser. I found the more I'm open about my faith and the truth of my conviction, the more I was protected.

Yeah—well, that wasn't always the case. In a relationship beginning I state my faith, my life as I live it, my goals and aspirations—capping it off with an absolute knowing I have contentment in my life that is palatable, and it comes from Christ. Some find it appealing, others are instantly repelled. But a girl has to have hope.

The ones that pursue me are oddly, irritably interested—but curious. They want reassurances on timelines of intimacy, thinking only about what hoops they need to jump through to break your resolve. Nice, huh? Sure, on some level it is flattering. But on the other hand, it's very sad.

It's the easiest thing I was able to shed. Lust was the main driver of mine for years. I gave myself away to feel worthy and affirmed. Once Christ moved in and filled my soul, I was full to the point of overpouring. I no longer needed the fix.

"Do not be conformed to this world, but be transformed by the renewal of your mind," Paul writes in Romans 12:2, *"that by testing you may discern what is the will of God, what is good and acceptable and perfect."*

I prayed for this transformation, and it came.

Sex has become expected. Commonplace. More often than not, sex happens before you even know their middle name. In between ordering appetizers and the main meal. Not a big deal. It was like that for me. Until I knew the truth.

CHAPTER 27

MY CAREER

APPRECIATION

The experience of the career and all it offered has been exceptional.

My two decades have been spent in corporate America working for and with Fortune 100 engineering executives. These have been leadership roles with global giants of manufacturing. I've sold water, air, technology, and everything mechanical in-between. I've survived the corporate ladder—certainly with some scratches—and prevailed against many odds. It hasn't been an easy path I've followed in business and life, but I'm still here and alive today.

The Lord has blessed and prepared me with a fast-paced career that is intellectually challenging and rewarding. In His time my career became His mission field. My career has been nothing short of a miracle. I will forever be thankful to Him for blessing me with dreams that reached the stars. Without His heights, reaching and pulling me through my journey, you wouldn't be reading this right now. It's that simple. Everything He does is for my good—even the trials.

The corporate world has allowed me to excel at growing my leadership abilities and setting goals. The discipline of desk work and travel suits a high-energy mindset. Being allowed to "own" the business I managed for the betterment of the overall team was an environment I thrived in. Learning from the best and brightest world-renowned experts was a privilege. And to think they invited me to learn, and I got paid for it.

I enjoyed being a road warrior, traveling up to 85% for 23 years. I had boundless energy and passion for my work, and I loved what I did. I thrived in this environment—because to win, you only had to compete against yourself to meet your quota and lead the team results in growth. My sales strategy never changed. Persistence. Find the hidden sales channels and make it happen.

The quality of the global corporations I've worked for—the teams, peers, superiors, clients, and industry friends I've had the honor of knowing and working with—has filled a place in my heart that is still here to this day. I would have never learned from or impacted so many without my career. For that, I am forever grateful.

To truly be up to date with my knowledge of all the newest technologies and future roadmaps for combating our global energy crisis has been a pleasure. Holistic knowledge of building mechanical and technical solutions has enriched my life. I realized I'm not that far removed from my father's intelligence. It was mind-blowing to realize I was smart. Like scary smart. Every part of sales made sense. It seemed easy. I saw the pattern of how things needed to work together.

The education I have received during my years of work has been invaluable. It has all been empowering and enlightening. Learning was always available and encouraged! Free education—what a concept. My favorites were chiller courses and factory tours. The smell of grease oil brought me back to dads shop. I asked so many questions that they nicknamed me "Columbo" in my early years. I needed to understand how things worked for those things to work out in my mind. I think differently from others. I have often asked the questions no one wanted to have asked, but everyone had the same question. I simply can't tell a half-truth to someone purchasing from me. I don't trust what the teachers want me to believe. I need to understand what's being hidden. I needed to know what was behind the back door so I wouldn't fall into a trap. I was unashamed to learn. I asked questions that drove out the truth of the matter. I never received ridicule asking technical questions, but I would drill in like a dog to a bone. My approach cleared up a lot of the questions for others or a confrontational distance from the educator.

All this information and education made me successful. Turns out when you are provided the proper tools, you can learn anything.

As rewarding as the experience was, it wasn't always rosy. Much of the corporate environment is cutthroat; you have to spend most of your energy not being sidelined.

CHAPTER 28

INSIDE THE GILDED BIRDCAGE

CONTENT WARNING:
TOXIC WORKPLACE &
PSYCHOLOGICAL TRIGGERS

The following chapter explores the realities of a toxic work environment, including manipulation, discrimination, abuse of power, and the deep emotional and psychological toll it can take. It is an unfiltered account of workplace trauma, exposing the struggles of injustice, betrayal, and the fight to maintain dignity in a corrupt system.

If you have experienced a toxic workplace or workplace abuse, please read with care. If this chapter becomes overwhelming, I encourage you to step away, process, and return when you feel ready.

This is not just a story of hardship—it is a testament to resilience, faith, and the strength to stand against corruption, no matter the cost.

Okay. Let's slow down a minute before we move on.

The past few decades of my career have flown by. I've been jumping ship from one Fortune 100 manufacturing company to the next. I've quickly learned new trades, built client relationships, and advanced my career. When I left, regardless of the circumstances, I left solid accounts, solid growth, and engaged clients behind. But alas—there was garbage in every wake of my leaving.

Each time I departed a company, I left with battle scars professionally, emotionally, and financially. The only big winners were the companies I worked for. My clients also received a great deal of benefit from my being there. There is a reason my clients followed me. The plus was that every time I moved jobs, I also increased my base salary and commission possibilities. Don't buy the hype that job movement hurts your earning capabilities!

I entered each global company new role full of hope and enthusiasm. I was always confident about being able to grow strategic accounts within the vertical I led. I was always excited, curious, and thrilled to enter a new team. It was a given that I was the only high school graduate on the team. Make new friends, engage with old clients, learn new technologies, and establish new sales for the company—that was what I set out to accomplish.

And I was always embraced readily during the honeymoon phase. I opened my rolodex and contacted all my past clients. I planned symposiums, plant tours, and face-to-face or team meetings. I put national or global platforms and projects in motion and streamlined the sales strategy.

My attitude? It was always: This time I will shine.

Every company I left had a story. Some I quit. Some I resigned from and was grateful for the opportunity. Some I was fired from. Some I sued. Some I got out of by the skin on my teeth. And I always got the same message from male leadership upon leaving: I wasn't liked. I was hard to work with. I was too demanding. I had great client skills and brought in great sales, but I was not worth all the frustration. I crushed my bonuses but still was not good enough. I needed to know my place. I was too focused on the clients—your paychecks don't come from the clients, they told me. Your warnings about upset customers are a reflection on you, not our leadership decisions. Of course each client matters—but you take it too far. You don't take "no" for an answer. You are unmovable at times. We know what's best. You don't have the right to question our decision. Any decision. You are a drain. You are not wanted. We are tired of hearing your voice.

Now, a reasonable person would learn, reflect, and adjust their behaviors. They would double down on pleasantries and deliver on the ever-changing expectations with a smile and a tight mouth. They would bite their lip at the first sign of chauvinism or favoritism and swallow hard when barbs are thrown. They would be silent when sabotaged, know their place, and be happy with a seat at the table. After all, we gave you a seat, so be happy with our scraps. They would accept company decisions that cost clients their money—even when those clients were not privy to "free" add-ons or "7% specification fees." They would accept others' work that wasn't accurate just to be part of their business strategy. They would do menial data entry so they wouldn't be focused on doing anything to show anyone up. They would sit back and not complain when shut out of client executive meetings with clients they had brought through the door. They would scribe without complaining, and they certainly wouldn't have any opposing views. They would be grateful.

Years of being beaten down had left a lifetime impression on me. Don't let anyone get on top. Don't give an inch. Question everything. Believe no one. Trust no one's intentions. Double-check everything. Do not trust others. Some may call this behavior paranoid, stubborn, insubordinate, or bossy. I call it survival as a woman in corporate America.

BUTTERFLY EFFECT

I entered a new company and started out strong. I was growing my territory and expanding it quickly. For the umpteen time, I'd moved globally and was finding projects easily. My influence was spreading through my client relationships across the globe. I had the clients' needs in my front pocket and was driving forward. My clients were happy. I was leading the charge and taking care of them. I was fearless.

A director of global sales was being shown as lazy and as an over-promoting showboat. I'd embarrassed him with my quick performance in his regions.

I did what he'd told leadership was not going to be easy. I unraveled years of his efforts to explain why the various global regions would not do well to justify his lackluster year-over-year sales. Years of his expertise, advice, and accountability were gone with a series of solid new projects, all of which were signed and implemented from the United States without his involvement or influence.

I was beneath his role and therefore inferior. I needed to stay that way. Little did he know I'd been raised as inferior. Little did he know I knew all the tricks.

I tried to involve him early in the projects, scheduling internal team/client strategy meetings. During our first few conversations, it was obvious he was embarrassed meeting senior clients for the first time. He had claimed he had a working relationship with them in his past reports to leadership. I actually felt bad for the guy. After the fourth call, he began objecting to me setting the meetings. He would set the meetings if he deemed them appropriate, he said. But I continued, as I always do.

I was invited to speak at a luxury brands engineering conference for EMEA, APAC in Malaysia. He was incensed; he wanted to know why I was invited and he wasn't. He said I didn't need to go since I wouldn't be respected, and he would go in my place.

It all reminded me of the Fish-a-Roo. And so, I thought: Screw that.

I asked, "Why wouldn't I be respected?" And he replied, "Because you're a divorced, single, middle-aged woman. "Men from those regions—(he was one)—don't respect such women." He said that despite the fact I had been invited by a brand executive in charge. He took it personally. It was a direct blow to his ego. That executive, who I had known for years, did not know who he was. Yet he felt it was his place to attend. In reality, it was just so he could gain control over me. So he told me, "No."

Game, set, match.

It took me three days to compile my evidence against him. I documented him trying to interfere with the projects I had in play, his inner company manipulation in the various regions, and his blatant acts of trying to misguide me.

I filed an HR complaint.

HR didn't know what to do with it. My months of complaining to my senior boss about the bullying and belittling behavior only frustrated my leadership. Work it out amongst yourselves—that was their attitude. But how do you work out prejudice that is so deeply ingrained that there is no give until submission? How do you gloss over prejudice against a woman? Against my very feminine existence? Against my perceived sins of being divorced, single, and independent? Against my total direct personality?

"How do you gloss over prejudice against a woman? Against my very feminine existence? Against my perceived sins of being divorced, single, and independent? Against my total direct personality?"

A woman, no less, and certainly nothing more than

that. Who is she to call me out? Who is she to deny me? Who does she think she is? Does she not know her place?

HR asked us each to state our complaints. He said women first, and I responded. I asked him, "Why are we on this HR call today?"

After 30 seconds of silence, he started. He said I didn't know what I was doing. I never kept him informed. I didn't respect his authority, and I was reckless. I was arrogant. I used clients against him. I was a goody two shoes. I was miss perfect. On and on he went. I sat in silence until it was my time to speak.

I asked HR about their policy with complaints of this nature. Since there was obviously a conflict of interest, how do we proceed? I put it back to where it belonged. My boss was speechless. HR was sputtering, and the bully was deflated. Resolving this as "just work it out" is not working for me any longer.

The plan was to work together for two weeks and come back with a new plan. He never attempted to call me or work together. I did not either.

Our second HR call was priceless. He was so openly angry at being dismissed that I was able to bait him. I pulled out documentation of his antics and asked him direct questions about project sabotage, which he couldn't avoid because I'd provided side emails of his counter-directing my direction on projects. He realized I had spies in his regions providing me with behind-the-scenes emails. They were tired of him as well. He was flabbergasted and extremely angry.

He fought back with a vengeance. And then I asked him why he felt I wouldn't be accepted to attend the

Global Engineering Conference. And that was when he said, "Because you are a woman."

I asked him if being a woman had anything to do with my intelligence and my knowledge of the market. He responded, "You don't understand what being a woman is. You are abrasive. You are not feminine. You are a bully. You are aggressive. You do not know when to sit back. You don't know your place."

Thirty seconds of silence went by. I again asked HR, "What is the policy for a complaint of this nature?"

One week later, the dude was gone. No call came from HR or my boss to check and see how I was. And there was no digging on their end to see if any other leaders in the organization had the same opinion of women. Nothing further. No follow up. Silence.

They wanted women like me not to tell. Not to act. Not to speak up.

> "They wanted women like me not to tell. Not to act. Not to speak up."

Many more of his type are currently living large with corporate executive careers today. Worse, this attitude might only be growing as foreign cultures become more and more prominent in U.S. companies and instill the same ingrained attitude towards women.

Second call. Behind the curtain of my truth.

I fought him with all the indignation I had. I would not let men hold me down any longer. Old hurts paved my way. This was a rightful dismissal based on facts. I beat him down in front of others and it felt good. Dude had a low view of women. Since biblical times, it's been much of the same. I can recount many instances of the same behavior. It happens over and over again. But at least he was brought down. Amen. Didn't play well for promotability in the end, but I didn't care.

I had to be heard.

GROUNDHOG DAY

Another new job.

I pushed my way in the door. I went after this role with something to prove. Within the first 60 days, I had completed my account plan for The Americas Hospitality strategy. I held my first internal leadership meeting to educate team leaders on a new direction to gaining market share with our technology and services. I asked executive clients (owners and brands) to join my first meeting. I wanted my leadership to learn directly from the industry decision makers what they were looking for from our company. Off to a good start.

A few months later they had hired a new guy in another P&L group to watch over one of my strongest global relationships. The initial handshake told me everything I needed to know. He didn't view me as his peer, but rather as someone he could use. He was outwardly dismissive from the get-go. A pro manipulator. I saw through his every motive.

The sexism offensives were blatant and consistent. He told our clients that we were working together as a team, but he was in charge. We were never a team. Dude was an asshole. And I don't do assholes.

I spent the next 2 years continuously bringing him into meetings with leadership to get some resolve and stop his sabotage. To say I spoke up about his antics would be an understatement. Simply put, I wasn't going to put up with being treated badly. And I wasn't going to be under his thumb or give him any passes.

He called me Jo in front of others to make it seem like we were close. Many times, I corrected him and told him to call me by my name. But this just made it more appealing to him. This same thing has happened to me time and time again. This behavior is one of control. He only gave me condensed versions of client interactions to keep me in the dark. If he ever had an executive meeting with clients, I wasn't invited. Instead, I'd hear about it from my clients and be mystified as he indicated I was part of his plans. He kept everything a secret from me. Often, he would slip up and say something only to assure me he had told me previously. Invites he "sent" didn't show on my calendar, and he would accuse me of missing meetings. I would get forwarded emails from my clients about important topics or meetings that he hadn't CC'ed me on. I knew this type of toxic work environment all too well.

To combat the frustration, I put my head down and worked. But trying to stay out of someone's way when you're assigned to the same account is impossible. You cannot stay away from someone who has made making you the irrational emotional woman a sport. I was distracted. I wasn't reading my Bible. A few years earlier I'd been volunteering in my church and going on mission trips. Now I was back fighting to be heard, scrambling to stay affirmed. I was living an isolated but faith-led life with daily prayers, but I had moved away from my strong daily devotion to Christ and gratitude. I had moved away from my community of believers. The world had snuck in, and I was too focused on worldly achievements to notice.

I always knew when I was on the way out. It was always one or two people, sometimes even an entire division, that wanted me gone. It almost became a game for me to see how long it would take to turn the tide.

Work had become a battleground. Again. Leadership wanted us to work it out. They did not stop the behavior. It was his word against mine. I was on my own. I was fired. I was told I was only 50% of the problem. It reveals how women are often told they are equally responsible for abuse simply because they didn't smile through it.

> "I was told I was only 50% of the problem."

They wanted me gone because they didn't like me. Get in line.

USED UP

Dinner boat on the Hudson. Live string music, nightclub singer, wine, drinks, duck and steaks served on white linen and fine china. Extensive fireworks over the Statue of Liberty as the boat cruised by—it was choreographed to precision. The bigwigs are here from overseas—which is funny because they are all four-foot-seven and 100 years old. I have created quite the coup by having 4 global executive clients accept this two-day boondoggle. Truthfully, my only ticket into this event was my clients and my tenacious attitude. See, women are not the favorite breed of this culture. My table was prime feeding ground for the corporate sharks. In a setting like this, the cultural differences meld after the fifth round of drinks. Halfway through dessert, the chairman comes over with three young interpreters. He sits, makes small talk, then waves his hand in front of the girls to one of my clients. In broken English, he compliments "A handsome, powerful, lucky American client" and tells him to "choose." I had worked my entire career carefully to craft a professional presence with my clients. And then within 30 seconds, he reduced my role with them to a prostitution provider. My client, whom was also my friend, declined. The chairman pushed again. Embarrassed, my client declined strongly. Although the homeliest and repugnant client of 9 at the table looked at the chairman and said what about me? – to which he was ignored.

The chairman of the global OEM company I was slaving for never acknowledged me sitting at the table with trusted clients. Different cultures bring different norms into our society.

It's a torrential storm. The rain is ruining the fireworks. The gale wind is blowing everyone to safety below. I go out alone. None of my party wants to join me. Only about 1% of the attendees made it to the viewing deck. The refreshment of the storm fills my void. The fireworks and views are inspiring.

I walk back in, my fancy dress soaked and my hair a mess—but internally, I am calm.

ISMs: Corruption. Dismissed. Humiliation. Taken advantage of. Shame. Sorrow.

Heavenly Virtue: Prudence.

PHYSICAL ABUSE IN THE WORKPLACE

A toxic teammate simply went too far to assert control over me. He turned to physical abuse to keep me in place. The abuse started in the taxi line. My client, a respected global Hospitality consultant introduced me to a high-ranking brand executive, who simply had on the most beautiful scarf. I complimented her, and we engaged in an easy conversation.

Suddenly, my left arm was pulled back hard, and I was pulled into a six-foot+, 250-pound man. He pulled so hard that I staggered into him forcefully. I was shocked and frozen at the same time.

The fact I was so friendly with her irritated him. He demanded to know if I had met her before. When I said no, he said I was making a fool of myself. I shook him loose and stepped away. At dinner, he was outwardly rude and aggressive to our male client. He was dismissive, too, mocking the client's livelihood when I intervened and changed the topic. At this point, he squeezed my upper left thigh hard under the table to shut me up. It mortified me. When that didn't appease him, he swiftly kicked me under the table to make his point. Suddenly the dinner was over. As I walked out the door I told my client what happened, I returned to my room and called my best friend. I was angry, ashamed and very upset. I've known lots of work bullies, but none

> *"I've known lots of work bullies, but none of them had ever become physical. This little man would not lose."*

of them had ever become physical. This little man would not lose.

I dissociated. I didn't fully remember the abuse until my client brought it up months later. That's how the body survives when the world pretends it's not happening. That's C-PTSD. It's not forgetting—it's *fragmenting*. It's when your brain protects you by filing memories away without a timestamp, because processing them in real time would destroy you. That exact abuse happened to me as a young mother. Suddenly you are frozen in your past. You don't scream. You don't run. You detach. You become polite at the table while your soul checks out. It's not weakness—it's the nervous system doing triage while no one else in the room is willing to help.

I brought the incident to HR, expecting some level of intervention. Instead, I was met with indifference. Your word against his, and he doesn't recall it. That was all they had to offer me. The clients voice was hearsay. No concern. Just a convenient dismissal that let the issue evaporate.

It was clear: The system wasn't built to protect women like me. It was built to keep men like him and toxic dysfunction in place. It was also clear the HR personnel didn't care or understand complex trauma and how it re-wires extreme duress in their employees suffering from PTSD. I was scorned for reporting the crime months later,.

Classic example of why women don't report abuse.

BURNING BRIDGES

I resigned from another corporate role. I had absolutely loved my position there, as I was working with a great team of peers. But there were major issues with leadership. Within 18 months, seven leaders who supported my division came and went. Basically, no decisions on long-term goals can be made if you have a revolving door of leadership all wanting to make their mark with yet another new direction from the C-Suite.

The last shift, however, opened a hole for me to be the global hospitality vertical leader. My president at the time called to tell me the role was mine. Later that day, on two team calls, my president and my VP announced my pending promotion to other leaders and my peers.

Finally. I was in seventh heaven.

As the excitement was settling in, I was asked to arrange CEO level meetings between our company and two global brands. It would be the first time the top executives from these organizations spoke to one another. It was also the first time my global company would engage with top leaders in this vertical. Big deal. I had spent weeks scheduling the meetings, pulling in every favor I had to make it happen. I spent 100+ hours working on a detailed two-page briefing of the accounts financial, stated energy goals, and initiatives. I included all large projects, relevant topics, and historical tidbits on how each brand influenced technology sales. To me, the brief was perfect.

Well, not quite. It seemed they had a template for this sort of meeting that I was not aware of. After receiving a call from the CMO informing me of the mistake, he sent me the format. It was juvenile—the worst sort of template. It required you to put each letter of every word in a separate text box. Not free flowing at all. The information they had room for on the template was all generic. There was no space for pertinent information about the history of the accounts or forward motions. It felt, to me, like a slap in the face.

I tried, but I didn't make it past the first intro paragraph. My mind would not let me focus. They needed it now. With my heart racing, I tried to complete it. The complexity of how my thoughts related to the template tangled my responses. Right in front of my PC, I melted down. I can't do it this way. This is crazy. I am not capable. My brain doesn't work like this. I won't.

I called the CMO and told him I wasn't going to complete the template and to please submit my brief. Later, I received the template—which the CMO completed himself. He said the boss needed it shorter. He took what he wanted from the brief and discarded the rest. You might as well print the Wikipedia page and call it good.

I figured it out after. The call was nothing more than an introduction. It wasn't about moving the current needle forward—it was a simple relationship meeting. There were projects being worked on at lower executive levels, and a nod from a high-ranking executive would have sped up the process. My need to move faster would have leaned into such an opportunity—not wasted it.

Also during this time, I was working on a project in Pacific Southeast Asia. This project had been installed incorrectly six years ago, well before my time at the company. For years, the regional brand engineering director had been trying to get my company to fix the issues. My company wasn't allowed to sell any new projects into this country if this warranty issue was not resolved. I set up bi-weekly calls, many at 4 a.m., to get all the team players working on the resolve. It was going to be very expensive to unravel all the warranty issues that had been denied for years. My top brass, upon hearing of the cost of repair, approved it only if I could get the brand to "give" us five projects as a quid pro quo. Ludicrous expectation. Global brands are held by shareholders—all projects were approved through a series of very regulated parameters. The "good old boys' club" doesn't work with bonded contracts. I said no—again. I would not embarrass myself asking or denying the truth of the situation by offering a shady deal that I found broke my ethical compass. We should have taken care of the client five years ago without expectations—because it was our fault the technology didn't work.

Two weeks passed without any info on my promotion. My boss assured me it was moving forward. I grew restless. I set a meeting with the president, who had offered me the role. He assured me it was still mine. Assured me HR was working on the job description. "Just keep doing what you're doing with all the accounts," he said.

October, November, and December passed without any word. I continued to ask and was told the same thing each time. All was good, it's coming. Keep doing what you're doing.

And then one day, while I was in Montana with my mom just cruising through LinkedIn job postings, I saw the job! My promotion! I was floored.

I set up a meeting with HR, but they acted like they had no idea who I was. They indicated I had not applied for the role. And I told them I hadn't applied—I was informed by my president and a C-level executive that I had the role. They asked me if I had anything in writing. No. I told them about the announcement at the global team meetings. They said they had no knowledge of that. I told them I would apply if that's what they needed, then was informed that I could not apply. I told them to call my president to confirm the announcement, which had gone out to 96 other teammates. I told them my clients had sent cards and flowers of congratulations.

That was the end of the conversation.

Pride drove my resignation. But if I'm honest, it wasn't just pride. It was self-respect. It was the refusal to be diminished—to be played like a fool by a system that rewards obedience over competence and silence over integrity. It was the unshakable belief that I was worth more than empty promises and corporate theatrics.

I had spent years proving my worth, pulling together impossible deals, fixing problems no one else wanted to touch, and bringing integrity into a space where backroom handshakes and shortcuts were the norm. But the moment I saw my own promotion listed as a job opening for the world to apply, the illusion shattered. This wasn't just an oversight; it was a statement. A clear, deliberate message that I was disposable. That the work I poured into, the clients who trusted me, the sacrifices I made—they didn't matter.

But I did.

If I had played the game—kept my mouth shut, bent the rules to meet executive demands, and sacrificed my values for the sake of career advancement—maybe I'd still be there. Maybe I'd be sitting in that so-called promotion, watching another version of me fight the same battles I had, convinced that if they just worked a little harder, they'd finally be seen. But I know now that in environments like this, hard work isn't enough. Ethics aren't rewarded. And loyalty is a liability.

So I walked. Not because I failed, but because I refused to succeed by their definition. Because I knew there had to be something more. Because burning a bridge sometimes means lighting the path forward.

> "Burning a bridge sometimes means lighting the path forward."

HONEST EVALUATION

What an ego-filled move. I was completely spun up in my mind, obsessed with control, gripping so tightly to my own plans that I failed to see the bigger picture. I had convinced myself that I was living a faith-filled life—outwardly, my actions reflected belief. But beneath it, I had slipped. Again.

I wasn't truly walking with Christ; I was charging ahead and expecting Him to follow. I had allowed my work to define me, to consume me, until my identity was tangled up in titles, deals, and proving my worth. When you work to live instead of living while you work, it's always gluttony. I had lulled myself into a false assurance, thinking I was still rooted in faith when, in reality, I had become lukewarm. And Christ doesn't stand in the lukewarm. He spits it out.

I asked for it.

There are lessons here—more than a few:
- Do the work the CEO asks. Every time. Even if it's absurd, even if it makes no sense—play the game or get played.
- Get everything in writing. Promises mean nothing unless they're inked on paper.
- Quit letting your issues impede your thinking. Ego, trauma, and pride make terrible business advisors.
- Ask for help. Stop thinking you have to hold everything together alone.
- Quit always having to be right and proving yourself. Sometimes, silence is the strongest stance.
- Basically, do the exact opposite of what your brain, emotions, worth, and knowledge base tell you to do. Because sometimes, the very things that built you can also break you.

And the biggest lesson of all? The grass isn't always greener.

Turns out the promotion I lost wasn't the real loss. It was the intimacy I traded with Christ in order to chase it.

CORPORATE WHISTLEBLOWING

My father taught me many things in life, but being forthright and principled in business dealings was his passion. He held strong and fierce when he knew he was right, and he refused to back down. He lived and died by the mantra of doing the right thing. Following his path, I hold the same principles for my word in all interactions I have. It just makes sense. It's easier that way. You never have to try to remember what happened because it was and always is the truth.

During one of my roles, I uncovered nationwide practices that raised significant ethical concerns. A prominent engineering firm in the marketplace was charging vendors a 7% "specification fee" as a condition to be included in their equipment bids. The practice, while framed as standard procedure, appeared to unfairly inflate costs for clients, many of whom were unaware of the hidden fees being passed along.

In my time with the company, I had been successful in selling equipment directly to end-clients, by-passing such intermediaries. This approach, while beneficial for end clients, seemed to draw disapproval from the engineering firm. Instead of engaging me directly, they approached a junior salesperson in a local branch and presented the "deal" to him. 7% specification fee and our Company can be included to bid every project they were working on.

Unaware of the broader implications, he escalated the offer to leadership.

When I learned of this, I placed a few phone calls and readily discovered the deception. In an internal meeting, I raised a critical point: How could we justify absorbing a 7% fee without impacting our pricing structure? The answer was unsettling. I was informed that instead of offsetting the fee, an additional 7% line-item cost was being added to our bids to the engineering firm.

"This isn't right. This is stealing." I said during the meeting. "If our clients don't know about this, they're being misled. Passing the liability of the engineering firm to admit the line item is complacency." Confronting the issue made it clear that the practice couldn't remain hidden any longer. The clients deserved transparency, and I felt a responsibility to act.

The turning point came during a professional dinner with executives from various industries. I addressed the issue directly, asking a senior executive of a real estate investment trust (REIT), "How do you feel about the 7% specification fees being charged to your projects?" His reaction was one of surprise. Turning to others at the table, I asked, "How much are you being charged by the engineering firm?" The responses were unanimous: 7%.

By bringing this practice to light, I prompted a legal investigation. I was told later that because I posed the question in public, they had no choice but to look into it. It was later confirmed that this fee was being systematically applied and passed along to the end clients without their knowledge. The investigation revealed a widespread issue that went beyond just one company and many industries. About a year later, at a client leadership meeting, I crossed paths with one of the executives who had been affected by the exposure. He expressed frustration, stating, "Do you know how much scrutiny I've been under because of what you brought to light? My superiors demanded to know why they had to hear about this from a vendor."

My response was simple: "You should be grateful. My truth saved your company of investors—Brands, and many others—millions in hidden fees. You should just say thank you."

I believed then—as I do now—that shining a light on deceptive practices is never the wrong move. But something else became clear that day: *Exposing deception doesn't just reveal corruption—it exposes the people who were comfortable living beside it.*

It wasn't about the money. It was about the truth being seen.

The fallout was significant. The engineering firm's practices were eventually dismantled, and legal consequences followed. This incident reaffirmed my commitment to integrity and the principle that silence in the face of wrongdoing is complicity. While speaking out came with professional risks, it also underscored the value of accountability and transparency in business practices.

> *"While speaking out came with professional risks, it also underscored the value of accountability and transparency in business practices."*

I acted not out of self-interest, but out of a firm belief that clients deserved honesty and fairness. My goal was always to ensure that the people we served could trust the systems and organizations they relied on.

Some may say that such actions come with consequences—and they do. But I firmly believe that integrity is worth

> *"Standing for what is right often means standing alone, but it's a stance worth taking."*

the price. If nothing else, I learned this: Standing for what is right often means standing alone, but it's a stance worth taking. My silence wasn't for sale.

> *"My silence wasn't for sale."*

What I did was undeniably right, even though it came at a significant personal cost. Choosing to speak up in an environment where silence and complicity are the norm was not an easy decision, but it was the right one. Resigning was painful, but it allowed me to preserve something far more valuable—my integrity. I said something because it was simply the right thing to do.

If you see something you believe is wrong, remember that it is each of our responsibility to speak up, regardless of the personal cost.

Bushido Virtue: Valor

JUSTICE

Boardroom meeting in one of D.C.'s finest hotels. In the basement, in the oldest part of the hotel, there is a red velvet and leather executive office straight out of the 1940s. Odd, but memorable. We're having a crisis meeting of the minds to protect my client and my company from taking it in the shorts for severe quality issues, which had many layers and players of admitted fault.

I've come prepared for battle. I have my knight-in-shining-armor teammate and a 500-page binder, affectionally known as "The Bible" of all correspondence for this screwed-up project. My opponents do not want me here. They would prefer I got hit by a bus on the way. Lord knows they don't want to be here either—but it's not their lucky day.

My client, who has a deserving reputation as the biggest ass on earth if you are opposing him, is beaming. He doesn't know how, or frankly give a damn how, I resolve his problems, but he knows I will. Being a woman in an all-male meeting allows me to state a few things:

1. Don't expect me to play nice.
2. Do not come ill-prepared.
3. Don't piss me off by trying to cover your own ass. I'm not in business to be anyone's friend.

My wolf pack of two leaves the room so the others can talk. My teammate turns around—he's dying of quiet laughter. With his knees on the ground, he asks me, "Where did that come from?" I look him dead in the eye and say, "I don't mess around."

Thank you D for having my back.

Heavenly Virtue: Fortitude.

Don't mess with a girl from Montana.

SPIRITUAL WARFARE IN THE WORKPLACE

I am called to love my neighbor as I love myself. To be generous of the heart. To be a servant to others. To build others up at the expense of myself. To have an open spirit of acceptance. To be an example of Godly honor. And, of course, to turn the other cheek.

Well, I found that even if I gave someone the shirt off my back—and my coat and my sandals, too—there was no satisfying their need to diminish me. My career, which I once loved, had become a daily war of trying to survive.

As I grew in Christ I became a bigger target. I openly shared my faith and made references that were biblical to tie into the conversation. I put scripture on my email signature and objected when asked to remove it. I carried my Bible in my computer case and often read it openly. I became a spiritual target in a corrupt environment.

I also know that evil is always trying to trip us up. (After all, we're not fighting a war of flesh and blood.) Evil tells lies and covers up deceptions. It is always maneuvering, working to cast doubt and shame on the Godly. Evil cannot strip us of Christ's acceptance, but it can surely distract us from our mission. And boy, did I get distracted.

> *"For our struggle is not against flesh and blood, but against the rulers, against the authorities, against the powers of this dark world, and against the spiritual forces of evil in the heavenly realms."*
>
> **Ephesians 6:12**

Each time a personal attack occurred, I felt like I was back in my first husband's home—as if I was once again being berated and having my every move judged. As if I couldn't just be myself. Or I was back in another marriage, being told how stupid I was and how lucky I was to have such a career. Back in mom's house—her telling me I wasn't smart enough and that I wouldn't succeed. The message was always the same: I had been lucky. I had no real talent. I just needed to be quiet. Do what you are told. Let me take from you.

It has always seemed many wanted to see me put in my place.

The more I proved myself with sales and client interactions, the worse it got. The more other teams accepted me as a peer, the more I was targeted. Being a target is one thing—being a bully's obsession is another. I took great pride in not allowing any insult to penetrate. By this time in my life, I had become pretty much coated in armor. Nothing got in.

Well, I'll have to correct that a bit. A lot did get in. The attacks fed my trauma, and my survival coping strategies would be all that was running my thoughts. After all, it's impossible to live in this world when you know you are not liked, accepted, or valued.

Emotionally and physically, each departure cut me to the core. The feelings of abandonment and past abuse plagued my thoughts. Depression and anxiety crept in and occupied my mind. I was sleeping nonstop or not at all. It was anyone's guess if my weight would drop or gain. Stress paired with fibromyalgia is a serious killer. The overall body aches became immobilizing. Brain fog sets in out of nowhere, and then suddenly you become a walking zombie. There was no desire to do extracurricular activities and no desire to shop for myself, feed myself, or reach out to others for help.

I can do this alone, I thought. After all, I'd always been alone.

Financially, each departure was easily overcome. For the past two decades I'd been making a great deal of money without batting an eye. Each 401K was healthy in deposits. HSA savings plans were topped out and my savings was flush. I had spent a great deal of money over the years on frivolous (and not so frivolous) materialistic needs, but I had never spent over my budget. With each departure, whether abrupt or planned, I had enough in the bank to last until my next job. It certainly helped that there were more than a few departures that paid me handsomely out the door. (Deservingly so.)

I figured I had fought to get in the door, so there was no reason not to fight on my way out.

CHAPTER 29

I AM A WOMAN

I am a woman, and it's not a bad word.

Bullies have been part of my life since the beginning. My mother was the first, followed by my brothers. School wasn't a reprieve either. A popular boy in eighth grade humiliated me in front of a crowd, saying I was so ugly his dog wouldn't piss on my leg. A snarky girl once held up a rock and jeered, asking if my mouth was bigger than the stone, vowing to prove it. The insults were relentless. Later in life, there were insecure husbands and sons who acted like crows on a telephone line—perched to judge, to pick at my spirit. Even friends I once welcomed into my flock turned out to be false allies.

By a young age, I had mastered the art of enduring humiliation and staying resilient. I was conditioned to withstand being downgraded, sabotaged, and told to stay in my place. Then, at nearly 40, I entered the corporate world. What I found wasn't shocking—it was just an extension of what I'd always known. The difference was that here, the stakes were higher, the games more sophisticated, and the players wielded their power with sharper precision.

The corporate world is a battlefield for women. Toxic masculinity thrives in its corridors, draped in policies that promise equality but operate on favoritism and exclusion. From the start, I learned that success required dismantling my sensitivity—or I would risk being devoured. In this space, being a woman meant navigating unspoken rules: Don't outshine the men, don't call out their mistakes, and certainly don't expect to be treated as an equal.

Sexism in corporate environments is rarely overt—it's subtle, pervasive, and insidious. It shows up in the tone of a male colleague's voice when he repeats your idea as if it were his own. It's there in the way leadership praises your hard work in private but ignores your contributions in public meetings. It's in the way clients' casual comments about your appearance are met with laughter by your male peers, even when you stand frozen in discomfort.

I experienced all of this and more. I was praised during the honeymoon phase of new roles, valued for my results, and admired for my connections. But as soon as I challenged a poor decision or demanded accountability, the tide shifted. I became "difficult," "too honest," and "too focused on clients." These criticisms weren't just about my performance—they were about my refusal to conform to the unspoken expectation that I should stay small, agreeable, and quiet.

The double standards were glaring. While my male colleagues were celebrated for being assertive, I was labeled aggressive. Their ambition was seen as leadership potential, while mine was seen as arrogance. They could make mistakes and move on; I was expected to deliver perfection or face judgment. These inequities weren't just frustrating—they were exhausting.

It wasn't just peers or managers; the system itself was designed to keep women like me off-balance. Promotions required proving yourself twice over, only to find the ladder had been pulled up before you. Access to high-profile projects often came with strings attached, demanding loyalty to gatekeepers who made it clear they held the power. Even networking events weren't safe—how many times had I stood uncomfortably at corporate dinners, enduring flirtations thinly veiled as professional camaraderie?

My early conditioning helped me survive this world. I knew how to deflect potshots and keep moving forward despite sabotage. But that resilience came at a cost. Years of enduring these dynamics left me with a hardened exterior, constantly braced for battle. It reinforced the toxic belief that I could only rely on myself—that trust was a luxury I couldn't afford.

And yet, even as I fought to survive, I felt the weight of the cumulative trauma. Each dismissal, each undermining comment, each microaggression carried echoes of my past. The corporate world amplified the same messages I'd heard growing up: You're not enough. You're not smart enough. You don't belong here.

But the truth is, I do belong here. I've earned my place, not through favoritism or shortcuts, but through grit, skill, and determination. The fact that I've endured so much doesn't make the system right—it makes me stronger. And while I've learned to navigate the labyrinth of corporate sexism, I also recognize the toll it takes on women who come after me.

And if you're weary from the battle—hear this: God did not create you to cower. He created you to carry light into dark rooms. To speak when others whisper. To stand when others kneel to fear. You are not alone in this fight. You were chosen for it.

SEXISM
....

Sexism isn't just a personal problem—it's a systemic issue. It's the unspoken culture of rewarding conformity and punishing dissent. It's the expectation that women must do more, endure more, and accept less. It's the quiet acceptance of toxic behaviors as "just the way things are."

To those who've faced these battles: I see you. I see the way you've had to fight for your voice and your place at the table. I see the way you've had to smile through the insults and play the game to survive. And I want you to know—you're not alone.

To those who have silenced, discredited and earned privilege from abuse; I see you as well. I see the way you make others squirm for your enjoyment and hold no accountability. And I want you to know—you're not alone. It's your pack mentality that keeps you alive.

Today, I fight differently. I stand firm in my faith, leaning on Christ to remind me of my worth when the world tries to diminish it. I see the games for what they are, and I refuse to let them define me. My journey has been one of resilience, growth, and unshakable belief in my value—not because others have validated it, but because I know my Creator has.

Women don't need to dismantle their sensitivity; they need to dismantle the systems that demand it. We don't need to conform; we need to transform. And most importantly, we need to keep showing up, with faith, determination, and the courage to call out the lies that tell us we're less than.

> "My journey has been one of resilience, growth, and unshakable belief in my value—not because others have validated it, but because I know my Creator has."

> "Women don't need to dismantle their sensitivity; they need to dismantle the systems that demand it."

Here are some signs of a work abuser:

1. They sabotage a woman's contribution to the team goal for their own benefit, reputation, and power.
2. They count on your silence. The conflict is that you're torn between speaking up and potentially jeopardizing your job and suffering in silence. Do it. Report it. Say the truth.
3. They love interfering in your work, which prevents work from getting done and ultimately costs future financial achievement.
4. The potential success of others threatens them. They want to stop you before you outshine them or reveal their shortcomings.

5. You simply intimidate them because you can back up what you promote.
6. They turn to physical abuse in a work setting. Again, they count on your silence.

You can do your best to manage the situation, but it's really the company's responsibility to be observant and responsive to the needs of their workers and the general work environment. Especially when a confident woman or man makes the complaint.

Unless every person speaks up and documents toxic workplace, sexual, gender, physical, or psychological abuse, the tides won't change. I believe women are feared. Men were raised to be dominant, whereas women are conditioned to be submissive. Trauma doesn't care about your gender and no doubt many leaders and teammates have it ruling their jealousy, cunningness, and anger at targets. Lots of covert abusers in corporations. The power balance implodes pretty quickly when a woman will not keep her mouth shut.

"The system was never designed to accommodate women like me—but I refuse to accommodate it."

The system was never designed to accommodate women like me—but I refuse to accommodate it. I will not shrink. I will not stay silent. And neither should you.

CORPORATE CHAUVINISM

The term "mediocrity rises to the top" could never be truer in corporate America. And it has never seemed truer than in the HVAC and technology industries. These centuries-old industries were built on the backs of innovators like Willis Carrier, Mark Honeywell, and George Westinghouse, all of whom would turn over in their graves if they saw how their organizations were being run today. Backbone, integrity, direct adult conversation, and aggressively rocking established paths of doing business the way it's always done need not apply to senior leadership positions. Instead, the leaders promoted are the ones that know how to play the game the best. Agreeable and nonassertive, ethically questionable, and sometimes all-out morons get promoted because they are pliable men or fearful women who are simply content having a seat at the table.

Chauvinists—oh, I have met many. Men of all walks of life—educated, successful, handsome, homely, white- and blue-collar, and lowlifes of all kinds. I've found that little men come in all sizes and shapes. They shake your hand, smile in your face, and believe that you are there for their amusement. Or they view you as a disposable nuisance they can't wait to crumple up like a piece of paper.

Their MO is the same every time. They are pleasant at first, posing and positioning themselves in front of their peers as the greatest guys in the world. But I feel the static the minute I meet them. It's like a current that gets under your skin from the very first handshake. It's immediate, palpable in the air as they smile and sum you up from feet to breasts. It leaves me feeling raped and gagged by an invisible force. I've found these men to be insecure slime in the worst form. They can't attack me as they would their wives or lovers with put-downs, outright ridicule, or unbridled resentment. Instead, they work inch by inch to discount your views, raise doubts of your intelligence, and obstruct your success. They find immense pleasure in silently and not-so-secretly stabbing you in the back. They consider you a threat to their existence and find extraordinarily stealthy ways to express the message that you are simply not wanted, not worthy, and not expected to last.

During my early years, I accepted the threat and tried to stay out of their way. But as my career and reputation grew, so did my confidence. I responded to the barbs politely at first, letting them know in my tone and posture that I knew what they were doing and to back the hell off. The braver ones viewed this as a challenge. The meeker ones resorted to water cooler gossip and criticism. To this day, I'm not sure which is worse: head-on encounters or having to watch your back. My work ethic, confidence, and intelligence are things a weak-minded male simply cannot tolerate. In fact, he will seek to destroy those qualities in me—even if it causes him to self-destruct.

My strong, fierce, no-nonsense nature drove the braver ones to feats of sabotage that cease to amaze me even to this day.

My first encounter was with a district manager who felt he had ownership over my existence. He took great pleasure in telling anyone who listened that I was uncontrollable and full of myself. Another time, with a senior director, I was asked to take notes as my team participated in a whiteboard exercise and worked on a presentation. It took everything in me at the time to answer with a defiant denial in front of my all-male peer group. I told him, "I want to engage and contribute and will not be distracted or silenced by scribing." It wasn't that I was too good to take notes—a task one of my male peers did with enthusiasm. It was that I knew he'd made the request to belittle me because he had an issue with my strength. I later pushed an HR suit against him for denying me a promotion and moved on to another position.

The worst kind of chauvinist is the perceived ally. It hurts unbearably to be turned out in the cold and abandoned by someone you trusted. The denial strikes the core of your insecurities and the thought that you're not good enough. I will remember those heartaches and confidence blasts until the end of my days. I gave none of these men the satisfaction of knowing they hurt me, and I know in my heart that they carry the desertion of my friendship with them like an anchor on their soul.

I had a CEO who was so disturbed by my presence that he could barely be in the same room with me. I was surrounded by a team that respected me and reveled in my friendship, and I knew that the sheer sight of me laughing and full of life left him sleepless. Every chance he could get me alone, he would try his best to intimidate me with threatening innuendos. Or he would try to impress me with his old Air Force accomplishments. He actually pulled out psych charts and showed me he had a higher "A" corporate hook. Finally, he lowered himself to verbally and loudly demanding my respect. It's laughable now to think back on his actions. I clearly remember wanting to compare penis sizes, as I know that if I had one, mine would be bigger.

But make no mistake—standing tall in the face of corporate chauvinism comes with a price. There were days when the exhaustion felt unbearable, when I questioned whether the fight was worth it. There were moments of deep loneliness, knowing that every step forward meant another enemy, another dagger in my back, another door slammed shut. The weight of always having to prove myself, of always being on guard, of never being allowed the luxury of vulnerability—it was heavy. But what they never understood is that the fire inside me burned hotter than the fires around me. Every battle, every betrayal, and every attempt to silence me only refined me. I did not break. I did not crumble. Instead, I emerged stronger, sharper, and utterly unshakeable. Because in the end, my presence was never the problem. Their fear of it was.

The truth is, this kind of behavior isn't just about ego or competition. It's about power—who has it, who controls it, and who is terrified of losing it. Men like these don't just resent strong women; they fear them. They see confidence and competence in a woman as a threat to their fragile hierarchy. Their authority was never built on true leadership but on the expectation that others—especially women—would yield.

For years, I tried to understand the root of this behavior. Was it insecurity? Was it the fear of irrelevance? Or was it simply ingrained entitlement, a conditioned belief that women must always be less—less vocal, less assertive, and less ambitious? Whatever the reason, their resistance only strengthened my resolve. They wanted me to shrink, but I grew. They wanted to silence me, but I spoke louder. And no matter how many battles I fought, no matter how many wounds I carried, I refused to bow.

But for every battle I fought, for every moment I stood my ground, there was always someone lurking in the shadows, waiting to twist the story. People like these never see themselves as the problem. They rewrite the narrative to protect their fragile egos, turning accountability into an attack and weaponizing perception against the very women they undermine. If you asked one of them about me, about the way they treated me, you wouldn't hear the truth. You'd hear something like this:

"Oh, here we go—another bitter woman blaming men because she couldn't hack it. Typical. Always the victim, always whining about how unfair life is instead of owning up to her own shortcomings. Maybe—just maybe—she wasn't as smart as she thought she was. Maybe people just didn't like working with her, and it had nothing to do with her being a woman. But no, she'd rather spin some dramatic sob story about how every man she ever met was out to get her. Comparing penis sizes? Real professional. No wonder she got 'sabotaged'—who the hell would want to deal with that attitude every day? She thinks she's some fearless warrior, but all I see is a woman so desperate to prove she's better than everyone else that she can't see the real problem—herself."

In those moments of isolation, when betrayal stung and doubt crept in, I had to anchor myself in something greater than corporate games and human validation. I had to remind myself that my worth wasn't defined by a man's opinion, a promotion, or a title. God defined it. He had placed me here, in these rooms, at these tables—not to seek their approval, but to stand firm in who He created me to be.

I think back on these men now—their smirks, their whispered conversations, their desperate attempts to make me small—and I realize that every single one of them lost in the end. Not because I outplayed them, but because I never needed their permission to exist in the first place. Their power was always an illusion.

And while they may have fought to keep me down, they never understood one thing: I was never fighting for a seat at their table. I was building my own.

If you're reading this and nodding, know this: your presence isn't the problem either. It's their fear of your light. Don't dim it. Don't wait for permission. Build your table.

THE WOMEN

I have had great male bosses, though they have been few and far between. They viewed me as no better and no less than my male counterparts. They wanted the entire team to succeed. They took the time to understand what lay beneath the suits in front of them and how to make a team a team. They made it easy to succeed because the rules were the same for all. Clear cut. No in between. No favorites and certainly no insecurity of women in business. They felt I was a strength. A worthy contributor. A boss that has your back. I would not have had the career I had without them.

The women I have encountered in leadership positions were no better than most of the men. Many had imposter syndrome; they felt they had to be like the boys to stay in their place. They didn't inspire other women. Instead, they looked down at all those trying to reach the ranks of the glass ceiling. One continually referred to me as the hospitality girl. One couldn't compliment me on anything except how well I dressed. Another had a great time with how I pronounced words—always correcting me for my good. She took every opportunity to try to humiliate me in a crowd. Good luck. They didn't know I was raised by a mother who had already beaten me down and prepared me well. Go ahead and live a life in a leadership position that you are fearful of losing. Me? I didn't care if I lost. That was the rub. How the heck do you intimidate someone when they already know all the tricks?

Most women in corporate leadership roles were in traditional departments like legal, HR, administrative, and marketing. Few were the lone female sitting at corporate engineering tables across from clients and raising the bar. Few surveyed mechanical rooms, walked roofs to determine microgrid placements, or rode in technicians' trucks to understand their daily tasks. Few took any interest in other women. Few wanted other women to rise, as it would throw off the delicate power balance.

I never had a woman as a mentor. In fact, I saw many of them for who and what they were.

Afraid. Careful and cautious. Absent of emotion because they frowned upon emotionality in corporate. Be quiet, don't tell, and don't ask. Be submissive and agreeable. Lower your drive.

Phooey. That was not for me.

I found great support and sisterhood from other working-class women like me. Most were my peers in other industries. They shared many of the battle scars I had. We confided in each other and helped grow each other's careers. We supported each other and discussed abuses they were experiencing, which only reinforced that I was not alone. Our stories were alike. It's amazing how little has changed for women working in male-dominated careers over the past century. So much needs to change, but the ones in charge of the rules are fearful of our strength. I hope by the time my granddaughter enters the workforce, the climb will be much easier. But I highly doubt it, as all the cultural influences just blur the deeper line.

Despite the barriers I encountered I still persevered. I made a difference. It wasn't a waste. You can make a difference as well if you stay true to yourself and refuse to be silenced.

CHAPTER 30

CPTSD COPING MECHANISMS VS. SURVIVAL IN A TOXIC WORKSPACE

Understanding the Parallels:

As stated, CPTSD (complex post-traumatic stress disorder) is developed through prolonged exposure to abusive or oppressive environments, often where escape is not immediately possible. A toxic work environment operates similarly—it traps individuals in a cycle of fear, manipulation, and survival mode. The ways individuals cope with CPTSD often mirror how they navigate workplace toxicity, as both require constant vigilance, self-protection, and strategic endurance.

CPTSD Coping Mechanism Survival in a Toxic Work Environment:

Hypervigilance–Constantly scanning the environment for danger and anticipating threats before they arise.

Always on guard – Watching for power plays, backstabbing, or manipulative tactics from colleagues or leadership.

Emotional numbing – Shutting down feelings to endure repeated emotional distress.

Detachment from work – Disconnecting from job responsibilities; refusing to invest emotionally due to constant devaluation.

People-pleasing – Seeking approval to avoid conflict or punishment.

Overworking to avoid retaliation – Taking on excessive tasks to stay in management's good graces and prevent criticism.

Avoidance of triggers – Staying away from situations that may bring up past trauma.

Avoiding key figures – Dodging meetings, interactions, or direct communication with toxic managers or coworkers, or intentionally looking for direct conversations to be heard.

Dissociation – Mentally escaping to survive extreme emotional pain.

Zoning out at work – Feeling mentally absent in meetings; disengaging as a protective measure against hostility.

Fawning (submissiveness for safety) – Agreeing with aggressors to prevent confrontation.

Compliance without questioning – Going along with unreasonable demands to avoid being singled out.

Fighting (dominance for safety) – Calling out aggressors and offering no compliance without questioning. Not going along with the flow; standing out.

Self-blame – Internalizing the belief that the trauma is deserved or self-inflicted.

Imposter syndrome – Feeling undeserving of success and believing any failures are personal inadequacies rather than systemic sabotage.

Chronic fatigue & burnout – Exhaustion from being in a state of perpetual stress.

Job-induced burnout – Physical and emotional depletion from constant workplace hostility and pressure.

Fear of authority figures – Associating power with past trauma, making interactions anxiety-inducing.

Intimidation by leadership – Struggling to advocate for oneself due to fear of retaliation or dismissal.

Survival mode thinking – Prioritizing short-term safety over long-term well-being.

Staying in a job out of fear – Remaining in toxic workplaces despite the harm because leaving feels risky or unsafe, or complete escape and quick abandonment of environment.

The overlap between CPTSD coping mechanisms and toxic workplace survival strategies highlights how damaging prolonged exposure to workplace toxicity can be. Many individuals do not recognize they are engaging in trauma responses because they have normalized dysfunction as "just part of the job."

A toxic workplace does not just make you hate your job—it alters your nervous system, your perception of safety, and your fundamental beliefs about trust and self-worth. The only way forward is to reclaim your agency, recognize the patterns, and refuse to let trauma dictate your future.

All of us—men, women, and everything in between—are subject to abuse. It's those who cry foul that get swept into the trash. The louder you ask for fair treatment, the harsher the consequences. This will not change unless we shed light on what is truly going on behind closed doors. Tell the truth of the matter instead of going along with the crowd. Many cannot afford to say adios. To the ones that stay, watch your backs, as you won't see it coming. And even if you do, you can't stop it.

BREAKING THE CYCLE: HEALING AFTER WORKPLACE TRAUMA

CPTSD and workplace toxicity both demand survival strategies, but survival is not living. The goal is not just to cope but to break free, heal, and step into spaces where you are valued, respected, and empowered.

- Recognizing workplace trauma as real trauma – Understanding that prolonged mistreatment in a job can create the same psychological damage as other forms of abuse.
- Setting boundaries – Learning to say no, limiting exposure to

> *"Recognizing workplace trauma as real trauma – Understanding that prolonged mistreatment in a job can create the same psychological damage as other forms of abuse."*

toxicity, and identifying non-negotiables in a healthy work environment.
- Seeking support – Finding a trauma-informed therapist, support group, or mentor to process the damage done.
- Detoxing from workplace PTSD – Taking a mental and emotional break before jumping into a new job to reset stress responses.
- Rebuilding self-worth – Undoing the internalized belief that mistreatment was deserved and reinforcing personal value outside of job performance.

VOMIT

As for me, I had no idea my trauma had anything to do with my work issues. I didn't understand what abuse was—I just knew how to take it.

I've been told: You're lucky you've had a successful career. You're fortunate you have a nice figure that you don't have to work for. You haven't had a hard day in your entire time here because all you've done is skate on the backs of others—and the industry. You're a taker. We gave you a good life. We pay you a nice paycheck. Your criticism of us isn't valid. You're getting too big for your britches, and I'm doing you a favor by knocking you down a few pegs. I don't need to compliment you or tell you you're doing a good job. You are little miss know-it-all. When your looks fade, you will have to use your charm to stay in corporate. You need to sit down in the far corner and shut up and not ask questions. You know how you are, you know how you get. You already know that, and I don't want you getting ahead of yourself. Your foot looks fine to me. You don't understand. You need to thank me for your bonus. No one likes you. We wouldn't want you to have a big head. Do you really want me to introduce you separately when I accidentally left you out of my team introductions? I can't believe you would ask. You are not to place another phone call. You are little miss perfect. Don't you want to hear my criticism and judgment? It's good for you to believe it coming from me. You misunderstood—I was just joking. What? I didn't mean it the way you repeated it. That's not what I said. You're too sensitive—I was kidding. You misunderstood my wording. Your opinions don't matter. You have no voice here. Why did you place that call? You are nothing—quit acting like you're not. I was joking. Accept the truth: You would be nothing without the opportunities we provided you. You're difficult to talk to. You owe us for the years we stuck by you. You were supposed to be a racehorse and you became lame. You're too much—too strong, too confident, and too arrogant. You don't understand your place here. You turn our conversations around on us—that's not what we were saying. You take everything so literal. I made a mistake—you get so defensive over everything. Your notes are wrong. It was a marketing mistake, that's why we left you off the organizational chart slide presentation. You remember it wrong. Get in line. I just want you to get along with your peers. I'm done hearing about this. Believe me when I say you're only 50% of the issue. Figure it out on your own. I'm very, very tired of hearing about this because now I will have to make changes. Can't you just ignore him? Just do your job. You walk just fine, why the exaggeration.. After all, we love you. We are like family, and we own you through an employment contract. I care about you and want the best for you. If only you could treat us like you do your clients. You are like my little sister. You need to know I am right about you. You're not that good. It's your word against his. He doesn't say it didn't happen, he doesn't remember. You should care about what I'm saying. This is on you, not me. I'm saying this for your own good. (*I wish I had $1 for every time I heard that one.*)

And yet, I am still here.

Get everything in writing. Keep a diary every day, print every email, and record calls when legally permissible. Documentation is the only way you are going to win this unwinnable battle. They will drum you out, but if you're prepared, they will write you a check on your way out the door. I was never one for just complaining—I was one who had the goods. Even small and insignificant details add up over the course of months to prove the pattern you have been experiencing. Personal records are a must. Stay organized and be ready to go into battle prepared.

This is a heavy burden. You can win the battles on the outside and still lose the war inside.

I knew how to survive. I knew how to fight. I knew how to build the armor that made me untouchable. But inside, I was still the imposter—still the girl who believed strength was the only way to deserve love. I could stand up to corporate bullies and walk out with a check, but I couldn't outrun the voice inside that said I was nothing without a fight.

CHAPTER 31

SUICIDAL IDEATION

CONTENT WARNING:
SUICIDE AND DEEP EMOTIONAL
DISTRESS.

....

This chapter contains discussions of suicide, trauma, and deep emotional pain. These topics are presented with honesty and rawness, reflecting real experiences. If you are struggling or find these themes distressing, please take care while reading. You are not alone—if you need support, reach out to a trusted friend, faith leader, or a professional resource.

If you or someone you know is in crisis,
help is available:

📞 National Suicide Prevention Lifeline: 988 (U.S.)

📞 Crisis Text Line: Text HOME to 741741

Your life matters. ♥

LOST IN THE WILDERNESS

... Then mom died.

My world spiraled. Mom and I had overcome years of fighting and dislike toward one another. We had become friends the past decade and created many memories. We had traveled to weddings, gone on gambling trips, and mom had even accompanied me on business trips to New York and D.C. to take in the sights and see the plays. For the past decade, I had spent the entire Christmas season home in Missoula with her only to turn around and return for the summers. We regularly spoke on the phone, sharing tales from our lives. To say I wasn't ready for her to go is a minimization. I had convinced myself that she loved me. And then my brother told me that upon her passing, mom had always spoken horribly about me. I reared my head and told him he should know the horrible things dad said about him. I know I shouldn't have hurt him while he was grieving, but I did. Hurt people hurt people. But his assurance of mom's never loving me nor accepting me was a direct shot to my heart, and it caused all my feelings of being unworthy to surface.

I returned to Missoula to tend to her with my siblings while she passed. Participated in spaghetti night with family, cleaned out the house, split up the property, and went on like normal. But nothing was normal. My life was never going to be the same. Pull myself out of bed and look at the computer screen. Make a few client calls, follow up on what was 100% necessary, and then crawl back into bed. Work was war. Try a vacation with a girlfriend and pretend I'm moving forward. Living a chore. Sleeping is impossible. I had no appetite. No thoughts were going in or out. Just numb. Stay numb. Numb the pain. Night after night, the same feelings of worthlessness.

> ISMs: Empty. Ill Health. Broken. Sloth.

SERPENT IN MY GARDEN

"What the true proverb says has happened to them: 'The dog returns to its own vomit, and the sow, after washing herself, returns to wallow in the mire."

2 Peter 2:22

Suicidal ideation is the experience of persistent or recurring thoughts about ending one's own life. It exists on a spectrum, ranging from fleeting, passive thoughts—such as wishing one wouldn't wake up—to active planning with intent. These thoughts often arise from deep emotional pain, hopelessness, trauma, or overwhelming circumstances where the mind begins to perceive death as an escape from suffering.

For many, suicidal ideation isn't necessarily about wanting to die—it's about wanting the pain to stop, feeling trapped in cycles of despair, or believing there's no other way forward. The pain just needs to stop. It can be fueled by mental health conditions like depression, PTSD, complex trauma, or even spiritual and existential crises. It's a battle between the desire to live and the exhaustion of continuing in pain.

This battle is one I have known intimately. It is not a stranger to me—it has walked alongside me since childhood.

For me, I always thought of suicide as an option. As a young girl, I questioned my mother why it was illegal. It seemed to me it's my body, and I could do with it what I wanted. After all—you do it in secret. No one has to know.

In my lowest hours, it's always my first thought of relief. In my waking hours, I always know it's there. The intent is not to provoke guilt or sorrow in others. It's not about "I'll show you." It's all about escape. The thought offers calm, and gathering tools offers relief.

It offers an option.

I hadn't entertained a suicidal thought since I accepted Christ a decade earlier. Yes, I had many struggles since, but this wave of pain—I never saw it coming. Mom's death brought back old feelings of abandonment as well as shame that I had failed. I had lost the hope of ever truly proving to my mother I deserved her love.

And yet, I knew that my suffering did not make me exempt from faith. If anything, it forced me to wrestle with what faith truly meant.

I realized I wasn't immune to suffering even though my love is for the Lord. Begging the Lord to take me home on my timeline is prideful. Who am I to throw away His gift like that? I was praying to the Lord for comfort, and the devil heard my words and broke into the conversation in my mind. It's called Spiritual Warfare.

The thought of leaving this world and the troublesome life behind is what I pray for. I had thought that my strong belief in Christ would take away this yearning, but it hasn't.

Although this time—the thought terrified me.

Because this time, I recognized the deception for what it was. The enemy does not offer escape—he offers destruction.

But I now see that faith does not remove suffering—it strengthens me to endure it. Christ did not run from suffering; He embraced it for our sake. And in my pain, He is near. I was praying to the Lord for comfort, but the enemy twisted my sorrow into temptation. He is the deceiver, always ready to exploit suffering and make death seem like relief when, in truth, it is his greatest lie.

The devil seeks to convince us that we are beyond hope, that suffering is pointless, and that escape is the only way. But the Lord says otherwise.

> *"My grace is sufficient for you, for my power is made perfect in weakness."*
> **2 Corinthians 12:9**

When I feel weak, He is strong. When I feel abandoned, He is present. When I feel like an imposter in my own faith, He reminds me that I am His.

Because sometimes, when you've lived as an imposter for so long, you forget how to live as yourself. But I refuse to believe the lie that my suffering is meaningless. If Christ endured suffering for me, then I will endure suffering for Him.

So today, I choose to fight—not in my own strength, but in His.

> *"He has called me to endure, and by His grace, I will. For I know that He who began a good work in me will carry it to completion."*
> **Philippians 1:6**

Act 3

CHAPTER 32

HEALING

FULL CIRCLE

....

...I made the call to Sabino at midnight and started my in-patient treatment through the Holiday season. I had decorated it for Christmas before I left so I could come home to a festive house. I filled my freezer with homemade comfort food. I had called many dear friends and asked them to send me Christmas cards so I could have them as gifts when I returned. I shared openly my struggles. I knew my decision to go into treatment was the right one and wanted my home in order when I returned.

Once home, I settled into retaining as much of the Sabino regime as I could: thankfulness, daily check-ins, muse meditation, and weekly phycologist meetings. Pancakes and bacon became my morning routine.

Sandwich for lunch and a full, balanced dinner. During my first month home I gained 10 pounds! How could this be? I did the math for my time at Sabino. I'd had 270 meals and somehow came home five pounds lighter. I got home and started cooking, and the weight started coming on. This is one of the unfair truths in life.

I made a commitment to myself. I promised to give myself grace. I allowed myself to explore my mental illness and heal. I committed to the healing process, and I started the journey to explore my deepest emotions and the pre-conceived identity I had suppressed for years.

When I started studying my mental illness and looked for the root of my brokenness, I found it right where it has always been—below the surface of a well-placed mask. My own mask. The mask I shared with others. The mask I had protected and varnished. The mask I never took off for fear the ugliness would show.

I didn't just come home from Sabino with routines—I came home with a quiet understanding that God hadn't left me alone in the wilderness. He was with me in every bite, every mirror glance, and every hard truth I dared to face.

That midnight call didn't just save me. It revealed I was never alone—not for one breath, not for one prayer, not for one brokenhearted cry. The wilderness was never empty. It was sacred ground.

VIEW FROM GETHSEMANE

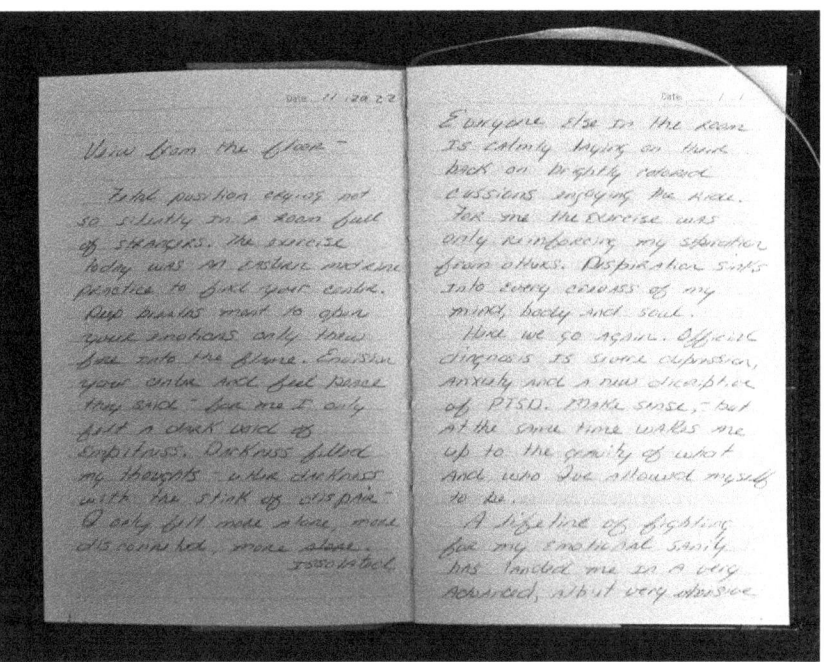

Excerpt — Day 2 of Sabino Recovery Journal — November 20th, 2022

The words below were never meant for an audience. I wrote them from the floor, in the dark, when I wasn't sure I would make it through the week. I'm leaving them here so you know where I started—and the ashes where Christ rose me from.

Fetal position, crying not so silently in a room full of strangers. The exercise today was an eastern medicine practice to find your center. Deep breaths meant to open your emotions only through fire into the flame.

Envision your center and feel peace they said, for me I only felt a dark void of emptiness. Darkness filled my thoughts, utter darkness with the stink of despair. I only felt more alone, more disconnected, more isolated. Everyone else in the room is calmly laying on their backs on brightly colored cushions enjoying The ride. For me, the exercise was only reinforcing my separation from others.

Desperation sinks into every crevice of my mind, my body and soul.

Here we go again. Official diagnosis is severe depression, anxiety and a new descriptive of PTSD. Makes sense, but at the same time wakes me up to the gravity of what and who I allowed myself to be. A lifetime of fighting for my emotional sanity has landed me in a very advanced trauma recovery center. I'm here of my own free choosing. It was this or total collapse. A lifetime of pain and past and present abuse by others and myself made me reach for help before I called it quits. The cover story, which rings of truth is moms death. Years of trying to gain her respect, praise and acceptance has suddenly come to an end. So much left unsaid. So much unknown. Did she love me. Did she know how? Feelings of years of active dismissals raise in my throat. Was I ever the daughter she envisioned or was I always a nuisance and a chore for her? From my end, the race for her acceptance is over. Now what? Who do I have to prove myself to? What to do without all her put downs, scrutiny and overt cruelty? The answer should be simple: rejoice, live, enjoy life without a critical eye and pungent mouth. Spend that inheritance she'd left me without guilt or judgment. Forget the many battles we've had when I started setting boundaries on her. 98 tall out of her shadow.

Live a better life.

But the pain is there. It hurts like 1000 cuts that have all broken lose all at once leaving a blood trail behind me. Pain at such intensity I can't see through it. Sorrow like the willing of a siren seeps through my entire body. How can this be when all I should feel is relief? Pain is all around me like the deep end of a pool. Can't touch the bottom, can't swim up to safety. Depression is such a complicated feeling, nothing simple about it.

> ISMs: Debilitating. Encompassing. Dark. Dangerous. Pain.
>
> Heavenly Virtue: Faith

I asked Christ for help, and He loves us deeper in our despair.

> *"The Lord is near to the brokenhearted and saves the crushed in spirit."*
>
> **Psalm 34:18**

I leave these words for those who know those dark places and that they may escape.

CHAPTER 33

DOUBT

HOW MUCH IS TOO MUCH?

*L*et's pause on this life of mine for a minute and think of your own stories. Think of a story you wouldn't want anyone to know. Stories of humiliation, shame, and guilt. Something tells me everyone reading this book isn't that different. We have all fallen short of ourselves on how we react to others and live our lives.

So how do we escape our shameful acts and correct our course? How do we know what we're supposed to do? How do we change our behaviors and thoughts? How do we become the person we know we are supposed to be? The truth is, we can't until we ask Jesus into our lives. We simply do not have that power alone. Jesus is the only one who can restore us to righteousness. By ourselves, we will fail. I was failing while looking like I was succeeding. Believing I was succeeding. Deceived by my own gaze.

Freedom comes from exposing our failures and weaknesses. Courage comes from vulnerability and accountability without fear. Only through being vulnerable can we experience the love of others and the grace of God. Untold secrets hold our healing by not exposing light to shame. Souls trapped in old thoughts and behaviors. Christ works to reveal all things.

It's easy to doubt and dismiss your talents, thoughts of new horizons, and daily peace. To discount your dreams and aspirations. The negative thoughts seep into your psyche and distract your goals. Who cares if I finish my story? What a stupid idea. Is it really something you can accomplish? Who cares if I take another job or not? Who cares about the life you're living, or your past? Your so-called illness and post-recovery? Your emotions? Who the hell cares about emotions?! We all know you're writing in your bikini by your pool while your dog's play. What is so important about you that you feel the need to write a book? No one wants to read about your debauchery!

Certainly, no one wants to hear about your acceptance of Christ. And nice try—trying to slip Him in in-between all the juicy parts. I don't believe in Him. Why should I believe a word you say? Really, who gives a shit? Who are you?

Doubt came into my mind, whispering its familiar poison. "You're making a mistake. You can't just walk away. What will people think? What will you do now? You're not young anymore—time is slipping away." I know that "I am more than a job. I am more than a paycheck. I am not bound by expectations anymore." But doubt mocks, "Oh, but you are. People are watching. They're whispering, 'She fell apart. She couldn't handle it. She's a mess.'" I hold my resolve, saying, "Let them whisper. My identity is in Christ, not in their shallow opinions." "That's cute," Doubt replies. "But faith doesn't pay the bills. You'll be back at a desk soon, groveling for a paycheck." My gut twisted at the thought, but I steadied myself. "I will walk forward, not backward. God provides." Doubt's voice darkened. "Liar. If that were true, you wouldn't be so mad about being discarded like a used tool. Admit it—you wanted them to see your worth, to regret letting you go." I exhaled sharply, examining the accusation: "I did. I did want that. But I don't need it." "Then why do you still wake up thinking about it?" Doubt pressed. "Why does it still make your stomach turn?" I swallowed hard. "Because healing isn't instant. But I won't be your hostage anymore." The voice lashed out, desperate. "This is just a phase. You're running on fumes. You'll slip up, and when you do, you'll realize you were never meant for more." A slow smile formed on my lips. "You don't get to define me anymore." "I don't have to," Doubt hissed. "You define yourself by your past. And your past is failure." I lifted my chin. "No. My past is proof of survival. My past is proof of God's redemption." "Redemption?" Doubt scoffed. "You've made too many mistakes for that." I let the silence settle before delivering the final blow. "Then why am I still standing?"

    Is what you've learned so far about my life of abuse and self-deprecation any worse than your own experience? Perhaps you think I had it pretty good compared to you. Perhaps you think I'm just a delicate flower and that I can't handle real abuse. I've had a great career with all that goes with it. You think, "I'll give you one day in my life if you want to know what real abuse is." Perhaps you think I've had it easy. I skated away just fine. Again, you think: Who are you to tell your story when mine is worse? Much, much worse.

Granted, you're probably correct. But abuse is not a competition. It's a known way of life. It's about survival.

How much abuse is worth complaining about?

We all learn to cope and adjust within our circumstances and surroundings. We figure out fast how to survive in order to stay a step ahead. I discovered through personal growth and therapy that our sense of individual perseverance often takes charge. Each of us abused cannot judge another, because we understand the effects that cause us to react differently than others. For those who have been abused, instinctive responses are our first go-to. (After all, our thinking is a product of how we learned to react to protect ourselves.) Denial comes next. This isn't really happening. Did he just say what I thought he said? Did he really just kick me hard under the table? Did he really tell me to shut up in front of others?

This is wrong. I know it's wrong. You can't tell me it's not wrong.

If you're ever wondered, "Have I been abused?" the answer is most likely yes. Abuse comes in many, many different forms. Trust me on this. If you have never wondered if you were abused, chances are you might be the abuser.

Any abuse is too much.

We all have the right to a peaceful existence. We have the right to our own personal boundaries, both at work and at home. We have the right to be respected and heard by others. Our parents and siblings aren't unhealthily shaping our views anymore. We aren't left to deal with rejection or fear by ourselves. We see the world from different angles when we understand abuse.

One head-slam into the headboard at 16 because you're objecting to his advances doesn't make him a predator. A simple theft of a cashiers till doesn't make him a thief. Spreading seeds of distrust of teammates doesn't make you toxic. Stealing from your wife and business doesn't make you a criminal. Feeding off people's emotions, skills, empathy and achievements doesn't make you a taker ...

But it does. And it adds up over a lifetime. We hold the key to understanding and learning. It's all about self-acceptance and recognition of others' actions towards you.

All we've ever wanted was to be loved and trusted. We just want a peaceful, simple life with someone who truly cares about us.

But what if your own mind is your worst enemy?

I found this to be the case whenever I was triggered. My sense of reason collapsed. Disassociation of my surroundings would settle in, and I would spend days staring off in silence. I was unable to quit ruminating and thinking about the past. Stewing. Over and over, the same thoughts of "coulda, shoulda, woulda" played in my mind. It was an endless cycle. Until I snapped out of it and moved forward. Dark times. The darkness would amplify due to drinking excessively, packs upon packs of cigarettes, no sleep or continuous sleep, and little food. Self-care would go out the window. Isolation would settle in. Lost in my own mind, unable to control my emotions. Stay numb or asleep so I don't have to feel anything.

Was my childhood really that bad? After all, I had a nice home, two parents, and a relatively wealthy upbringing. No parents beating on each other, no relatives in prison, and no influence of alcoholism or drugs. No one violated me while I slept. A few slaps? Really?

It was cold and unforgiving. Cruel and dysfunctional. Was that enough to completely shape my feelings about my place in the world?

Maybe I just needed to toughen up. Shake it off. Grow a pair.

People all over the world have rotten jobs, bad spouses, and mean mothers. My career seemed to work out okay for me. My exes didn't beat me to a pulp. Sure, my family was cruel with my emotions, depriving me of affection, and condescending. But is that enough to shape my identity?

The answer is yes. I suffered greatly and the pain was immense. The abuse was intentional. I was subjected to a constant barrage of criticism just for being who I was. Judgment of my feelings, actions, and basic life expectations. And it lasted my whole life, even after I left them all behind. Invisible fences. I was free but still in a cage in my mind—until I broke the chains.

Doubt is the weight that keeps us bound, convincing us that our past defines us and our pain is ours to bear alone. But Christ shatters those chains, revealing that our worth was never in question—only our belief in it. In Him, doubt dissolves, and the truth of who we are is restored.

I show what survival looks like when trauma becomes normal—and how healing only begins when the truth is no longer denied.

Who are you listening to?

CHAPTER 34

COURSE CORRECTION – BREAKING STRONGHOLDS

ANGER

At Sabino I learned about anger.

I never thought much about anger. I Never considered it a stronghold.

Anger was an emotion I rarely expressed. I do not hold grudges. I do not seek revenge. I am not jealous or envious. If I was telling someone my direct truth, it wasn't anger that fueled me; it was honesty. I don't get mad unless you poke me with a stick. I am not saying I am all roses and buttercups, but I'm pretty good natured.

As a trauma coping strategy, I had suppressed my instinct of anger to survive in my surroundings my entire life. I had pushed it all down. I didn't understand this emotion. Therapy helped me comprehend the extreme abuse of emotional neglect I have endured. Through ART sessions and EDMR I was able to dig into this block of injustices and feel the pain. I achieved closure and released the shame of failing myself. I had not protected myself. I was open to abuse.

I began to understand the importance of angers emotional distress and how I can work to process this emotion in a healthy way. It had been suppressed, and I saw the depth of my jaded mindset and the waves of toxic abuse over a lifetime—it was all under the spotlight. I had to allow the positivity of anger to grow.

That was a big jump for me.

Anger is a healthy response to injustice, fear, or torment. Anger lets you know that something is afoul. When you feel anger, it's not a bad thing. I was surprised by the anger that learning of complex trauma brought up. It caught me by surprise. I felt it and released it. I didn't know this emotion, and it scared me. I didn't realize anger was a good emotion that signaled to your psyche that something was wrong.

All I knew is that it wasn't allowed. Smile. Be nice. Do it our way and be quiet about it. No one wants to hear your voice.

And boy, did I get mad. Mad that I allowed what happened to me growing up to happen. Furious I put up with so much abuse from others. I was furious with myself.

Mad I played into my own self-abuse to numb or feel anything.

Mad I discounted myself and my morals.

Mad I stayed so long in abusive relationships with spouses and toxic friends.

Mad I spoiled my children.

Mad I was a wet rag for so long.

Mad I looked the other way.

Mad I didn't see clearly what my life had become until it was almost too late.

Mad at any perceived injustice.

Mad at any changes I didn't make or have control over.

Mad nothing had changed at work—and that it had only gotten worse.

I came home from gaining my CPTSD diagnosis with a big ball that needed unraveling. I continued to work past anger by examining it all and journaling. Feeling every twinge of anger and then choosing a reaction vs. not pushing it aside.

I didn't always win.

At work, passive aggressive behavior became my go-to. Just trying to get along became a challenge. My anger at the injustice of the system I was working in had now taken over all my emotions. It was like unleashing a beast.

If I'd had a spouse or someone living with me, they would have probably been my battering post. But all I had was work. I was once known for my pleasant demeanor, helpfulness, and willingness to adapt. Now I was spiteful, childish, and argumentative. Any distraction would set me into a flurry, and no infringement would go without a debate. Wake up angry, go to bed angry.

I needed to make some big changes. Being fired from my job was a relief. A blessing. I was thankful. Being fired allowed me time to heal. Time to breathe and reflect. They did me a huge favor. I had prayed to be out. Finally, I was free to choose my next direction. I was learning to trust myself, and this revelation was a huge step in the healing process.

I had a renewed spirit. Christ was guiding my path as He'd always done. Sure, my company had played games with me. Sure, I'd again been used for my connections and relationships, then dismissed. But is that enough to justify how I had been acting? No. Look in the mirror, Joanne. I was the problem child. It was my need to feel heard that got in my way. It was my need to feel recognized and esteemed that caused me to self-destruct. It was me. I needed to change.

Or not.

I'd survive without the paycheck. I'd survive without the self-importance of a big career. I'd survive without expending all the mental energy it took to do my job effectively while watching my back. I would walk through this new door with confidence, excited for what the Lord has for me. After all, I didn't really have a choice. I finally had to face myself with a clear mind and admit my pride was still running my life.

I resisted the voice in my head telling me to get a new job quickly because it was expected, and I had an expiration date. I shot down self-deprecating thoughts. I remained calm when fears arose, and I shook off all my ruminations.

But still, the doubt screams: Let me in! Let me foil your plans. Let me distract you and tempt you. Let me silence you.

No, I say: I'm still learning and growing. I won't be silenced into submission of my faith, skills, or worthiness.

I am chosen for greatness. I am now free. Just to be me. Just how I like to follow.

> *"I am doing a great work and I cannot come down. Why should the work stop while I leave it and come down to you?"*
>
> **Nehemiah 6:3**

CHAPTER 35

TRUST IN CHRIST'S PLAN

PRIDE

I retired seven years too early by worldly standards.

The Lord knew what I needed. My mental health needed to begin healing in peace without daily conference calls and travel. It was a stupid idea to think I could just go back into work with all the triggers. Correction: It was insane of me to think work was a good plan. It's like an alcoholic working in a bar—I would have never healed if I stayed. My physical health and soul health needed strengthening, and my identity health needed revamping. Spiritual knowledge and growing discernment answered the question of "why me?" He assured me I was valuable. I knew my worth on a different playing field, and so did Christ. He answered my prayers. Corporate doors closed.

My inner peace was restored. I finally put down one of my last strongholds.

Christ showed me that I could trust Him. Everything is in His timing and plan. It was time for me to write the book that has been within me for years. —I just listened instead of fighting Him. I finally trusted. He has much in store for me. My fear of losing relevancy in the world and my self-worth surrounding my identity needed to go.

The spiritual healing of my head, heart, and soul had to begin. Unafraid, I started to peel back the layers.

"To whom much is given, much will be required."

Luke 12:48

I was arrogant in my estimation of myself. I was prideful, believing I was in control of my career and not Christ. I misinterpreted me getting each new role as Christ's path instead of my own ego. I took His denial of me going to seminary as my approval to keep one foot in the corporate world. Each time I worked hard, I assured myself I was working for the Lord in the corporate mission field. What a load of crap.

All I was doing was continuing to feed my own pride, which was disguised as justification I felt from my big important job and paycheck. I lied to myself that I was not concerned with money and storing riches on earth. I pretended because I went on missions and served in the church that I had my priorities right. I hadn't even considered putting down the job and my unhealthy obsession with work. Never even considered that it was me with the log jammed so far up my eye that I couldn't see. I idolized money just as my mother did. My paycheck had become my identity.

I might have put down the shopping, excessive drinking, whoring, and all the other endless ways I used to feed my flesh over a decade ago—but when it came to work, I thought I could handle it. Worse—after this long, I felt I deserved it. After all, we all need a paycheck, right? I can make $300 an hour or $20, so who wouldn't choose the higher for the same or less effort with your current skills?

Even if it cost you your health. Even if it cost you your peace. Even if it caused relationship struggles. Even if it distracted you to a point you were neglecting self-care. Stick to the paycheck like glue because it provided your fuel, oxygen, and air to survive. The chase of money is the hardest stronghold to break.

Stepping out of the corporate world is the best advancement I've ever made for myself and my mental health. The gilded gold birdcage is there to keep you from leaving. The rock-star lifestyle and all that goes with it is hard to turn your back on. But the security it offers is a lie. There is no security in the corporate world. It is a fable. All of us—are subject to abuse. It's those who cry foul that get swept into the trash. The louder you ask for fair treatment, the harsher the consequences. This will not change unless we shed light on what is truly going on behind closed doors. Tell the truth of the matter instead of going along with the crowd. Many cannot afford to say adios. To the ones that stay, watch your backs, as you won't see it coming. And even if you do, you can't stop it.

Leaving it all behind has been my prize for surviving.

Living through it has become my strength.

So I laid it down. Not in defeat—but in deliverance. I gave up chasing false worth and let the Shepherd carry me out of the fire I kept walking back into.

> *"For I know the plans I have for you,"* declares the Lord, *"plans to prosper you and not to harm you, plans to give you a future and a hope."*
> **Jeremiah 29:11**

He wasn't punishing me. He was preserving me. Pulling me out before I burned to ash. My identity wasn't buried in a job title—it was sealed in Him. And now, instead of running myself into the ground, I rise every day to write truth, to walk in peace, and to know the kind of joy I never found in a paycheck.

Trusting Christ's plan didn't cost me my life. It gave me one.

PLACING TRUST IN MY HEART

Choosing a trauma treatment center to end my suffering instead of continued pain aided in my recovery and provided me a path to healing from a mental illness I never understood. Deep reflection was required. Deep connection with the Lord was demanded. I took another hard look at myself and my past rejections and an honest inventory of my true motivations. Through the healing cycle, I gained a solid realization of my relationships.

As I began to trust myself, I looked deeply into ingrained friendships that had ran their course and caused me pain over the years.

I realized my trust issues did me a favor in the corporate environment. You can believe nothing said to you is meant to promote you. They work to keep you off-balance, jumping through invisible hoops. I took risks, pushed back, or overly gave because I wanted to feel validated. I had a blind eye on my friendships. Had I employed the same skepticism on my friends, I may have spared myself some pain.

I realized my inability to feel true connection was on me—and then I understood clearly. It wasn't just about corporate manipulation or the transactional nature of the workplace; it extended into my personal life and into the friendships I had assumed were built on mutual love and respect. I had spent years collecting friends, yet I had been blind to the reality that some of my friendships weren't rooted in genuine care, but in quiet expectation.

A handful of lifelong friends had a negative reaction to my newfound strength in understanding my people pleasing tendencies and new consciousness of complex trauma and boundary setting. Some had been living off my generosity for years without complaints—until finally I stood my ground and set boundaries. Like my children, they had grown to expect me to furnish their extracurricular adventures or lift them out of financial or emotional struggles.

For decades, I paid the way for many people. Need an airplane ticket? Sure, I have points. Can't afford your own room? I have points for that too. Need $5000? Sure—you'll pay me back right? They won't save up to ski, have dinner, golf, or pay their fair share, but they are the first in line for your invitation. You have money, they say—I don't want to part with mine. I need to leave early, it's your fault. You are paying for the transfer to the airport—right? I did bring money, but I didn't offer anything because it goes so fast, and I need to save mine. Yours is better. You have more. After all, I had to pay for my own checked bags.

When I did object or ask for anything back in exchange, boy did they balk.

Why don't they just be honest? Why don't they just say:

"I don't like you questioning me. I don't like you asking me anything that I deem confrontational. I don't want to have an honest conversation with you because you turn my gaslighting around on me and I have no other tactics aside from imposing guilt and shame. You think you own the truth and that nothing I say can change it. You're being unreasonable. You are just seeing it from your perspective. You are just a dictator. I know it's your house but I feel the entitlement to invite others on an adventure you're paying for. Sabino was a crock of shit. Can't we just go back to how it was before? I don't like the new you."

And then there was my personal favorite—"I thought Christians were supposed to be nice. You're not nice. I liked you better without all these new ideas and influences. You're not well. We don't like you thinking you are well. You needed me when you were sick, remember? When you were low, I could use you. Who are you to say get lost? Your thoughts, feelings, and sudden expertise at understanding trauma is not appreciated. In fact, Sabino was a waste. It didn't do you any good—you're still the same. You've been brainwashed. You will die alone. I'm done."

Hah! To be honest, you're done because I told you the gig was up. And you didn't doubt *that* conviction of my truth.

It feels great to say no and enforce it. To have so many act like they didn't see it coming or feel wronged is very telling of their character—or, better said, their lack of character. If you keep kicking the dog, you should expect to get bitten. It's only a matter of time.

If you recognize yourself in actions or reactions in any of this, you might be inclined to hold the other side of the story. Perhaps this is just a version and you could alter the circumstances, but the result would be the same. One was giving, the other was taking. "You're leaving out the before and after," some might say. After all I've done for you! This isn't fair! YOU asked ME to go places. You're the one who made it so easy to take from you. You are little miss moneybags, only now you're singing a different tune. You're the one who had surgery and needed a friend. You're the one who called me crying, and I was there for you. You're the one who arranged all the resources to clean out mom's house, so I didn't have to lift a finger. You're the one I always had in my back pocket if I needed anything. You're the one who assumed leadership of the adventures, meetings, parties, and family gatherings. You greedy SOB—you never said there would be a day of reckoning. I was happy using you and giving nothing back. Sure, I took your love and talents and treated it all like crap. Sure, I took what you offered without even thinking of giving anything in return. Sure, I comforted you in times of trouble and knew you'd be there for me as well. I even allowed all your Christian talk that I had thought was just a phase. I knew when you returned from treatment that you'd be triumphant and full of force. But I never thought you'd get a backbone. I never thought you'd actually say, "No. No more."

And I certainly didn't think you ever needed anything from me because you act like you don't need anything from anyone. This is your own fault. You caused this. This is all on you. *Great, Now I will need a new back-up plan. Thanks.*

Being honest is the most Christian thing I can offer you. My generosity does have limits, and your time is up. Do the work. Pay your own way. It's called life. Do not ride off my coattails any longer. I see you. I see clearly who you are. You were never my cheerleader.

You are the one that doesn't value friendship. You are the one that has no loyalty and no perspective beyond your own needs. You are the one that gossips and feels envy. If I didn't fit your mold it was because I was never supposed to. I am unique. I am versatile. I do not hold my form in your hands because I cannot be held in place by deception. I get to be me.

And you – you are who you are. But even you have the power to ask for change.

SELF-REFLECTION: A HOUSE SWEPT CLEAN

Maybe you've read this chapter and felt the sting of recognition. Maybe you've been carrying people who wouldn't carry you. Maybe you've been offering loyalty to those who only loved the version of you they could control.

If so, I want to tell you something simple and true:
You are allowed to change.
You are allowed to grow past the roles you once played.
You are allowed to grieve the friendships that can't survive your healing.
You are allowed to say no—without explanation, without guilt.
I know what it's like to be the strong one, the generous one, the one who always brings the comfort, the connection, the credit card. And I also know what it feels like to realize...
they were never showing up for you—only what they could get from you.
But here's the hope:
Cleaning house makes room for joy.
Saying no makes room for yes.
Letting go makes space for God to fill.
The loss hurts—but the peace that follows is real.
And you deserve to live in that peace.
If this chapter stirred something in you, I want to encourage you to take one small step:
Look around your life. Ask yourself:
Who truly sees me? Who values me without needing to diminish me?
Then start there. Sweep a little. Clear a shelf. Crack a window.
Let light in. Consider, who drains me—and who pours into me?
You don't have to burn bridges in anger.
Sometimes, the most sacred ending is a quiet closing of the door.

Let God rebuild what others tried to dismantle.

Let Him show you the beauty of boundaries—and the blessing of becoming *undeniably you*.

And if you're the one who's taken more than you've given—

This is your moment to change that, too. Healing doesn't just belong to the wounded. It belongs to the willing.

This isn't about blaming people or cutting everyone off.

It's about naming what's real—so God can start rebuilding what's been broken.

Not all friendships are meant to survive your healing or your conviction to Christ.

And that's okay.

Let this chapter be your mirror.

Let this pain become your turning point.

And let truth—not guilt—lead your next step.

STOPPING THE INSANITY

Okay. Now let's get to the good part. The part about the awareness that comes with accepting you have childhood trauma. You stop feeling crazy. You understand why you've reacted so strongly to certain things.

It is important to oust doubters and negative influencers during the early part of your recovery. Distractions are not your friends. Dive in hard. Eliminate interruptions. Put yourself first. Examine and understand the truth. Dig in.

Stay in therapy, stay to your routine. Seek community. Stay curious reading and researching trauma to stay educated. Keep your head in the Bible. Pray.

For me, it was like veils had been ripped off my eyes. I began to see the motives and habitual actions of my friends, family members, and colleagues as clear as the light of day. I saw both their good and bad motives, their motives for their own standing and self-worth. Second to accepting Christ, the revelation and understanding of complex trauma survivorship changed my life course. I had not realized the impact.

Unacceptable actions from others had carried on for years. Actual inhumane treatment that you wouldn't treat a stranger the way some people I loved treated me. To zealously put me in positions of great embarrassment and shame, even if it embarrassed them as well. My abusers thought that the way they felt about me was how everyone felt about me.

When you adapt this healing mindset to how you examine others' actions, you see the abuse triggers in their tactics to minimize you as clearly as you've ever seen. The abuse from when it first started springs forward. And then another ludicrous request comes in for more generosity from a family member or friend. You combust. No, I'm done. I see you. I see you for who and what you are.

Understanding my life's trials and triumphant moments with clarity has served me well. So well, in fact, that I feel free to finally take flight.

A LIFE NO LONGER BORROWED

> *'I have lived too long on borrowed strength—giving away my power to keep the peace, making myself small so others could stand taller."*

There is no going back. No unseeing, no undoing, no pretending that the past didn't happen or that the truth can be softened to spare anyone's comfort. I have lived too long on borrowed strength—giving away my power to keep the peace, making myself small so others could stand taller, and paying the way in more ways than just career sacrifice and financial generosity. But that part of my life is over.

I have taken back what was always mine: my time, my heart, and my boundaries. My faith is not a shield for others to manipulate, nor is it a leash to keep me bound to their expectations. It is my foundation, my guide, and my absolute truth.

> *"Healing was never about getting back to who I was before the pain. That person is gone."*

Christ knew my healing was never about getting back to who I was before the pain. That person is gone. Healing is about becoming someone new—someone I was meant to be all along but was too weighed down to fully embrace. The woman who now stands is no longer weighed down. She is whole. She is full of wisdom. And she is never returning to a life of quiet suffering.

For those who could not love or respect me unless I stayed broken—your time is up. For those who resented my generosity but still took all they could—your time is up. For those who expected my silence—your time is up.

I walk away from the past without bitterness, only clarity. I see the deception now and feel thankfulness. And with this sight, I move forward—not as the woman I was, not even as the woman I have become, but as the woman I am still yet to be.

And that woman—me—owes nothing but truth to the world and to herself and The Lord.

CHAPTER 36
ARE YOUR SECRETS LIVING THRU YOU?

*Y*ou have taken in all my secrets. Some perhaps you didn't wish to know. Now, I have to turn the mirror on to you.

Are your habits destroying your well-being and peace? Are your learned coping defenses clouding your judgment? Is your life so filled with abuse of all forms that you have just gotten used to defeat? Are you explaining the abuse away? Are you ignoring the abuse? Are your opinions valued, and your voice heard in all or most personal interactions? Are you respected? Do you respect yourself? Are close family members, friends, and co-workers—who are so used to exploiting your flaws and faults—fighting the boundaries you are setting in place? Have you come face to face with your own willful abuse of your body and soul and decided you are ready for a change? Are you afraid of change? Has the fear of change crippled you from taking action? Have you dared to reflect on your past choices and identified a pattern of self-abuse and self-abandonment? Have you ever considered that past or present abuse may be contributing to your anxiety, depression, ill-health, numbing behaviors, and sadness? Have you earnestly explored how your family, circle of friends, and co-workers treat you? Have you taken accountability for your own actions and asked others for forgiveness? Have you forgiven yourself? Has such a thought even crossed your mind?

Have. You. Forgiven. Yourself?

> *"Have. You. Forgiven. Yourself? Have you ever considered that forgiving yourself and asking for forgiveness is the first step to healing?"*

Have you ever considered that forgiving yourself and asking for forgiveness is the first step to healing?

OR—are you good? Is your life bearable and upsetting the status quo will disrupt your comfort and conditional security? Is it easier just to let things go on as they always have than to object to others' treatment of you? Is it just easier to bite your tongue and endure being continually sabotaged by others? Is it you who sabotages yourself into complacency? Is it easier just to take the beatings and try harder tomorrow? Hope things will get better by doing nothing? Is it you who is afraid to explore a new life? Is it you who is scared of change and doesn't believe it can happen? Is it you who is scared of exploring your faults and finding truth? Honesty is all we have when we take a hard look in the mirror. It takes courage.

OR—are you uncomfortably recognizing yourself as an abuser? Maybe you don't like that word. It sounds so accusatory. So calculating and needy. Abuser—makes it sound like you enjoy using others to get what you need. (And maybe you do.) Is it you who casts guilt and shame or spreads discord and division? Is it you who, in your insecurity, is envious, petty, and jealous? Is it you that uses people to feel superior? Is it you that dominates and controls others through any means necessary? Is it you that makes fun of others in front of groups to humiliate and silence them? Is it you that gossips about others in an effort to feel better about yourself? Is it you that uses others for your own personal gain? Is it you that feels entitled to trap others in your world of emotional dominance? Is it you that slaps, hits, kicks, or rapes to feel powerful? Are you the mocker? The liar? The thief? The backstabber? The bully? Maybe you're the boss. The boss that takes his teams accomplishments like a softball to the chest with a plastic badge. The boss that yells or completely ignores, issues threats or hides behind policy to silence an employee? Is it you that has no internal peace and can't stand to see others happy, healthy, and confident? Is it you that kicks people when they're down and badmouths them when they are up? Is it you right now that hears my words and only think it's judgmental piousness and not a call for personal reflection? Perhaps it's you that thinks this is a personal attack? Is it you that believes they have no call to action? Is it you that believes others need controlling and nothing you're doing is wrong? Is it you who likes everything the way it is and is resistant to others changing around you? Is it you holding others in a cage? If any of this is you, know that you too have the power for miraculous change. It's called accountability to stop abusive practices. This is your punch in the nose to see the light and change behaviors. It's called self-confidence. Ask Christ to gain some.

OR—is it you who knows the profound mercy of acquiring Faith in Christ but still can't seem to maintain peace? To possess joy? Is it you who prays at night while tears soak the pillow? Is it you who combs through the Scriptures, looking for encouragement and direction? Is it you who earnestly prays to the Lord asking for more forgiveness and understanding daily? Is it you who feels discouraged when The Lord is silent, but still holds hope? Is it you who encourages others when they are hurting even though you yourself are hurting just as deeply? Is it you who knows that The Lord works all things for our good? Is it you that knows the Lord has marvelous plans for your life? Is it you who knows the sacrifice He made on the cross so we could live free from fear and sorrow? Is it you that knows that trials are good for us as we hold unshakable faith in Jesus Christ? Is it you who understands everything is in The Lord's timing and He is patiently waiting for you to completely trust Him? To honor Him. To commit to Him with all of your heart. Is it you that trusts the process and has faith to patiently wait upon The Lord? Is it you who is so bold in your faith that you profess it from the mountaintops? He rejoices in your weakness as much as He does your strength. Is it you that can feel His pleasure in your love of The Father and commitment to serve Him with all your heart? If so, this is called abundant faith.

We all have the power to rise above, seek wisdom, and acquire the truth. You just have to be honest with yourself and start the process of healing. It all starts and ends with forgiveness.

My story is mine. It's not yours. My personal relationship with Christ is my own. My life has been mine, and I hold no others responsible for any of the failings or success. I lived it. I learned from it. I forgave myself, I started healing and I recovered. You can as well. We all have a story to tell and a marvelous life to live.

Acquire the Truth of your circumstances by searching for it. The Truth will set you free.

Are you ready to start your journey?

CHAPTER 37
IT'S BEEN AN HONOR

So, you've read all I was willing to share. There is more—there always is—but for now, this is enough. If you were hoping for names, companies, or confessions I refused to give, well, go ahead and be disappointed. I didn't need to clear my plate on such a public stage. But if my faith, my traps, and my healing can save others from suffering in silence and shame, then the effort is worth the reward.

Perhaps you only want to believe the "bad" stories in this book. The truth of my debauchery is easier to take in and think about. You've read about all my struggles, all my shame, and all my secrets. Perhaps you've experienced some of the same. Maybe my trials seemed too out there to believe. Maybe you think I'm an actor, a fraud.

Whatever you've felt while reading this, I'm fine with it. I didn't write this book to be believed by everyone—I wrote it because it is my truth. And if, after considering all my actions, you still believe I'm deceived, I'm good with that too. Because I would not be here without Christ's love and support.

I wrote this book quickly as the words and stories poured out of me. I wrote this for you—the ones who are being beaten down, the ones beating themselves down, the ones afraid to make bold choices. I wrote this for the 16-year-olds who have yet to discover they are in a trap. I wrote this for those who have had an abortion, suffered abuse from others, or abused their body with alcohol, sex, or drugs. I wrote this for those who have been raped and stripped of their innocence. I wrote this for you, sitting in a home of silent abuse. I wrote this for those who are hurting themselves, searching for comfort in all the wrong places.

I got you.

But ultimately, I wrote this for those who wonder, "Is there anyone else out there like me?"

The answer is yes. You are not alone. We are not alone.

I am strong. I no longer hide in the darkness, begging for scraps to feel worthy. I will never again discount my boundaries or morals—in life, love, or business—to make others more comfortable. Nor should you.

Who is bold enough to speak up? To tell their ugly stories without shame? To look deep within themselves and face the hard truth of their situation and actions? Who is brave enough to start the journey to healing?

Who is willing to tell their truth—even if it's just to themselves?

Who is willing to admit they need help?

Who is willing to admit that someone in their life is lying and deceiving them daily, making them feel they must hide their true self to avoid scorn and ridicule?

Who are you people-pleasing?

Who are you running from?

Who makes you feel frozen in your circumstances?

Who needs a different life so badly but can't see a way out no matter how hard they try?

Who needs change so desperately that it's all they think about? Dream about? Pray about?

I believe real change—true, lasting change—is possible through Faith in Jesus Christ. Changing the way you think is hard. In fact, any change takes substantial work. And most times, change is false. We are the best liars to ourselves.

You do well for a while—walking away from past traps—but the world seeps back in, pulling you under again, causing you to backslide. Only when you reach the point where staying silent is worse than speaking your truth—only then—do you begin to walk in heavenly freedom.

> "Only when you reach the point where staying silent is worse than speaking your truth—only then—do you begin to walk in freedom."

That is the revelation of Christ.

As for me—shedding light on my failures has been a true honor and privilege. To have the freedom to expose myself without fear is His reward. If even one of my stories has left you with a longing for self-evaluation, then it has value. If my trials have been used for good, then I am stronger than all my past failures.

> *"The world's been trying to silence me for years. But I refuse."*

If you think I'm a hypocrite and wish I'd shut up—get in line. The world's been trying to silence me for years.

But I refuse.

CHAPTER 38

THE TABLE IS SET

Today when I look at my life, I am thankful—for my future.

First off, the fact that you're reading this book means it's published and available on audiobook, with an accompanying workbook. That exact goal has been in my mind since 2013. My next? Buying my book in an airport bookstore. I see it. I've seen it for years. I believe it, and always have.

The writing part came easily. The editing? That took forever. I prayed for discernment at every step, asking God for the right words. It was worth the wait.

I never considered letting someone else narrate my story. It's my story. I was born with a speech disorder—rhotacism—what my mother called a "thick German tongue." To be clear, Mom's term was outdated, offensive, and rooted in ethnic stereotyping—but that was Mom. Today we understand speech disorders like mine as articulation disorders, and they're treated with therapy—not ridicule, like in my childhood.

Pronouncing R's and L's has been a lifelong struggle. I've been teased and corrected my entire life for how I speak, for my word choices, and for using malapropisms—saying the wrong word that sounds close to the right one, often with some unintentional humor. Hearing my voice on the audiobook triggered all of that past mocking. I hear the slurs. I hear the mispronunciations. But I did it anyway. In spite of myself. And it was rewarding.

My life is content. I am full.

I've found acceptance in my surroundings and life circumstances. No more deadlines. No more quotas. No more packing. No more flights. Now it's gardening and writing. No more dysfunction—just caring friends and family. I found a sweet, small church—Lewisville Lighthouse—where I attend Celebrate Recovery and Bible study with solid believers. I continue to see my psychologist, rheumatologist, chiropractor, and podiatrist as part of my physical and mental health routine. I walk my dogs. I clean my house. I cook my own food. I plan real vacations—not corporate boondoggles with strangers. This better life? It still feels new. And it's exciting.

I opened a Hospitality Technology consulting company: Gailwinds Group, LLC. Gail is my middle name. I always hated it because I thought it was a boy's name. But when I had to name my company, I instantly thought of wind. My style was never a gentle breeze. It's a gale wind. It came to rip the lies off the walls, to tear down what was built on silence, and to make space for truth to take root. You can brace against it—or you can let it free. But either way? The wind is here.

I currently consult on private projects—everything from sales strategy plans and HVAC systems to complex building technology with a focus on construction and energy-saving measures (ESM). It's good to step back into a trade I love. My education gave me a far-reaching knowledge of the industry. Now, I sit on the other side of the table—deciding which products get bought. I know the players. I know the games. I was that puppet master. It's hard to slip anything past me now. Again, I work for my clients. Again, I'm at the table. But now? I'm having fun.

I also opened Gailwinds Publishing and Bountiful Events. My workbook will be the template for many workshops and seminars. It is my desire to help as many with my story and inspire hope and change. I'm planning Virtue of Honor book retreats in Costa Rica at a resort I purchased for exactly that purpose. Bringing survivors together in a calm setting is powerful and healing. Speaking to my life's lessons assures others they are not alone in their struggles.

Mostly, though, I get to tell my story. I get to educate. I get to offer hope. I get to be me.

I educate industry leaders on the impact of complex trauma and workplace abuse, highlighting how trauma-informed awareness can transform leadership, improve organizational health, and confront longstanding patterns of dysfunction. Through keynotes and workshops, I help professionals recognize the behavioral and structural roots of unhealthy environments—equipping them to lead with clarity, accountability, and empathy. I sit in rooms filled with young women searching for peace and purpose. I share what survival looks like, and teach strength. I enjoy working with professionals to put a name to trauma survival and help overcome domestic violence shame.

I'm teaming with an esteemed producer, Andy Costa—who perfected my audiobook—to create my story into a documentary of hope. I'm helping launch a Christian, R-rated testimonial series on YouTube called *The Naked Truth*. Perfect fit for my background if you ask me.

Every time I speak, I carry the power of Christ. And mostly—I pray. I pray that my words point to the traps I fell into, and that they help other survivors stand in strength. The Lord has set me up for big things. Bigger than I ever asked for. Bigger than my brain could have imagined. I believe He will deliver.

But don't forget—as you're reading this, it's not me or my story chasing you to make changes.

It's the Lord who's pursuing you.

I asked Him for the desires of my heart, and I received more than I ever deserved in the form of peace and contentment. And you? You can ask, too. No matter what your past has been. No matter where you are. No matter your circumstances. If you ask—He will answer.

I am not only a survivor. I am a witness. And the table is set.

I am Joanne, and I hold many names: Chosen. Adopted. Ambassador for Christ. Child of God. Friend. Servant of Christ. Redeemed and Forgiven. God's Workmanship. Flawed but Free.

And now, I ask you—who are you?

To me, you are my guest. Did you realize this table was set for you? This book was written for you from the very first word. Are you ready to blow up your life to have freedom? Are you ready to be curious?

THE TABLE IS SET

Will you join me at the table?
Will you tell your stories unashamed?
Will you live a better life?
I double dare you.

CHAPTER 39

FREEDOM

TO BE ME

Freedom of speech. Freedom of time. Freedom of expression. Freedom of honesty. Freedom of flair. Freedom from hiding intelligence. Freedom from ridicule. Freedom from fear. Freedom of food. Freedom of self-acceptance. Freedom from self-abuse. Freedom from co-dependency. Freedom from substance abuse. For too long, the world tried to convince me that these freedoms were out of reach. That I had to earn them. That I had to beg for them. That I had to wait for permission. But the truth? I was born free to make a choice. And so were you.

Free to dream. Free to simply be. Free to take time to know myself. To unlearn the lies, to strip away the expectations, and to break every chain that was never meant to hold me. Time to explore my boundaries. Time to really understand what drives me and what lights my fire. Time to no longer apologize for the light inside me. Time to catch my breath. To be still. To stop surviving and start living. To hear my calling. To change a lifespan of bad choices. To walk away from every cycle that tried to keep me bound. To contribute to others' lives. To inspire. To grow. To be inspired. To be curious. To be all that I can be on my own terms.

Because that is the birthright of a child of God.

"It is for freedom that Christ has set us free. Stand firm, then, and do not let yourselves be burdened again by a yoke of slavery."

Galatians 5:1

This freedom? It's not a reward. It's a responsibility. A priceless gift for accepting the strength and light I was elected upon at birth. A timely honor for coming to grips with trauma's effects on me. Not as a victim. Not as someone broken. But as someone rebuilt—stronger, wiser, and unshakable.

Freedom to kick that trauma's ass daily. Not just once. Not just in theory. Every. Single. Day. Freedom to heal. Not because the world says it's time, but because I say so. Because God has already made a way.

Freedom to quit fighting. Because the fight has already been won. Understanding I've fought for every freedom I've always known was mine in the first place. That no one had the right to take it. That I was never as weak as they wanted me to believe.

Free to fall and get back up. Free of shame, guilt, and punishment placed on me by others. Their judgment is not my identity. Free of my own unrealistic expectations. Because grace covers even me.

Freedom to understand that becoming stronger, healthier, and smarter just takes backbone, God, and therapy.

And now? Now I see it clearly.

Be free. Stay free. Believe you are free. Know you are free. Daily. Not just in moments of clarity. Not just when it's easy. But daily.

Complex trauma, daily life, painful trials—they are not a prison.

They are the threshold of transformation.

So, take your freedom. No more waiting. No more apologizing. No more asking permission.

Your past trauma is not a life sentence. It's the start of your revolution.

Now go live like it.

> *"Complex trauma, daily life, painful trials—they are not a prison. They are the threshold of transformation. So, take your freedom. No more waiting. No more apologizing. No more asking permission. Your past trauma is not a life sentence. It's the start of your revolution. Now go live like it."*

"Whom the Son sets free is free indeed."

John 8:36

Lisa

Wanda

www.ingramcontent.com/pod-product-compliance
Lightning Source LLC
Chambersburg PA
CBHW020827160426
43192CB00007B/549